N4MB3R CRUNCHE7

WRITTEN BY SI SPURRIER

ARTWORK BY PJ HOLDEN

COLORS BY JORDIE BELLAIRE

NUMBERCRUNCHER

ISBN: 9781782760047

Published by Titan Comics
A division of Titan Publishing Group Ltd.
144 Southwark St.
London
SE1 0UP

First edition: January 2014.

10 9 8 7 6 5 4 3 2 1

Printed in China.

Titan Comics. TC0055

TITAN COMICS

EDITOR STEVE WHITE
DESIGNER ROB FARMER

Titan Comics Editorial Andrew James Jon Chapple
Gabriela Houston
Production Supervisors Kelly Fenlon, Jackie Flook
Interim Production Assistant Peter James
Art Director Oz Browne
Studio Manager Selina Juneja
Circulation Manager Steve Tothill
Marketing Manager Ricky Claydon
Marketing Assistant Tara Felton
Publishing Manager Darryl Tothill
Publishing Director Chris Teather
Operations Director Leigh Baulch
Executive Director Vivian Cheung
Publisher Nick Landau

What did you think of this book? We love to hear
from our readers. Please email us at:
readercomments@titanemail.com, or write to us
at the above address.

To receive news, competitions, and exclusive
offers online, please sign up for the Titan Comics
newsletter on our website:
www.titan-comics.com

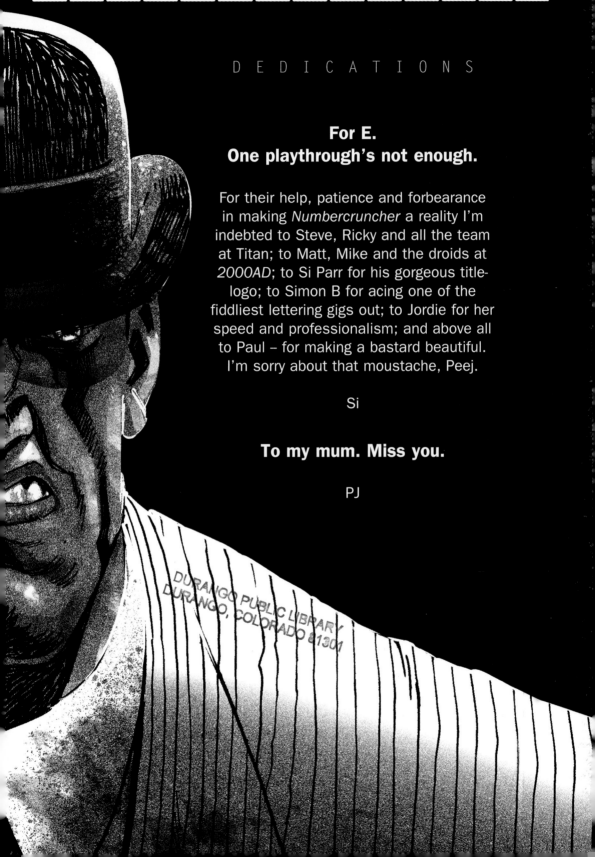

N4MBERCRUNCHER

DEDICATIONS

**For E.
One playthrough's not enough.**

For their help, patience and forbearance
in making *Numbercruncher* a reality I'm
indebted to Steve, Ricky and all the team
at Titan; to Matt, Mike and the droids at
2000AD; to Si Parr for his gorgeous title-
logo; to Simon B for acing one of the
fiddliest lettering gigs out; to Jordie for her
speed and professionalism; and above all
to Paul – for making a bastard beautiful.
I'm sorry about that moustache, Peej.

Si

To my mum. Miss you.

PJ

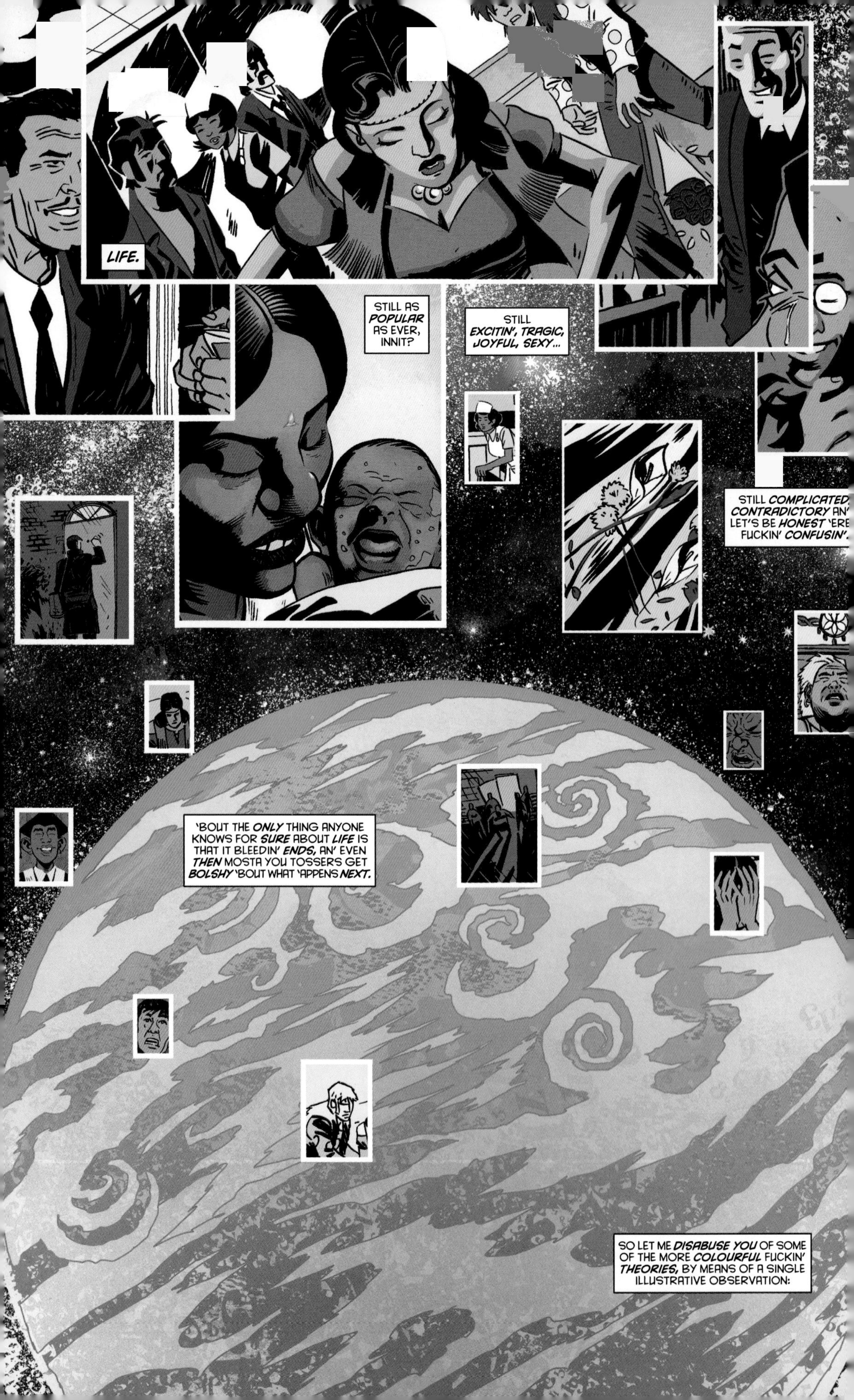
LIFE.
STILL AS POPULAR AS EVER, INNIT?
STILL EXCITIN', TRAGIC, JOYFUL, SEXY...
STILL COMPLICATED, CONTRADICTORY AN' LET'S BE HONEST 'ERE FUCKIN' CONFUSIN'.
'BOUT THE ONLY THING ANYONE KNOWS FOR SURE ABOUT LIFE IS THAT IT BLEEDIN' ENDS, AN' EVEN THEN MOSTA YOU TOSSERS GET BOLSHY 'BOUT WHAT 'APPENS NEXT.
SO LET ME DISABUSE YOU OF SOME OF THE MORE COLOURFUL FUCKIN' THEORIES, BY MEANS OF A SINGLE ILLUSTRATIVE OBSERVATION:

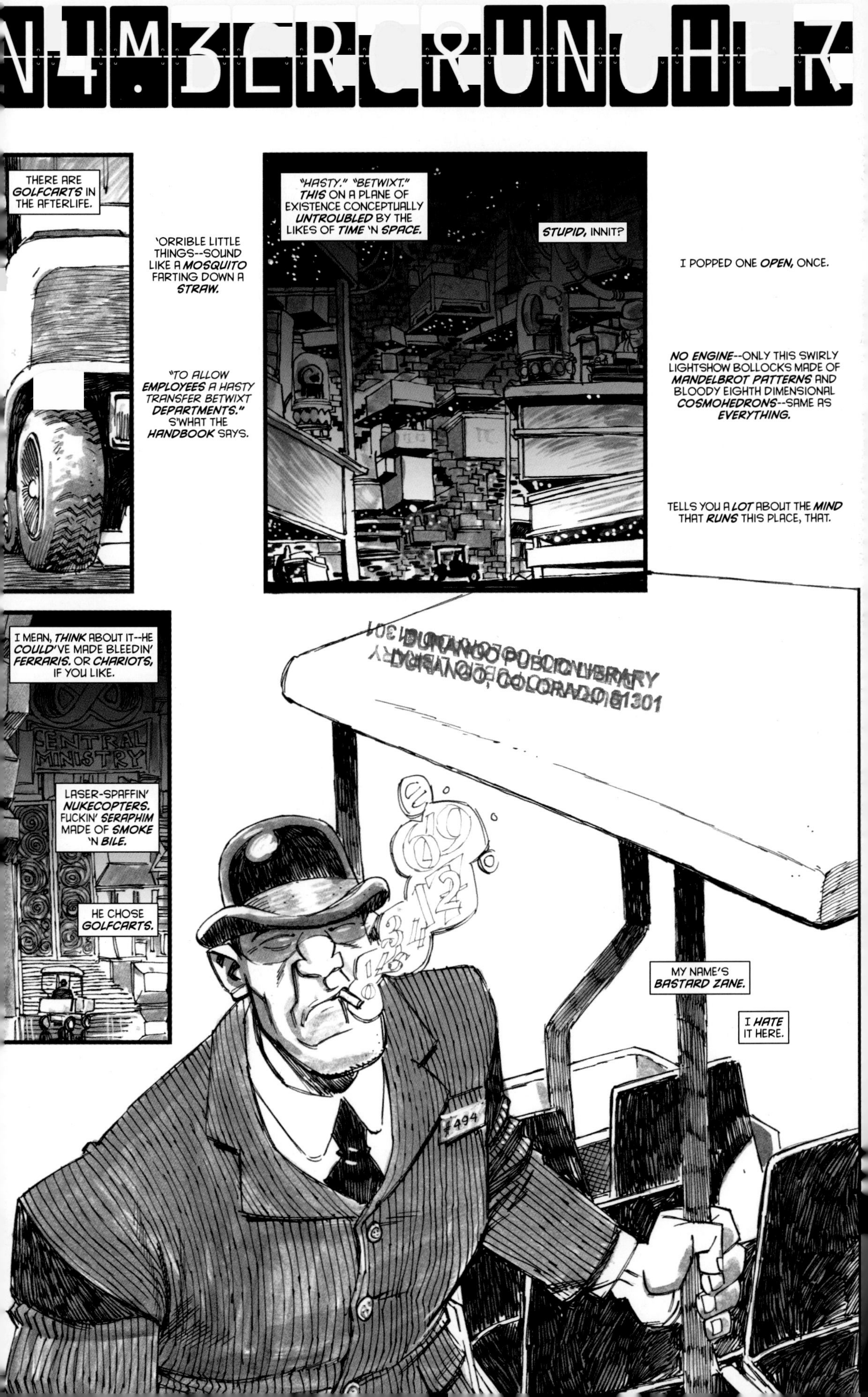
THERE ARE GOLFCARTS IN THE AFTERLIFE.
'ORRIBLE LITTLE THINGS--SOUND LIKE A MOSQUITO FARTING DOWN A STRAW.
"TO ALLOW EMPLOYEES A HASTY TRANSFER BETWIXT DEPARTMENTS." S'WHAT THE HANDBOOK SAYS.
"HASTY." "BETWIXT." THIS ON A PLANE OF EXISTENCE CONCEPTUALLY UNTROUBLED BY THE LIKES OF TIME 'N SPACE.
STUPID, INNIT?
I POPPED ONE OPEN, ONCE.
NO ENGINE--ONLY THIS SWIRLY LIGHTSHOW BOLLOCKS MADE OF MANDELBROT PATTERNS AND BLOODY EIGHTH DIMENSIONAL COSMOHEDRONS--SAME AS EVERYTHING.
TELLS YOU A LOT ABOUT THE MIND THAT RUNS THIS PLACE, THAT.
I MEAN, THINK ABOUT IT--HE COULD'VE MADE BLEEDIN' FERRARIS. OR CHARIOTS, IF YOU LIKE.
CENTRAL MINISTRY
LASER-SPAFFIN' NUKECOPTERS. FUCKIN' SERAPHIM MADE OF SMOKE 'N BILE.
HE CHOSE GOLFCARTS.
#494
MY NAME'S BASTARD ZANE.
I HATE IT HERE.

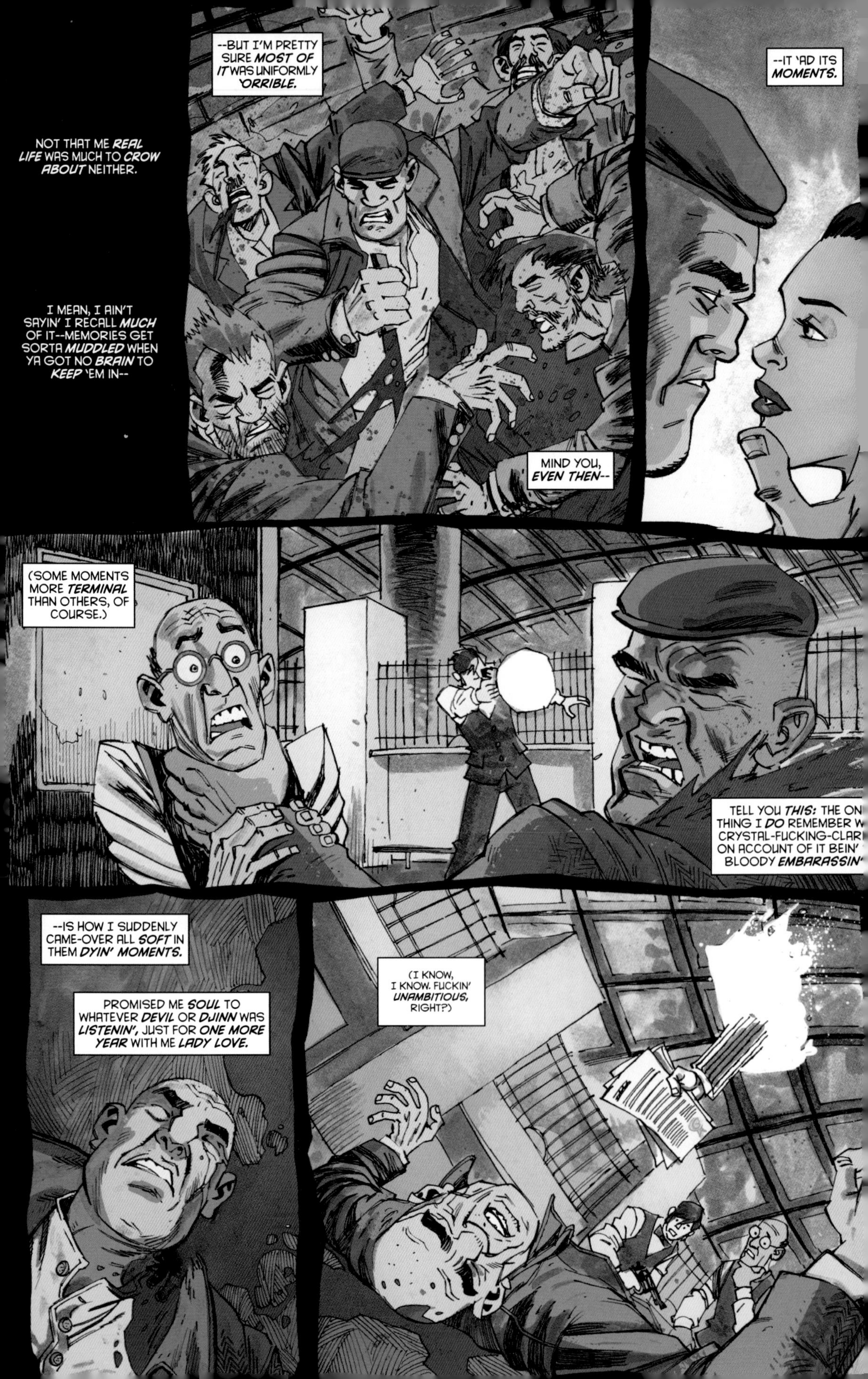
NOT THAT ME REAL LIFE WAS MUCH TO CROW ABOUT NEITHER.
I MEAN, I AIN'T SAYIN' I RECALL MUCH OF IT--MEMORIES GET SORTA MUDDLED WHEN YA GOT NO BRAIN TO KEEP 'EM IN--
--BUT I'M PRETTY SURE MOST OF IT WAS UNIFORMLY 'ORRIBLE.
MIND YOU, EVEN THEN--
--IT 'AD ITS MOMENTS.
(SOME MOMENTS MORE TERMINAL THAN OTHERS, OF COURSE.)
--IS HOW I SUDDENLY CAME-OVER ALL SOFT IN THEM DYIN' MOMENTS.
PROMISED ME SOUL TO WHATEVER DEVIL OR DJINN WAS LISTENIN', JUST FOR ONE MORE YEAR WITH ME LADY LOVE.
(I KNOW, I KNOW. FUCKIN' UNAMBITIOUS, RIGHT?)

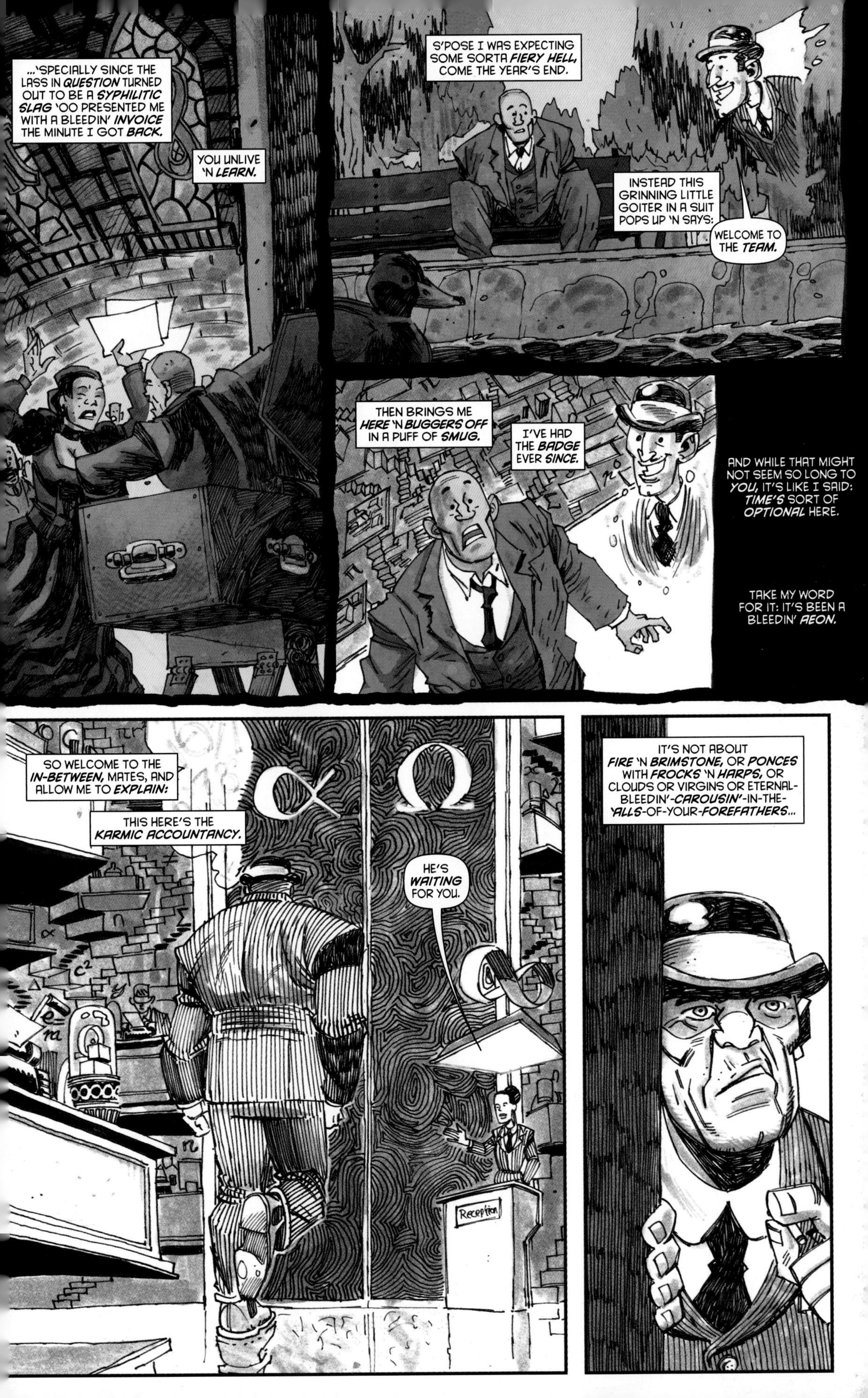
...'SPECIALLY SINCE THE LASS IN QUESTION TURNED OUT TO BE A SYPHILITIC SLAG 'OO PRESENTED ME WITH A BLEEDIN' INVOICE THE MINUTE I GOT BACK.
YOU UNLIVE 'N LEARN.
S'POSE I WAS EXPECTING SOME SORTA FIERY HELL, COME THE YEAR'S END.
INSTEAD THIS GRINNING LITTLE GOITER IN A SUIT POPS UP 'N SAYS:
WELCOME TO THE TEAM.
THEN BRINGS ME HERE 'N BUGGERS OFF IN A PUFF OF SMUG.
I'VE HAD THE BADGE EVER SINCE.
AND WHILE THAT MIGHT NOT SEEM SO LONG TO YOU, IT'S LIKE I SAID: TIME'S SORT OF OPTIONAL HERE.
TAKE MY WORD FOR IT: IT'S BEEN A BLEEDIN' AEON.
SO WELCOME TO THE IN-BETWEEN, MATES, AND ALLOW ME TO EXPLAIN:
THIS HERE'S THE KARMIC ACCOUNTANCY.
HE'S WAITING FOR YOU.
Reception
IT'S NOT ABOUT FIRE 'N BRIMSTONE, OR PONCES WITH FROCKS 'N HARPS, OR CLOUDS OR VIRGINS OR ETERNAL-BLEEDIN'-CAROUSIN'-IN-THE-'ALLS-OF-YOUR-FOREFATHERS...

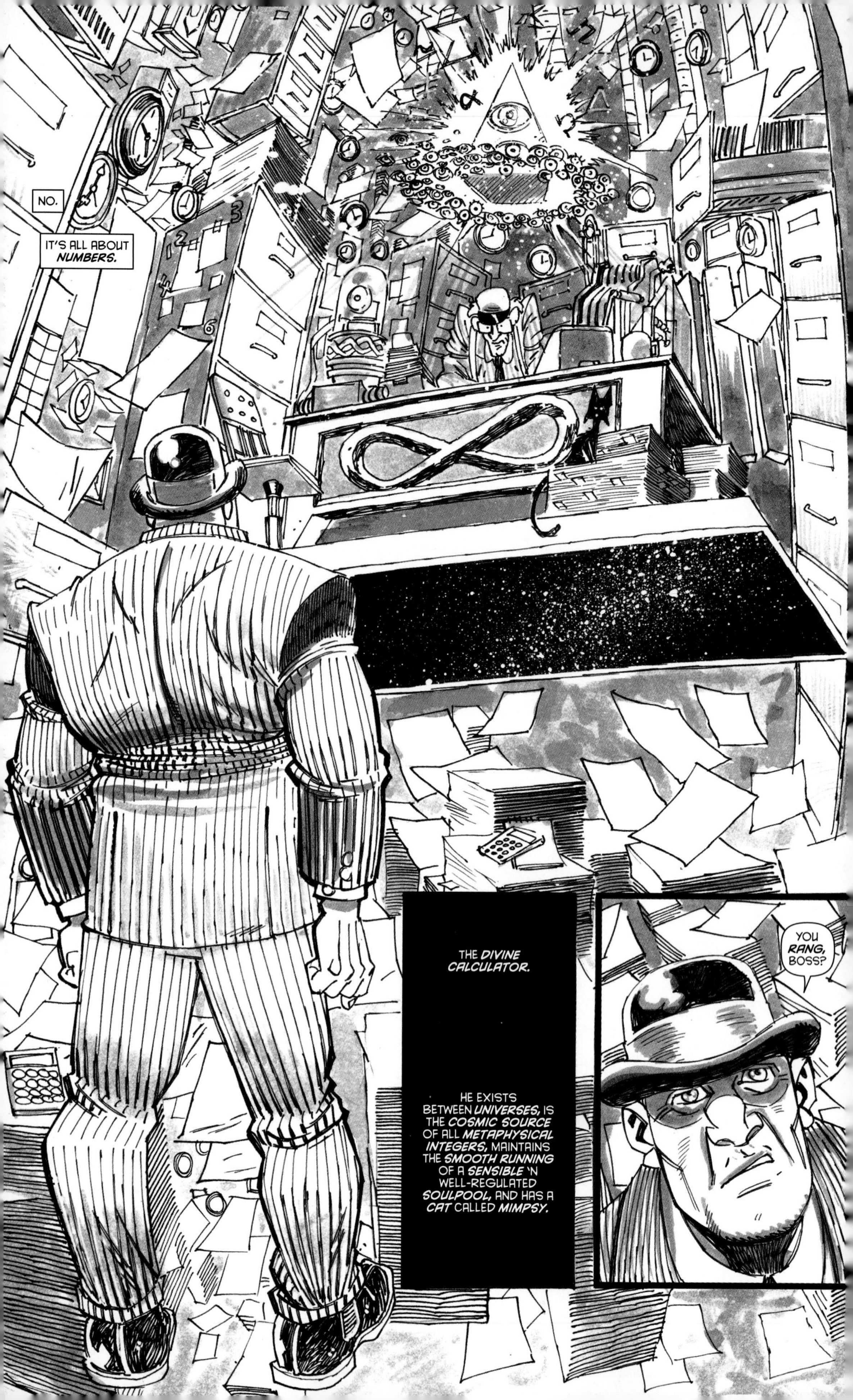
NO.
IT'S ALL ABOUT NUMBERS.
THE DIVINE CALCULATOR.
HE EXISTS BETWEEN UNIVERSES, IS THE COSMIC SOURCE OF ALL METAPHYSICAL INTEGERS, MAINTAINS THE SMOOTH RUNNING OF A SENSIBLE 'N WELL-REGULATED SOULPOOL, AND HAS A CAT CALLED MIMPSY.
YOU RANG, BOSS?

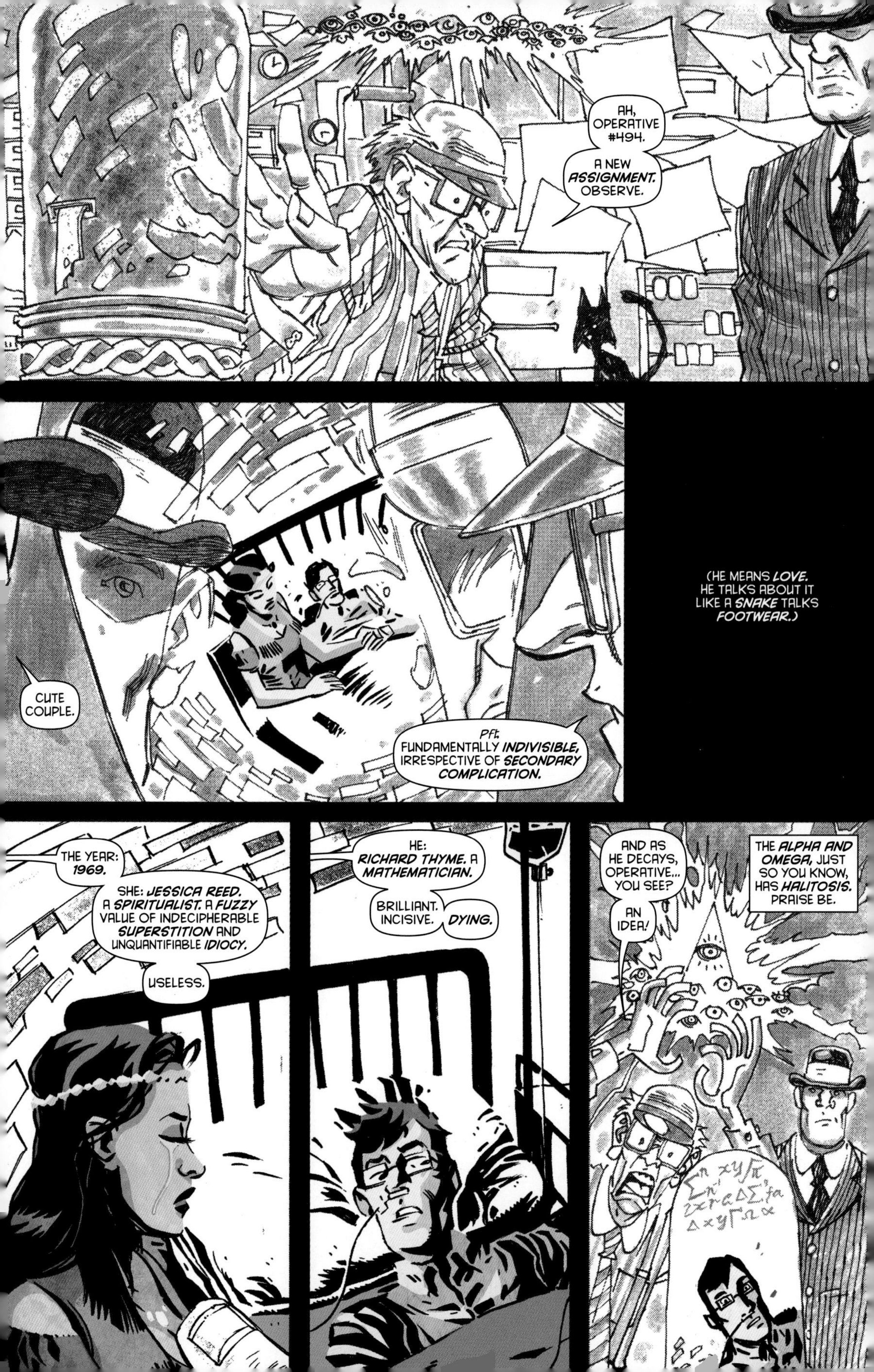

AH, OPERATIVE #494.
A NEW *ASSIGNMENT.* OBSERVE.
CUTE COUPLE.
Pft. FUNDAMENTALLY *INDIVISIBLE,* IRRESPECTIVE OF *SECONDARY COMPLICATION.*
(HE MEANS *LOVE.* HE TALKS ABOUT IT LIKE A *SNAKE* TALKS *FOOTWEAR.)*
THE YEAR: *1969.*
SHE: *JESSICA REED.* A *SPIRITUALIST.* A *FUZZY* VALUE OF INDECIPHERABLE *SUPERSTITION* AND UNQUANTIFIABLE *IDIOCY.*
USELESS.
HE: *RICHARD THYME.* A *MATHEMATICIAN.*
BRILLIANT. INCISIVE.
DYING.
AND AS HE DECAYS, OPERATIVE... YOU SEE?
AN IDEA!
THE *ALPHA AND OMEGA,* JUST SO YOU KNOW, HAS *HALITOSIS.* PRAISE BE.

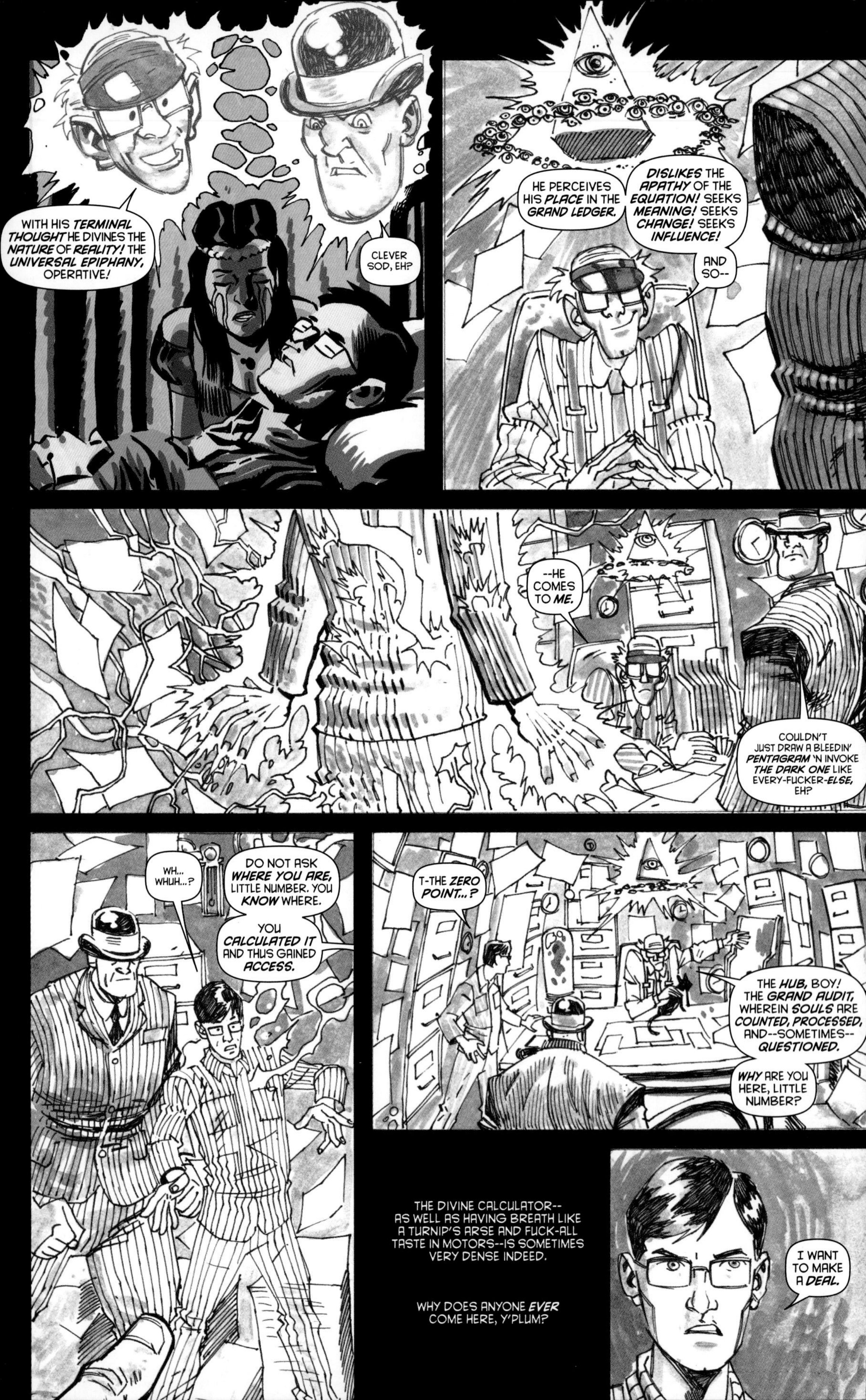
WITH HIS TERMINAL THOUGHT HE DIVINES THE NATURE OF REALITY! THE UNIVERSAL EPIPHANY, OPERATIVE!
CLEVER SOD, EH?
HE PERCEIVES HIS PLACE IN THE GRAND LEDGER.
DISLIKES THE APATHY OF THE EQUATION! SEEKS MEANING! SEEKS CHANGE! SEEKS INFLUENCE!
AND SO--
--HE COMES TO ME.
COULDN'T JUST DRAW A BLEEDIN' PENTAGRAM 'N INVOKE THE DARK ONE LIKE EVERY-FUCKER-ELSE, EH?
WH... WHUH...?
DO NOT ASK WHERE YOU ARE, LITTLE NUMBER. YOU KNOW WHERE.
YOU CALCULATED IT AND THUS GAINED ACCESS.
T-THE ZERO POINT...?
THE HUB, BOY! THE GRAND AUDIT, WHEREIN SOULS ARE COUNTED, PROCESSED, AND--SOMETIMES--QUESTIONED.
WHY ARE YOU HERE, LITTLE NUMBER?
THE DIVINE CALCULATOR-- AS WELL AS HAVING BREATH LIKE A TURNIP'S ARSE AND FUCK-ALL TASTE IN MOTORS--IS SOMETIMES VERY DENSE INDEED.
WHY DOES ANYONE EVER COME HERE, Y'PLUM?
I WANT TO MAKE A DEAL.

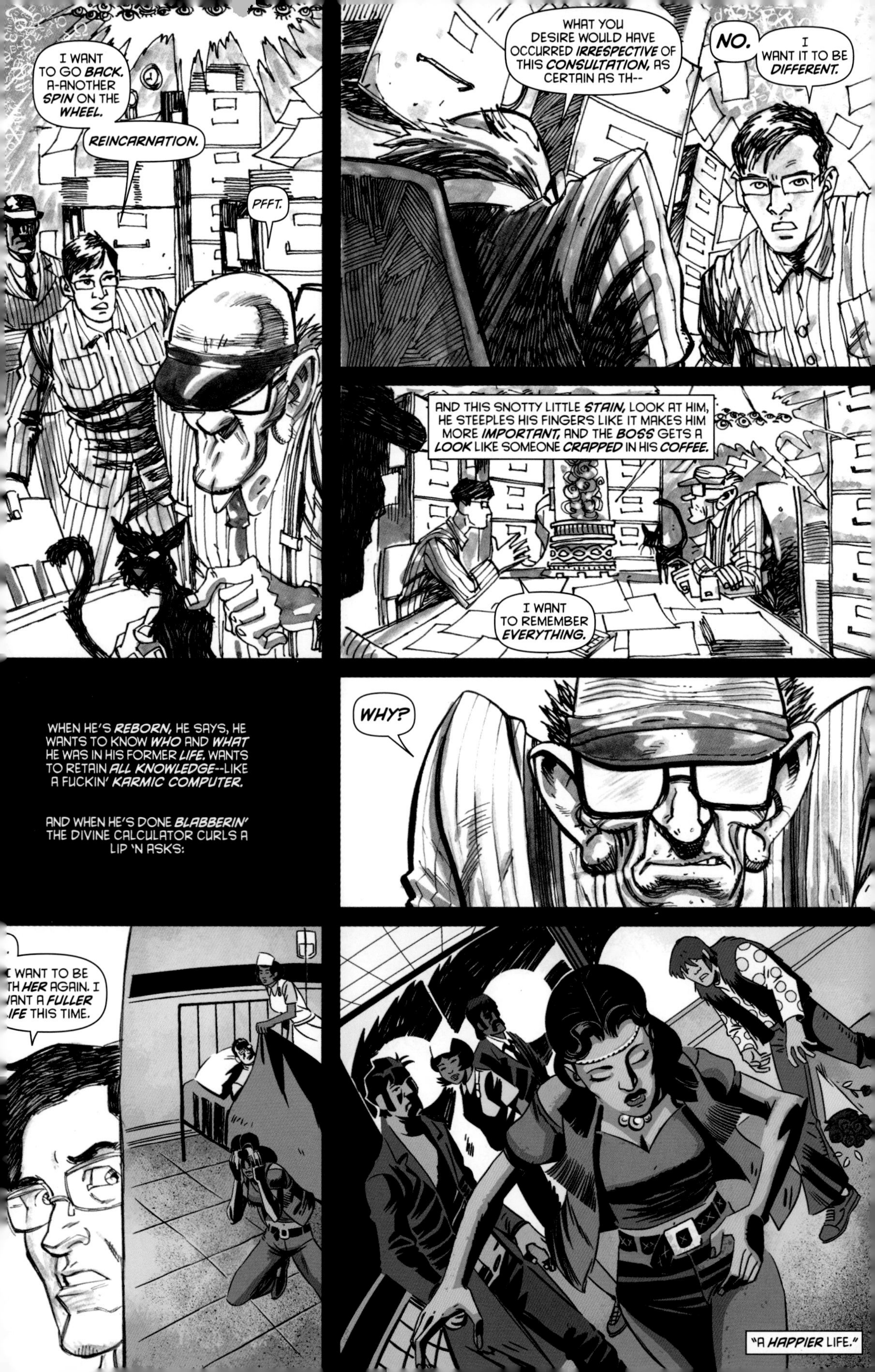
I WANT TO GO BACK. A-ANOTHER SPIN ON THE WHEEL.
REINCARNATION.
PFFT.
WHAT YOU DESIRE WOULD HAVE OCCURRED IRRESPECTIVE OF THIS CONSULTATION, AS CERTAIN AS TH--
NO.
I WANT IT TO BE DIFFERENT.
AND THIS SNOTTY LITTLE STAIN, LOOK AT HIM, HE STEEPLES HIS FINGERS LIKE IT MAKES HIM MORE IMPORTANT, AND THE BOSS GETS A LOOK LIKE SOMEONE CRAPPED IN HIS COFFEE.
I WANT TO REMEMBER EVERYTHING.
WHEN HE'S REBORN, HE SAYS, HE WANTS TO KNOW WHO AND WHAT HE WAS IN HIS FORMER LIFE. WANTS TO RETAIN ALL KNOWLEDGE--LIKE A FUCKIN' KARMIC COMPUTER.
AND WHEN HE'S DONE BLABBERIN' THE DIVINE CALCULATOR CURLS A LIP 'N ASKS:
WHY?
WANT TO BE TH HER AGAIN. I ANT A FULLER IFE THIS TIME.
"A HAPPIER LIFE."

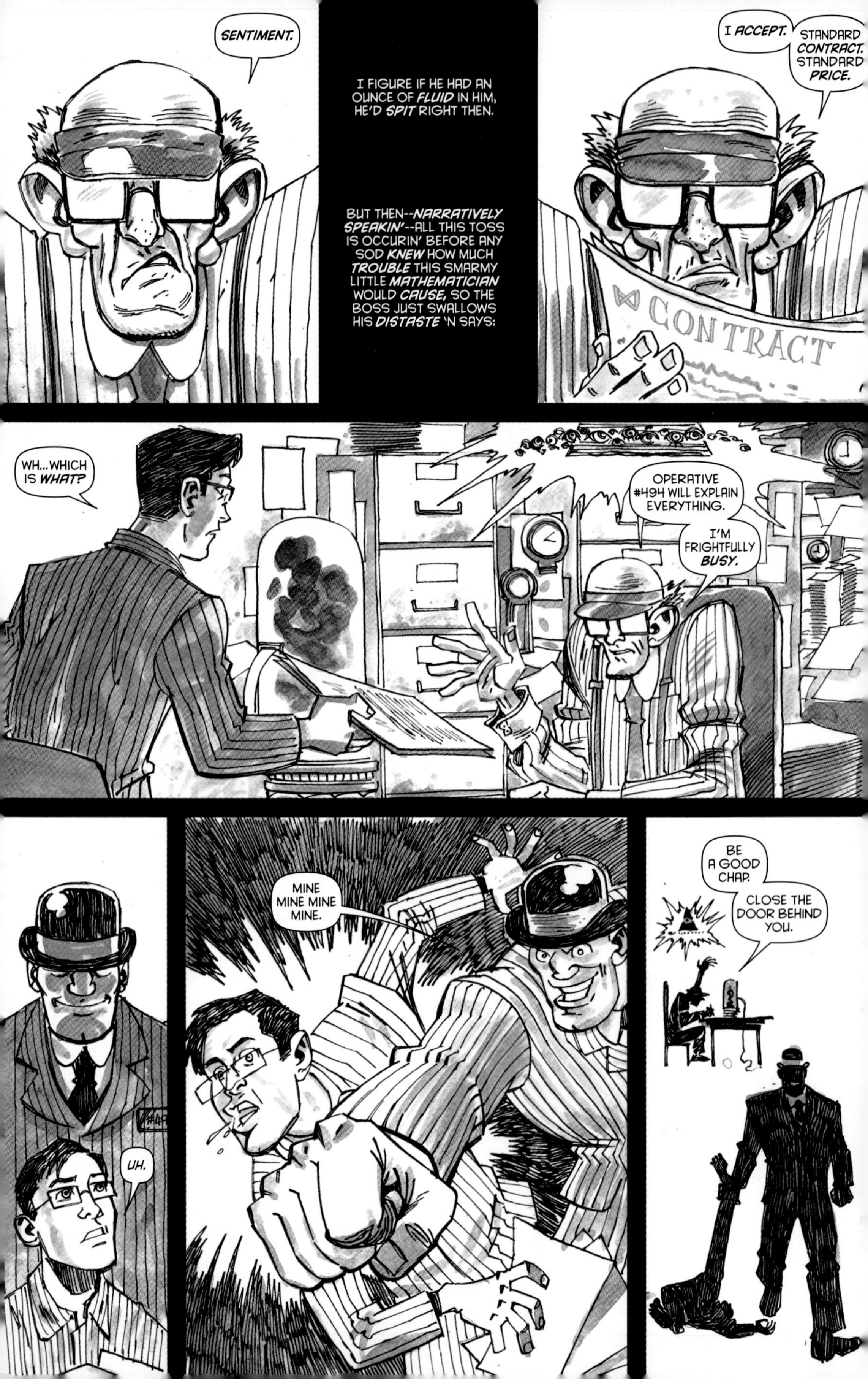
SENTIMENT.
I FIGURE IF HE HAD AN OUNCE OF FLUID IN HIM, HE'D SPIT RIGHT THEN.
BUT THEN--NARRATIVELY SPEAKIN'--ALL THIS TOSS IS OCCURIN' BEFORE ANY SOD KNEW HOW MUCH TROUBLE THIS SMARMY LITTLE MATHEMATICIAN WOULD CAUSE, SO THE BOSS JUST SWALLOWS HIS DISTASTE 'N SAYS:
I ACCEPT.
STANDARD CONTRACT. STANDARD PRICE.
CONTRACT
WH...WHICH IS WHAT?
OPERATIVE #494 WILL EXPLAIN EVERYTHING.
I'M FRIGHTFULLY BUSY.
UH.
MINE MINE MINE MINE.
BE A GOOD CHAP.
CLOSE THE DOOR BEHIND YOU.

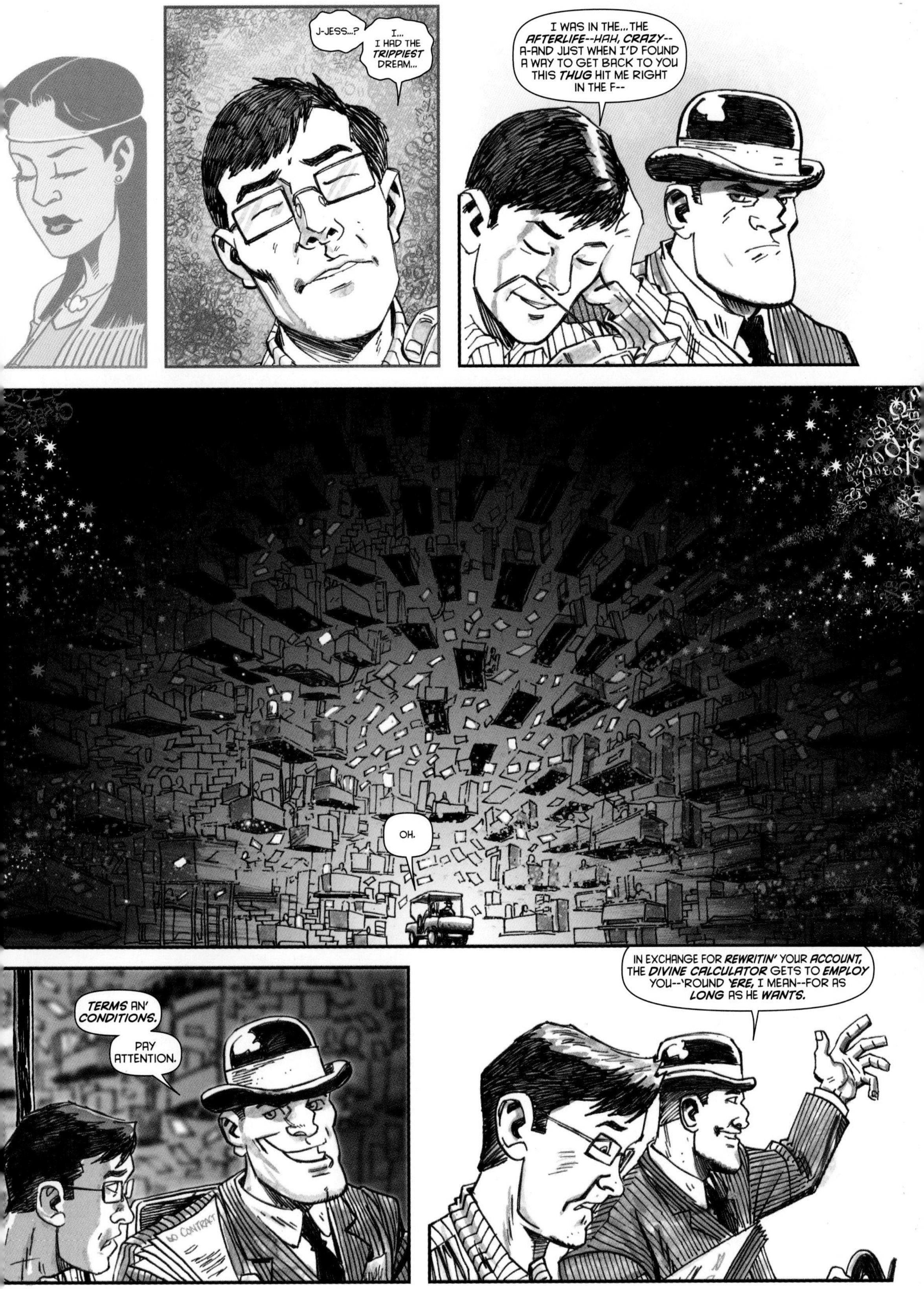
J-JESS...?
I... I HAD THE TRIPPIEST DREAM...
I WAS IN THE... THE AFTERLIFE--HAH, CRAZY-- A-AND JUST WHEN I'D FOUND A WAY TO GET BACK TO YOU THIS THUG HIT ME RIGHT IN THE F--
OH.
TERMS AN' CONDITIONS.
PAY ATTENTION.
IN EXCHANGE FOR REWRITIN' YOUR ACCOUNT, THE DIVINE CALCULATOR GETS TO EMPLOY YOU--'ROUND 'ERE, I MEAN--FOR AS LONG AS HE WANTS.

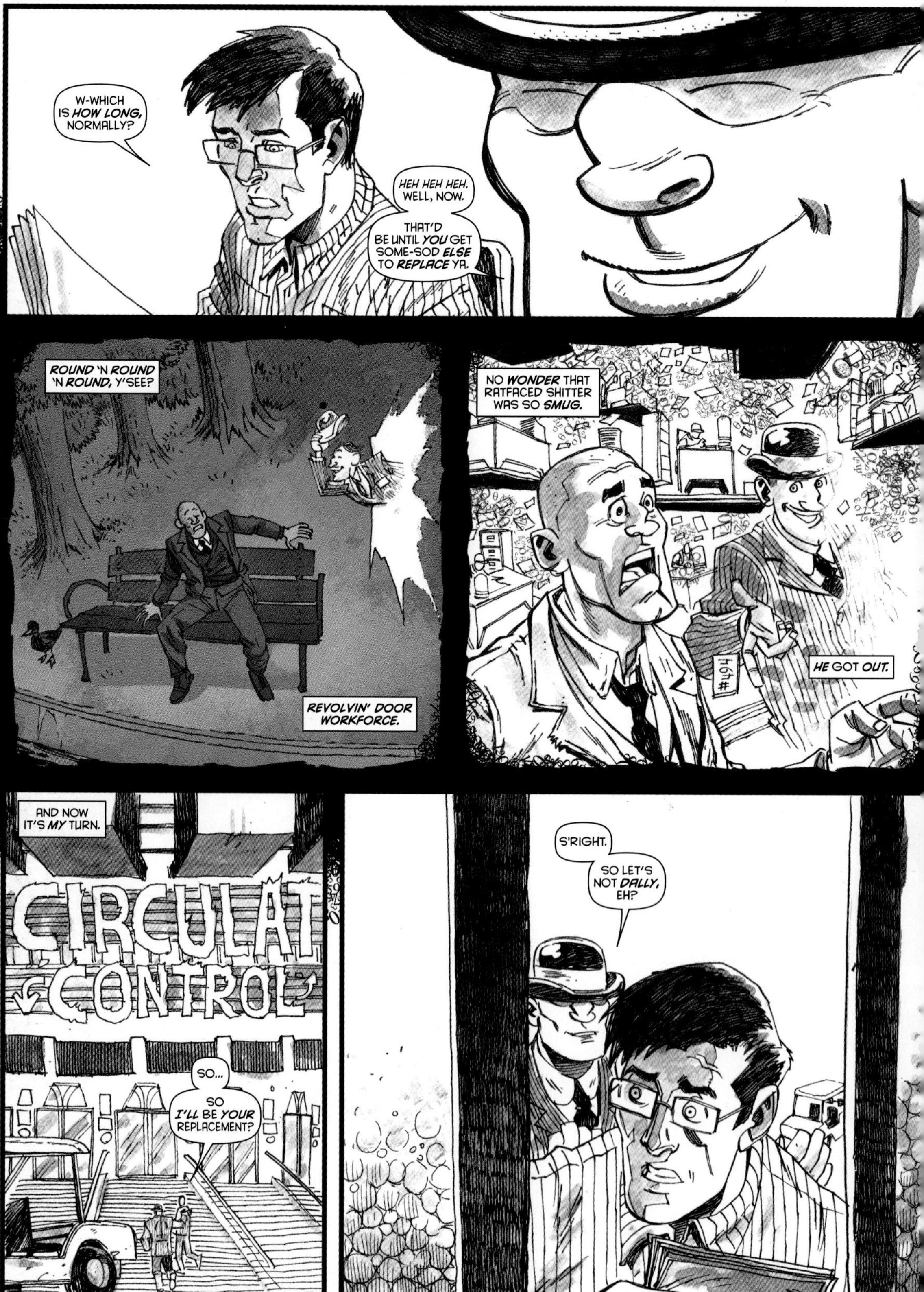
W-WHICH IS HOW LONG, NORMALLY?
HEH HEH HEH. WELL, NOW.
THAT'D BE UNTIL YOU GET SOME-SOD ELSE TO REPLACE YA.
ROUND 'N ROUND 'N ROUND, Y'SEE?
REVOLVIN' DOOR WORKFORCE.
NO WONDER THAT RATFACED SHITTER WAS SO SMUG.
HE GOT OUT.
AND NOW IT'S MY TURN.
CIRCULAT
CONTROL
SO...
SO I'LL BE YOUR REPLACEMENT?
S'RIGHT.
SO LET'S NOT DALLY, EH?

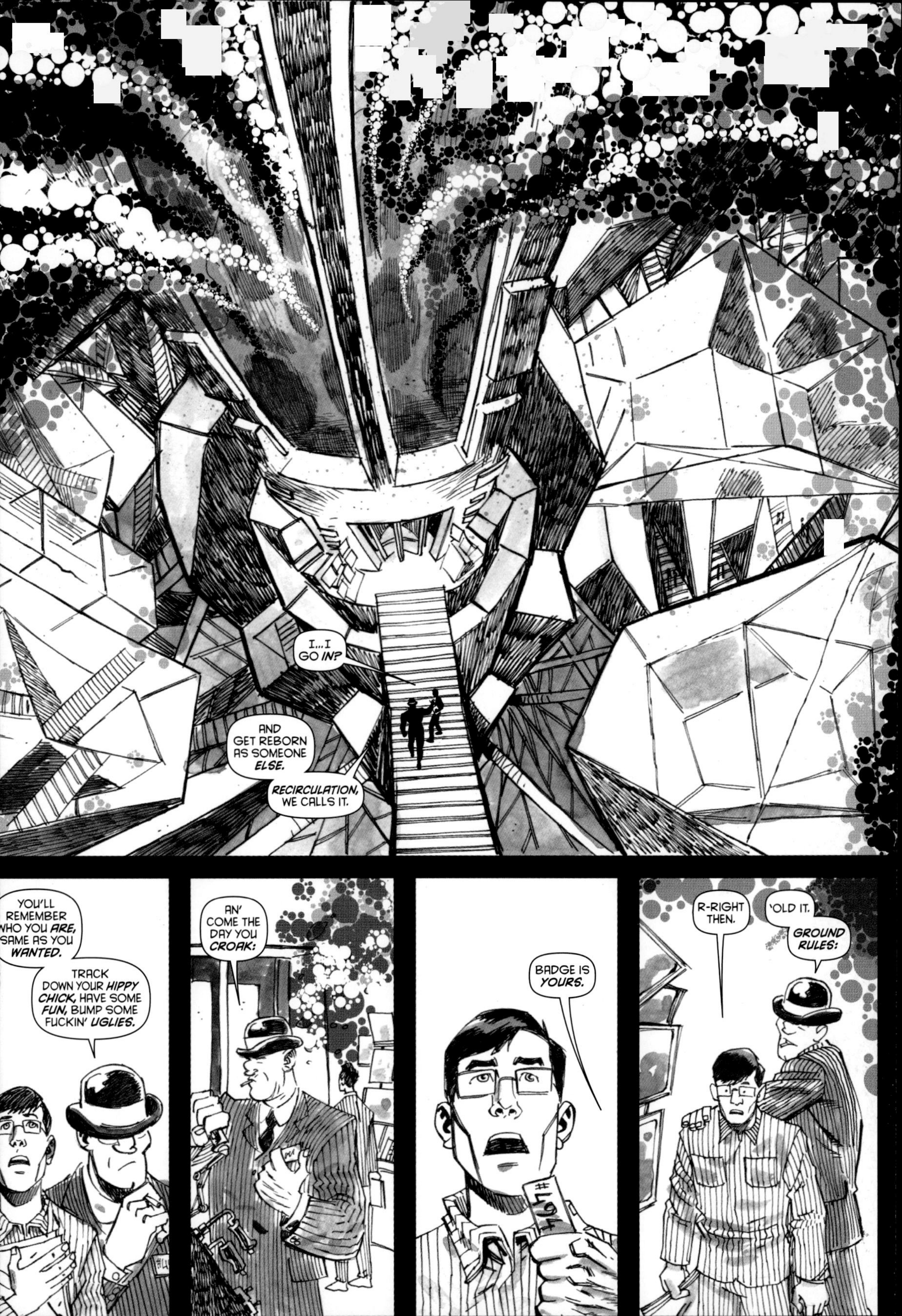
I... I GO *IN?*
AND GET REBORN AS SOMEONE *ELSE.*
RECIRCULATION, WE CALLS IT.
YOU'LL REMEMBER WHO YOU *ARE,* SAME AS YOU *WANTED.*
TRACK DOWN YOUR *HIPPY CHICK,* HAVE SOME *FUN,* BUMP SOME FUCKIN' *UGLIES.*
AN' COME THE DAY YOU *CROAK:*
BADGE IS *YOURS.*
R-RIGHT THEN.
'OLD IT.
GROUND RULES:

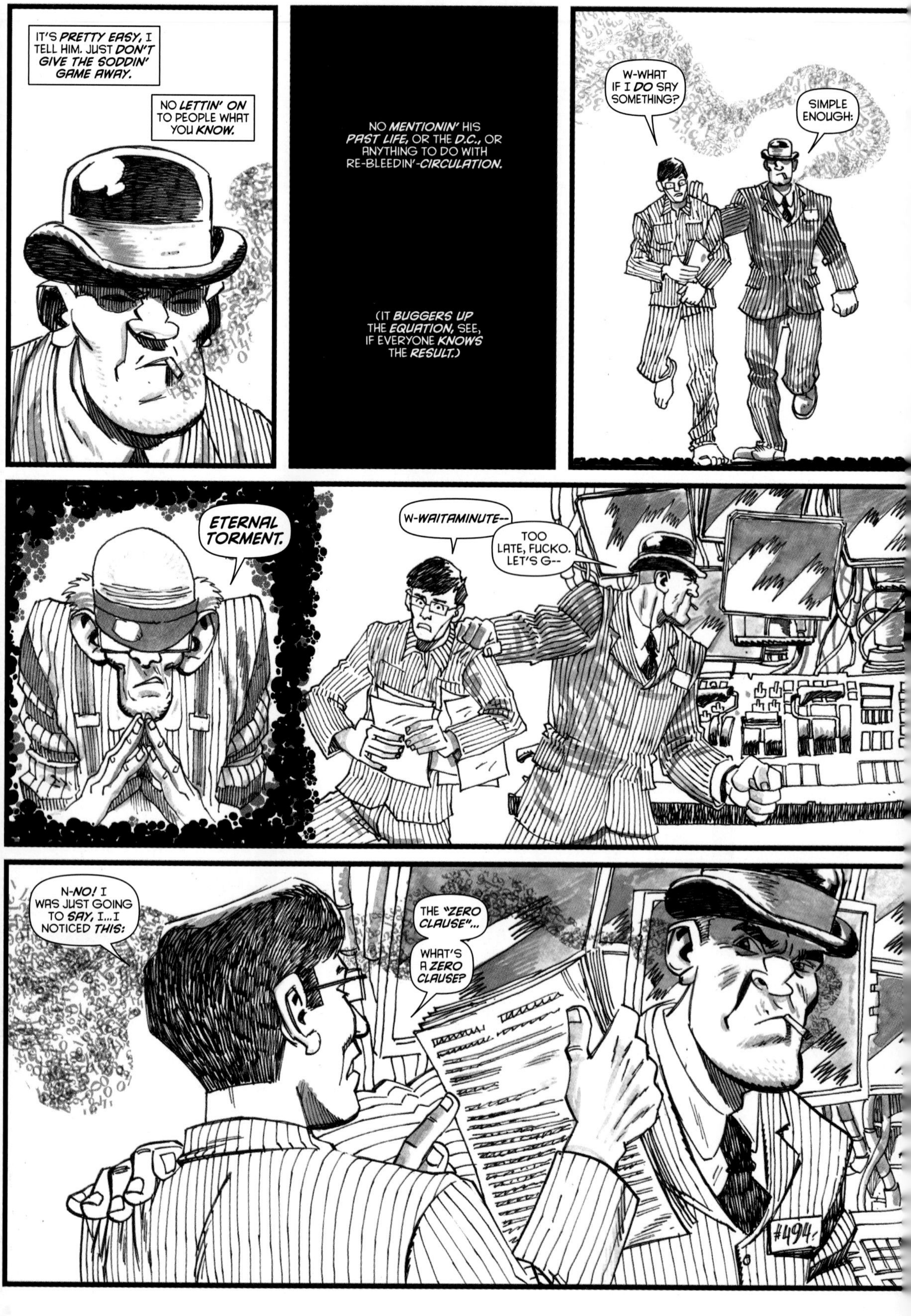

IT'S PRETTY EASY, I TELL HIM. JUST DON'T GIVE THE SODDIN' GAME AWAY.
NO LETTIN' ON TO PEOPLE WHAT YOU KNOW.
NO MENTIONIN' HIS PAST LIFE, OR THE D.C., OR ANYTHING TO DO WITH RE-BLEEDIN'-CIRCULATION.
(IT BUGGERS UP THE EQUATION, SEE, IF EVERYONE KNOWS THE RESULT.)
W-WHAT IF I DO SAY SOMETHING?
SIMPLE ENOUGH:
ETERNAL TORMENT.
W-WAITAMINUTE--
TOO LATE, FUCKO. LET'S G--
N-NO! I WAS JUST GOING TO SAY, I...I NOTICED THIS:
THE "ZERO CLAUSE"...
WHAT'S A ZERO CLAUSE?
#494

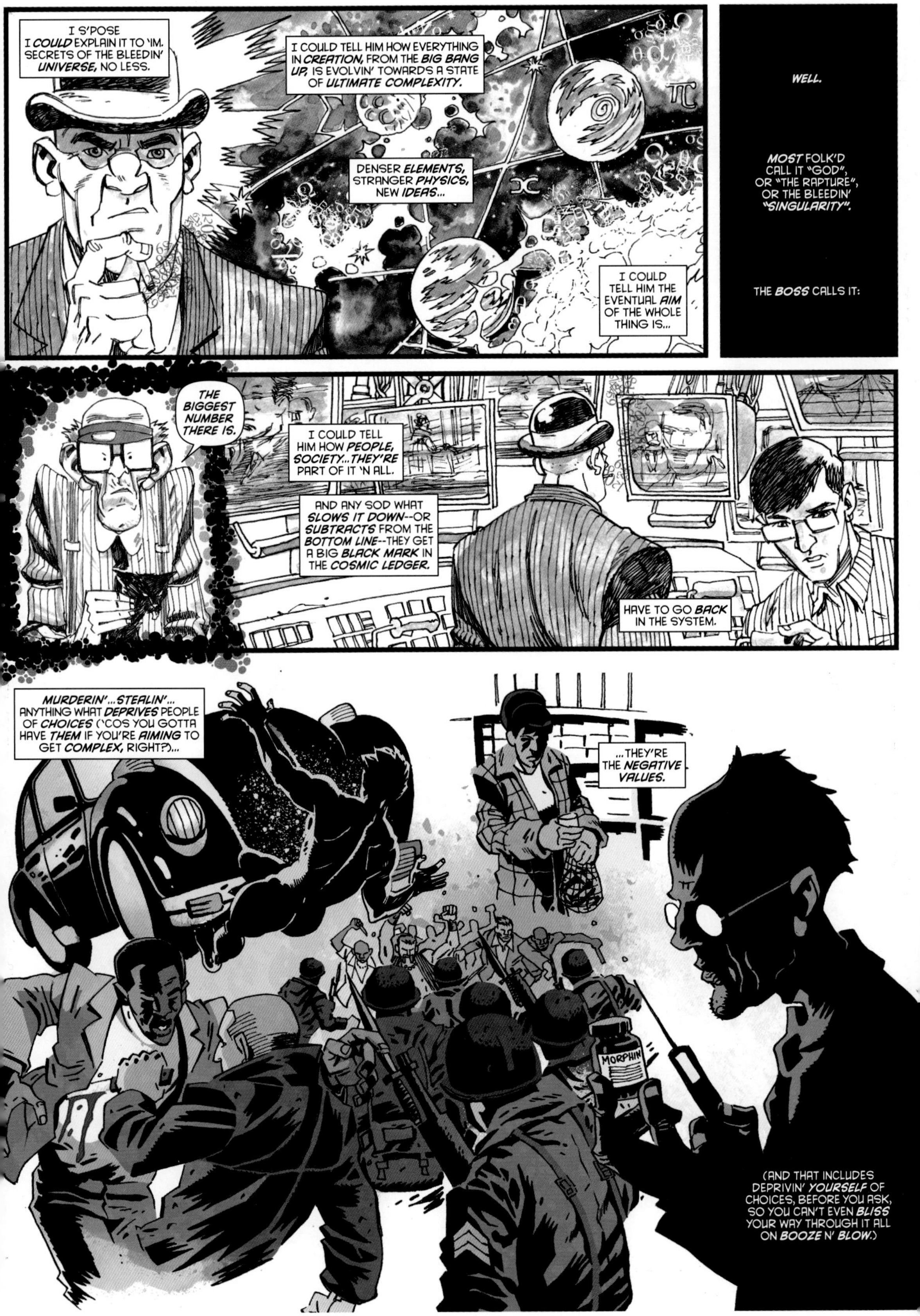
I S'POSE I *COULD* EXPLAIN IT TO 'IM. SECRETS OF THE BLEEDIN' *UNIVERSE,* NO LESS.
I COULD TELL HIM HOW EVERYTHING IN *CREATION,* FROM THE *BIG BANG UP,* IS EVOLVIN' TOWARDS A STATE OF *ULTIMATE COMPLEXITY.*
DENSER *ELEMENTS,* STRANGER *PHYSICS,* NEW *IDEAS*...
I COULD TELL HIM THE EVENTUAL *AIM* OF THE WHOLE THING IS...
WELL.
MOST FOLK'D CALL IT "GOD", OR "THE RAPTURE", OR THE BLEEDIN' *"SINGULARITY".*
THE *BOSS* CALLS IT:
THE BIGGEST NUMBER THERE IS.
I COULD TELL HIM HOW *PEOPLE, SOCIETY...THEY'RE* PART OF IT 'N ALL.
AND ANY SOD WHAT *SLOWS IT DOWN*--OR *SUBTRACTS* FROM THE *BOTTOM LINE*--THEY GET A BIG *BLACK MARK* IN THE *COSMIC LEDGER.*
HAVE TO GO *BACK* IN THE SYSTEM.
MURDERIN'...STEALIN'... ANYTHING WHAT *DEPRIVES* PEOPLE OF *CHOICES* ('COS YOU GOTTA HAVE *THEM* IF YOU'RE *AIMING* TO GET *COMPLEX,* RIGHT?)...
...THEY'RE THE *NEGATIVE VALUES.*
MORPHIN
(AND THAT INCLUDES DEPRIVIN' *YOURSELF* OF CHOICES, BEFORE YOU ASK, SO YOU CAN'T EVEN *BLISS* YOUR WAY THROUGH IT ALL ON *BOOZE* N' *BLOW.*)

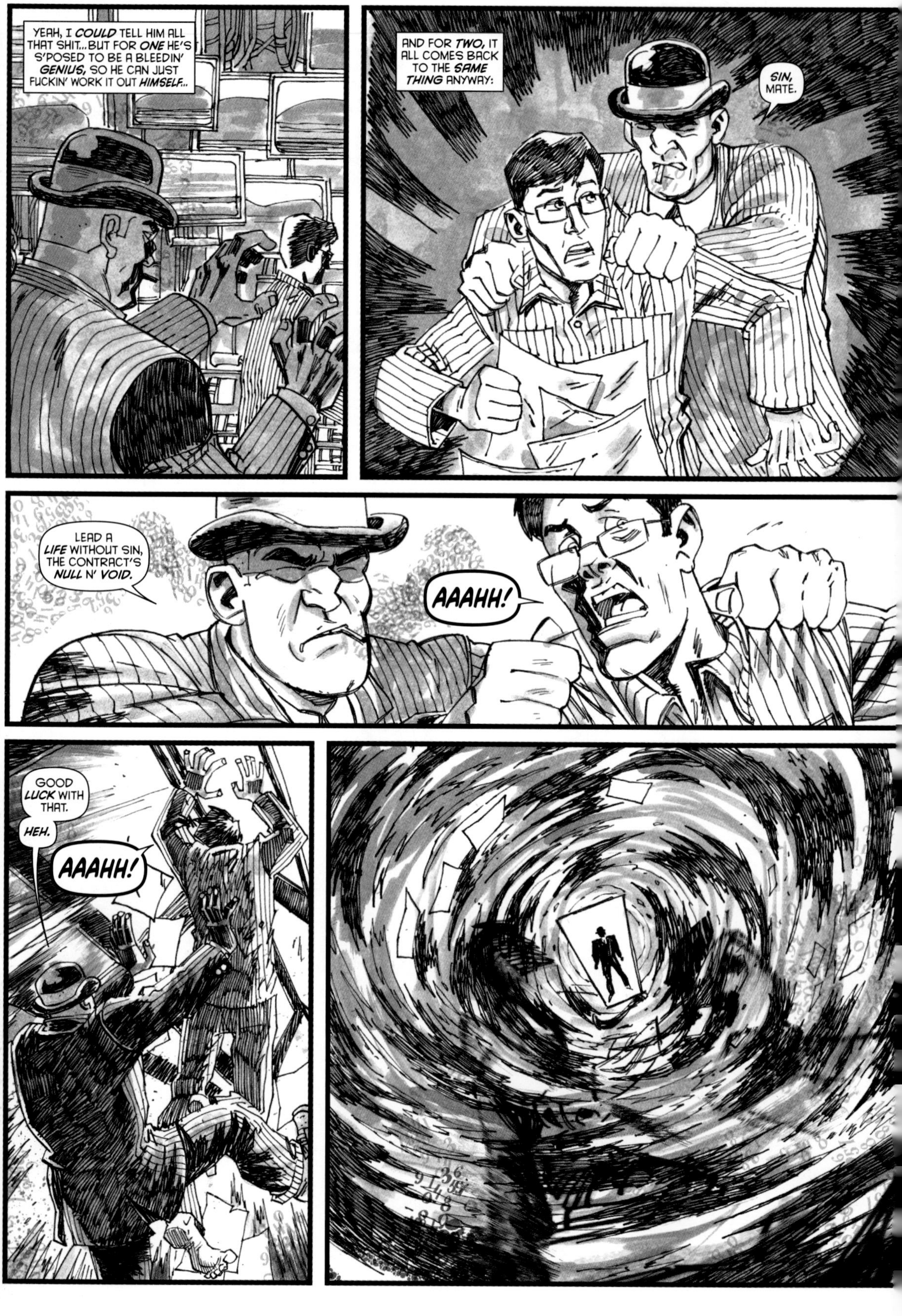
YEAH, I COULD TELL HIM ALL THAT SHIT...BUT FOR ONE HE'S S'POSED TO BE A BLEEDIN' GENIUS, SO HE CAN JUST FUCKIN' WORK IT OUT HIMSELF...
AND FOR TWO, IT ALL COMES BACK TO THE SAME THING ANYWAY:
SIN, MATE.
LEAD A LIFE WITHOUT SIN, THE CONTRACT'S NULL N' VOID.
AAAHH!
GOOD LUCK WITH THAT.
HEH.
AAAHH!

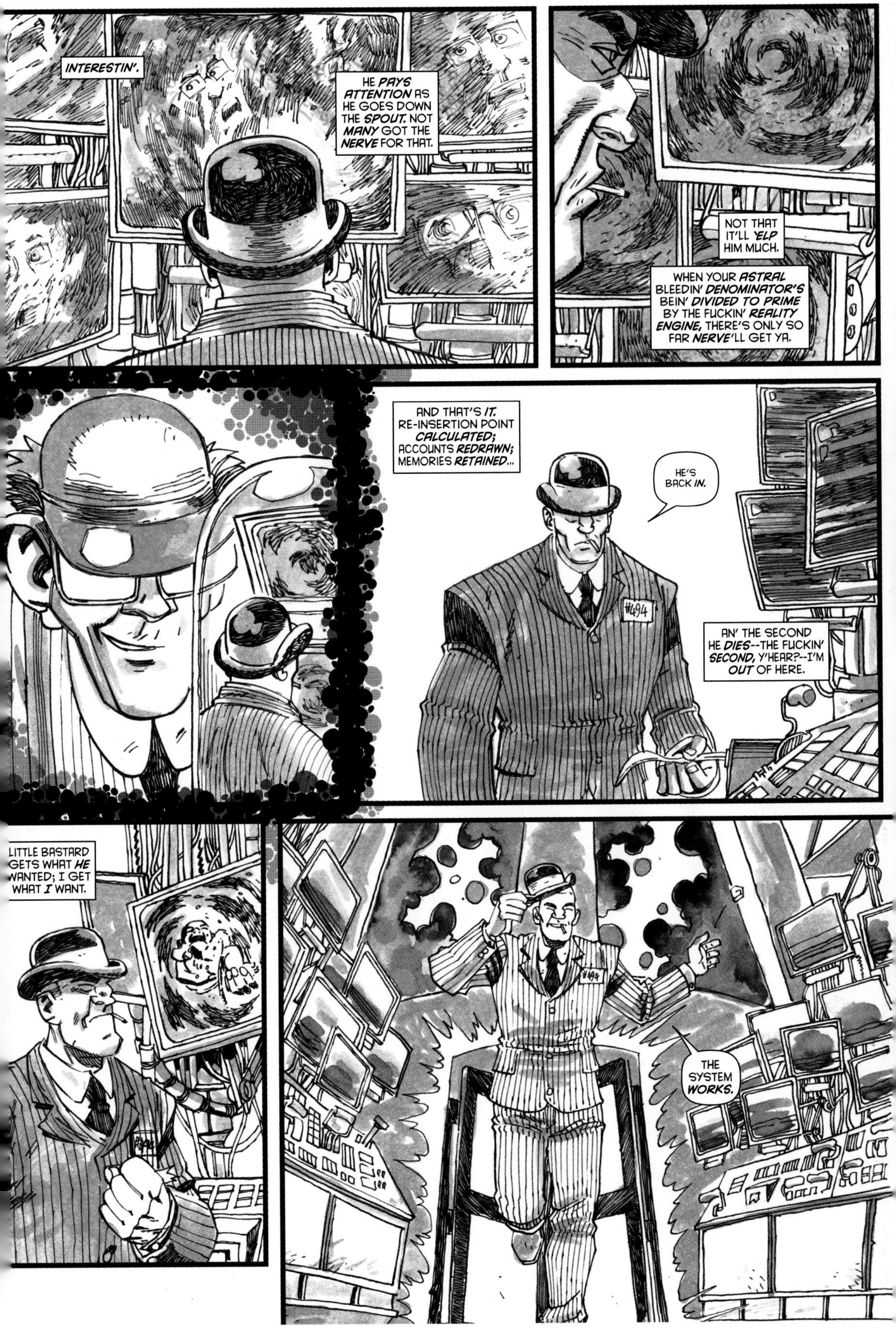
INTERESTIN'.
HE PAYS ATTENTION AS HE GOES DOWN THE SPOUT. NOT MANY GOT THE NERVE FOR THAT.
NOT THAT IT'LL YELP HIM MUCH.
WHEN YOUR ASTRAL BLEEDIN' DENOMINATOR'S BEIN' DIVIDED TO PRIME BY THE FUCKIN' REALITY ENGINE, THERE'S ONLY SO FAR NERVE'LL GET YA.
AND THAT'S IT. RE-INSERTION POINT CALCULATED; ACCOUNTS REDRAWN; MEMORIES RETAINED...
HE'S BACK IN.
AN' THE SECOND HE DIES--THE FUCKIN' SECOND, Y'HEAR?--I'M OUT OF HERE.
LITTLE BASTARD GETS WHAT HE WANTED; I GET WHAT I WANT.
THE SYSTEM WORKS.

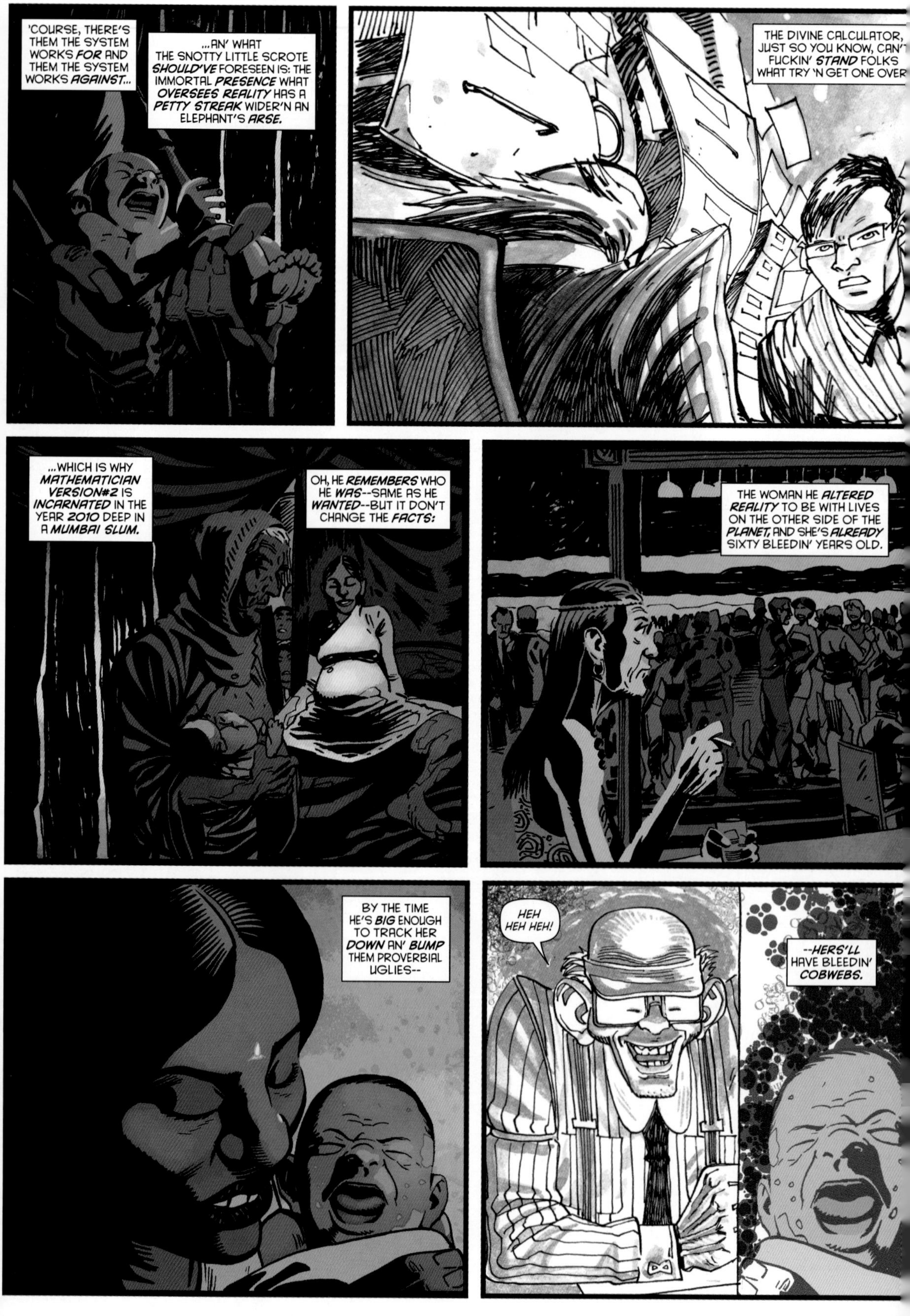
'COURSE, THERE'S THEM THE SYSTEM WORKS *FOR* AND THEM THE SYSTEM WORKS *AGAINST*...
...AN' WHAT THE SNOTTY LITTLE SCROTE *SHOULD'VE* FORESEEN IS: THE IMMORTAL *PRESENCE* WHAT *OVERSEES REALITY* HAS A *PETTY STREAK* WIDER'N AN ELEPHANT'S *ARSE.*
THE DIVINE CALCULATOR, JUST SO YOU KNOW, CAN'T FUCKIN' *STAND* FOLKS WHAT TRY 'N GET ONE OVER
...WHICH IS WHY *MATHEMATICIAN VERSION#2* IS *INCARNATED* IN THE YEAR *2010* DEEP IN A *MUMBAI SLUM.*
OH, HE *REMEMBERS* WHO HE *WAS*--SAME AS HE *WANTED*--BUT IT DON'T CHANGE THE *FACTS:*
THE WOMAN HE *ALTERED REALITY* TO BE WITH LIVES ON THE OTHER SIDE OF THE *PLANET,* AND SHE'S *ALREADY* SIXTY BLEEDIN' YEARS OLD.
BY THE TIME HE'S *BIG* ENOUGH TO TRACK HER *DOWN* AN' *BUMP* THEM PROVERBIAL UGLIES--
HEH HEH HEH!
--*HERS'LL* HAVE BLEEDIN' *COBWEBS.*

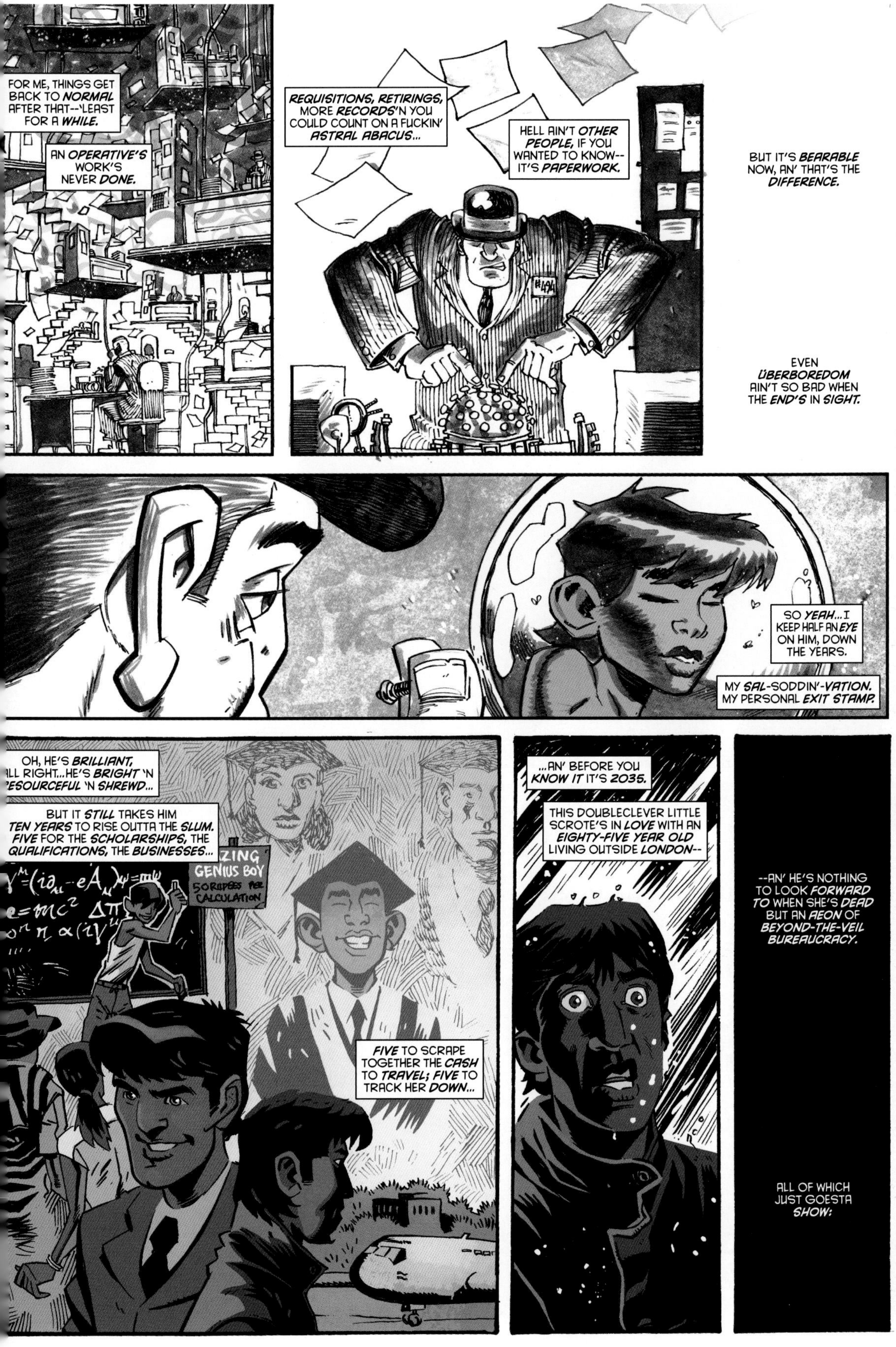

FOR ME, THINGS GET BACK TO NORMAL AFTER THAT--'LEAST FOR A WHILE.
AN OPERATIVE'S WORK'S NEVER DONE.
REQUISITIONS, RETIRINGS, MORE RECORDS'N YOU COULD COUNT ON A FUCKIN' ASTRAL ABACUS...
HELL AIN'T OTHER PEOPLE, IF YOU WANTED TO KNOW-- IT'S PAPERWORK.
BUT IT'S BEARABLE NOW, AN' THAT'S THE DIFFERENCE.
EVEN ÜBERBOREDOM AIN'T SO BAD WHEN THE END'S IN SIGHT.
SO YEAH...I KEEP HALF AN EYE ON HIM, DOWN THE YEARS.
MY SAL-SODDIN'-VATION. MY PERSONAL EXIT STAMP.
OH, HE'S BRILLIANT, LL RIGHT...HE'S BRIGHT 'N ESOURCEFUL 'N SHREWD...
BUT IT STILL TAKES HIM TEN YEARS TO RISE OUTTA THE SLUM. FIVE FOR THE SCHOLARSHIPS, THE QUALIFICATIONS, THE BUSINESSES...
ZING
GENIUS BOY
50 RUPEES PER CALCULATION
FIVE TO SCRAPE TOGETHER THE CASH TO TRAVEL; FIVE TO TRACK HER DOWN...
...AN' BEFORE YOU KNOW IT IT'S 2035.
THIS DOUBLECLEVER LITTLE SCROTE'S IN LOVE WITH AN EIGHTY-FIVE YEAR OLD LIVING OUTSIDE LONDON--
--AN' HE'S NOTHING TO LOOK FORWARD TO WHEN SHE'S DEAD BUT AN AEON OF BEYOND-THE-VEIL BUREAUCRACY.
ALL OF WHICH JUST GOESTA SHOW:

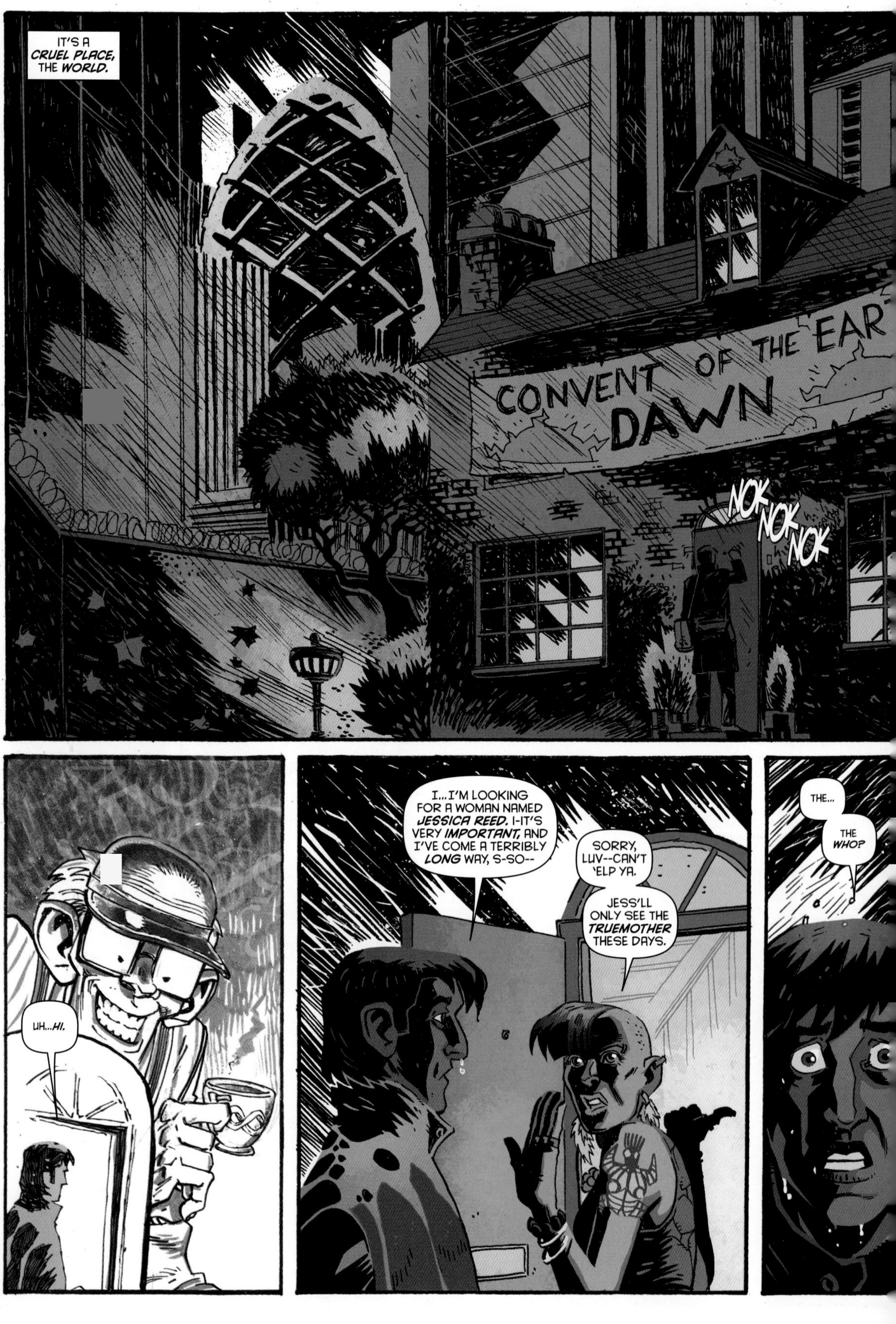
IT'S A CRUEL PLACE, THE WORLD.
CONVENT OF THE EAR
DAWN
NOK NOK NOK
UH...HI.
I...I'M LOOKING FOR A WOMAN NAMED JESSICA REED. I-IT'S VERY IMPORTANT, AND I'VE COME A TERRIBLY LONG WAY, S-SO--
SORRY, LUV--CAN'T 'ELP YA.
JESS'LL ONLY SEE THE TRUEMOTHER THESE DAYS.
THE...
THE WHO?

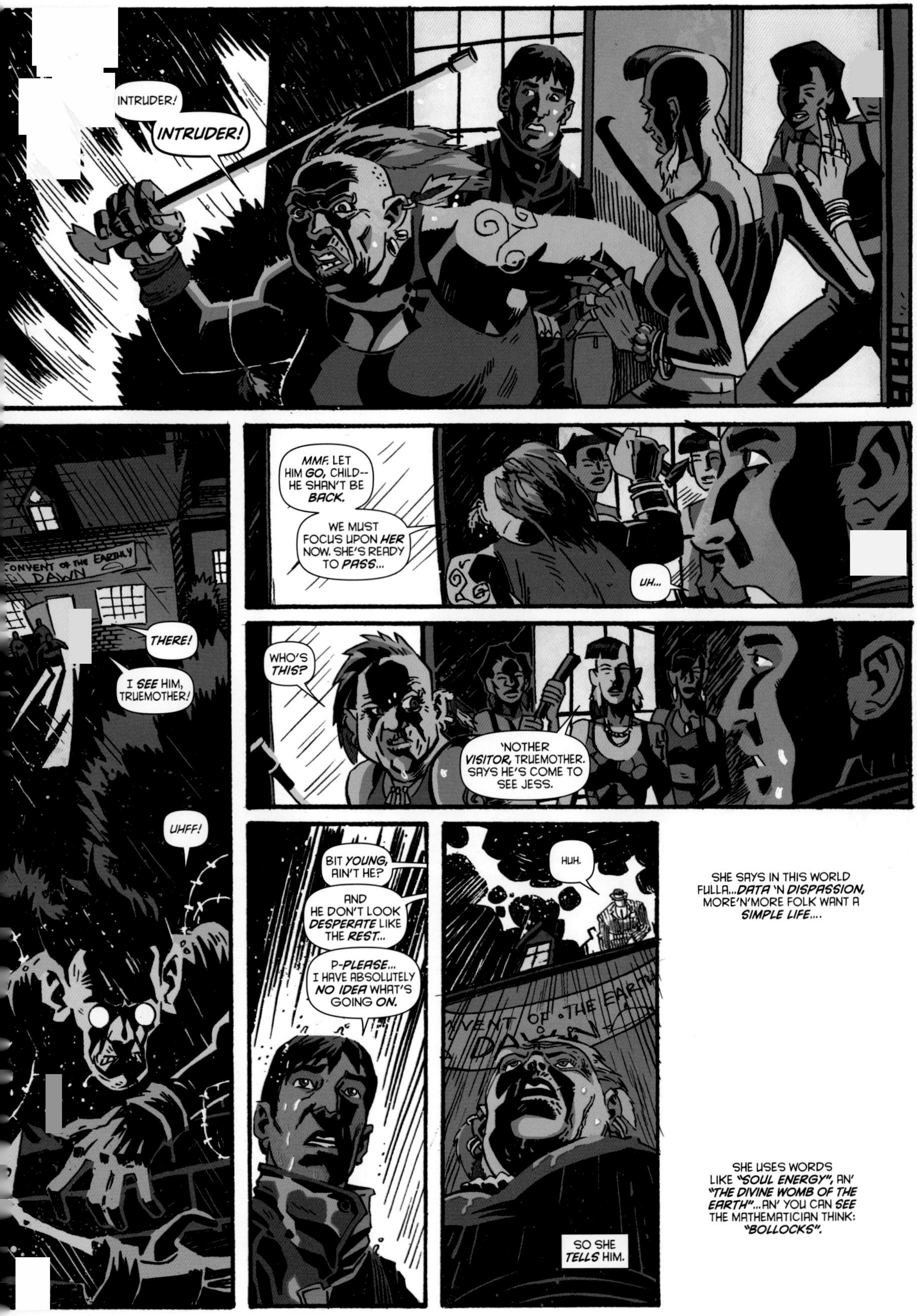
INTRUDER!
INTRUDER!
THERE!
I SEE HIM, TRUEMOTHER!
UHFF!
MMF. LET HIM GO, CHILD-- HE SHAN'T BE BACK.
WE MUST FOCUS UPON HER NOW. SHE'S READY TO PASS...
UH...
WHO'S THIS?
'NOTHER VISITOR, TRUEMOTHER. SAYS HE'S COME TO SEE JESS.
BIT YOUNG, AIN'T HE?
AND HE DON'T LOOK DESPERATE LIKE THE REST...
P-PLEASE... I HAVE ABSOLUTELY NO IDEA WHAT'S GOING ON.
HUH.
SO SHE TELLS HIM.
SHE SAYS IN THIS WORLD FULLA...DATA 'N DISPASSION, MORE'N'MORE FOLK WANT A SIMPLE LIFE....
SHE USES WORDS LIKE "SOUL ENERGY", AN' "THE DIVINE WOMB OF THE EARTH"...AN' YOU CAN SEE THE MATHEMATICIAN THINK: "BOLLOCKS".

SHE SAYS SHE AN' HER *FLOCK* ARE PURSUIN' A MORE *SPIRITUAL*, MORE *REWARDIN'* LIFE, AN' FOR *THAT* THERE'S JUST ONE *RULE:*

NO MEN.

KLUMP

POOR SOD.

CAN'T 'ELP FEELIN' *SORRY* FOR 'IM.

BRAIN LIKE *HIS* AIN'T DISSIMILAR TO A *MACHINE*--ALL ANGLES'N'*ALGEBRA*...

NEVER *DEVIATES*. NEVER GETS *DISTRACTED*...

SHOOTIN' *STRAIGHT* AN' *TRUE* AT ITS *TARGET*.

J-*JESS*...?

THEN COME THE DAY ALL THEM *LINES* 'N *LAWS* GET THE *ENGINE* WHERE IT WANTS TO *GO*...

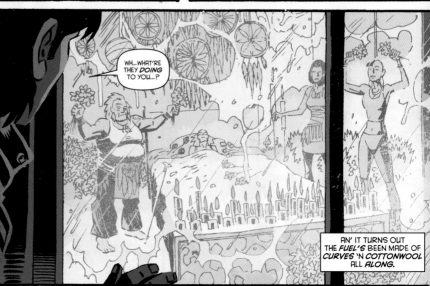

WH...WHAT'RE THEY *DOING* TO YOU...?

AN' IT TURNS OUT THE *FUEL'S* BEEN MADE OF *CURVES* 'N *COTTONWOOL* ALL *ALONG*.

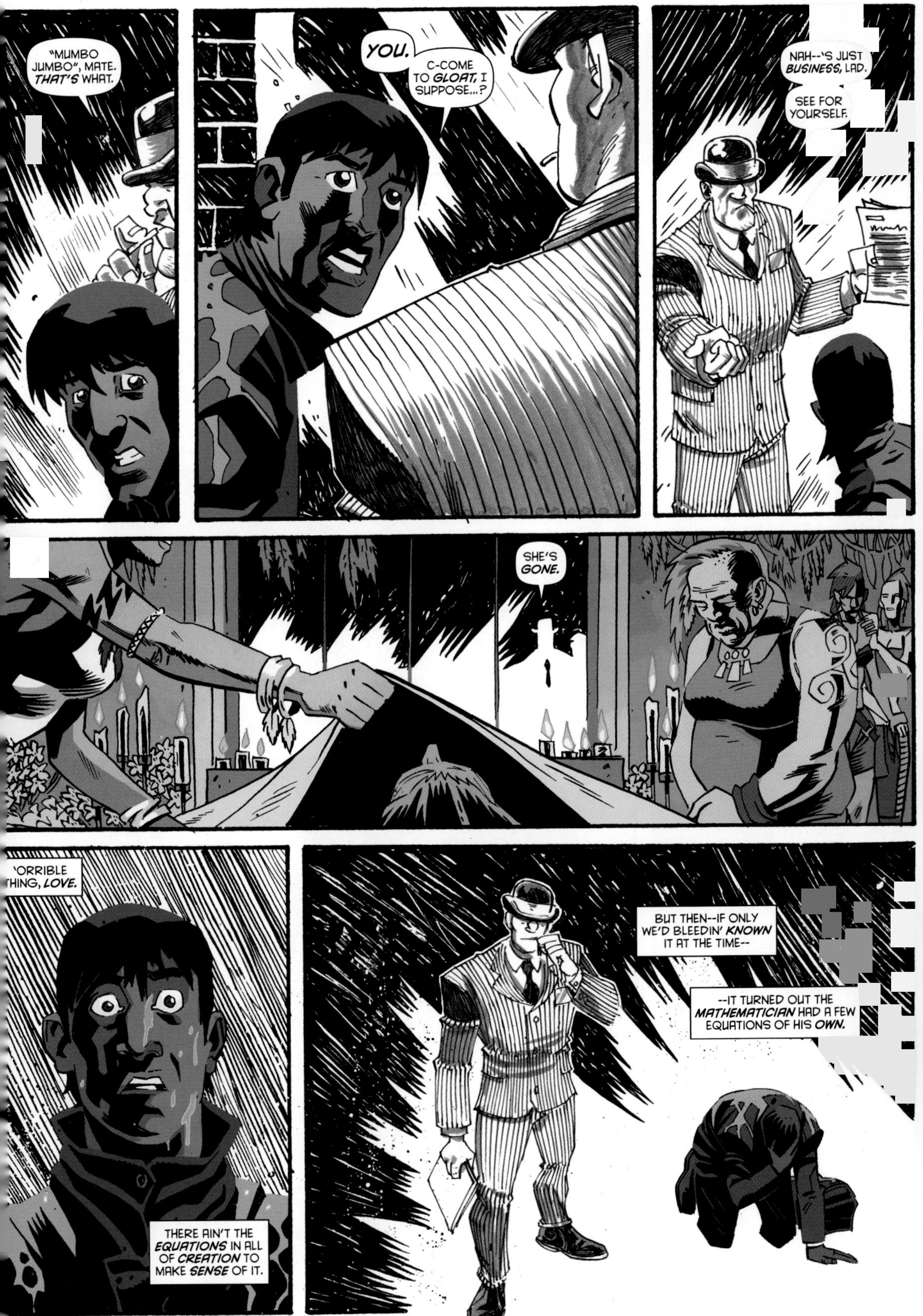

"MUMBO JUMBO", MATE. THAT'S WHAT.
YOU.
C-COME TO GLOAT, I SUPPOSE...?
NAH--'S JUST BUSINESS, LAD.
SEE FOR YOURSELF.
SHE'S GONE.
'ORRIBLE THING, LOVE.
THERE AIN'T THE EQUATIONS IN ALL OF CREATION TO MAKE SENSE OF IT.
BUT THEN--IF ONLY WE'D BLEEDIN' KNOWN IT AT THE TIME--
--IT TURNED OUT THE MATHEMATICIAN HAD A FEW EQUATIONS OF HIS OWN.

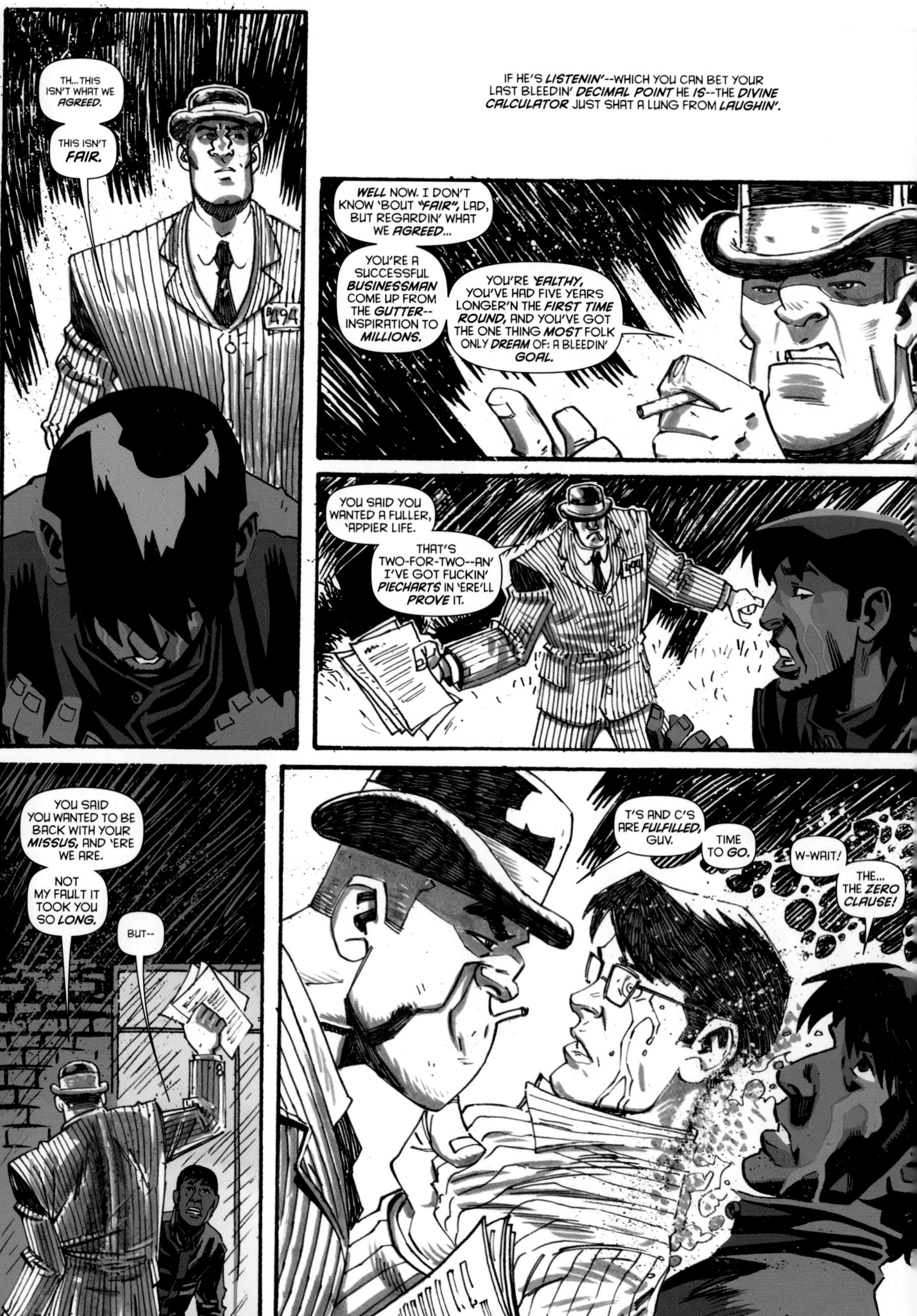
TH...THIS ISN'T WHAT WE AGREED.
THIS ISN'T FAIR.
IF HE'S LISTENIN'--WHICH YOU CAN BET YOUR LAST BLEEDIN' DECIMAL POINT HE IS--THE DIVINE CALCULATOR JUST SHAT A LUNG FROM LAUGHIN'.
WELL NOW. I DON'T KNOW 'BOUT "FAIR", LAD, BUT REGARDIN' WHAT WE AGREED...
YOU'RE A SUCCESSFUL BUSINESSMAN COME UP FROM THE GUTTER--INSPIRATION TO MILLIONS.
YOU'RE 'EALTHY, YOU'VE HAD FIVE YEARS LONGER'N THE FIRST TIME ROUND, AND YOU'VE GOT THE ONE THING MOST FOLK ONLY DREAM OF: A BLEEDIN' GOAL.
YOU SAID YOU WANTED A FULLER, 'APPIER LIFE.
THAT'S TWO-FOR-TWO--AN' I'VE GOT FUCKIN' PIECHARTS IN 'ERE'LL PROVE IT.
YOU SAID YOU WANTED TO BE BACK WITH YOUR MISSUS, AND 'ERE WE ARE.
NOT MY FAULT IT TOOK YOU SO LONG.
BUT--
T'S AND C'S ARE FULFILLED, GUV.
TIME TO GO.
W-WAIT!
THE... THE ZERO CLAUSE!

I'VE LED A *GOOD* LIFE! I HAVEN'T EXPLOITED ANYONE, O-OR...OR *HURT* PEOPLE...OR *CHEATED.*

I NEVER BREATHED A *WORD* ABOUT *RECIRCULATION!*

AND?

YOU SAID IF I DIDN'T *SIN* THEN THE CONTRACT'S *NULL* AND *VOID!*

BUT YOU *DID* SIN, SONNYJIM.

YOU SINNED THE SECOND YOU WAS *BORN.*

IT WAS THE *RETAINED MEMORIES,* DONE IT.

HE *INCARNATED* WITH AN 'EAD FULL OF *LOVE* AND *LUST,* POOR GIT, FOCUSED SO TIGHT ON *ONE THING--* ONE *WOMAN--*THAT HE DIDN'T PLAY HIS *PART* IN THE *BIGGER EQUATION.*

WASN'T A PRODUCTIVE, UNPREDICTABLE, *COMPLEX* LITTLE NUMBER.

OBSESSION, LAD. YOU ROBBED *YOURSELF* OF CHOICES.

SO:

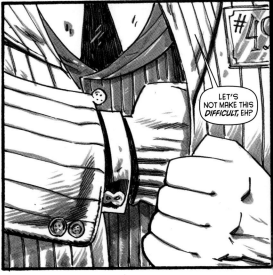

#49

LET'S NOT MAKE THIS *DIFFICULT,* EH?

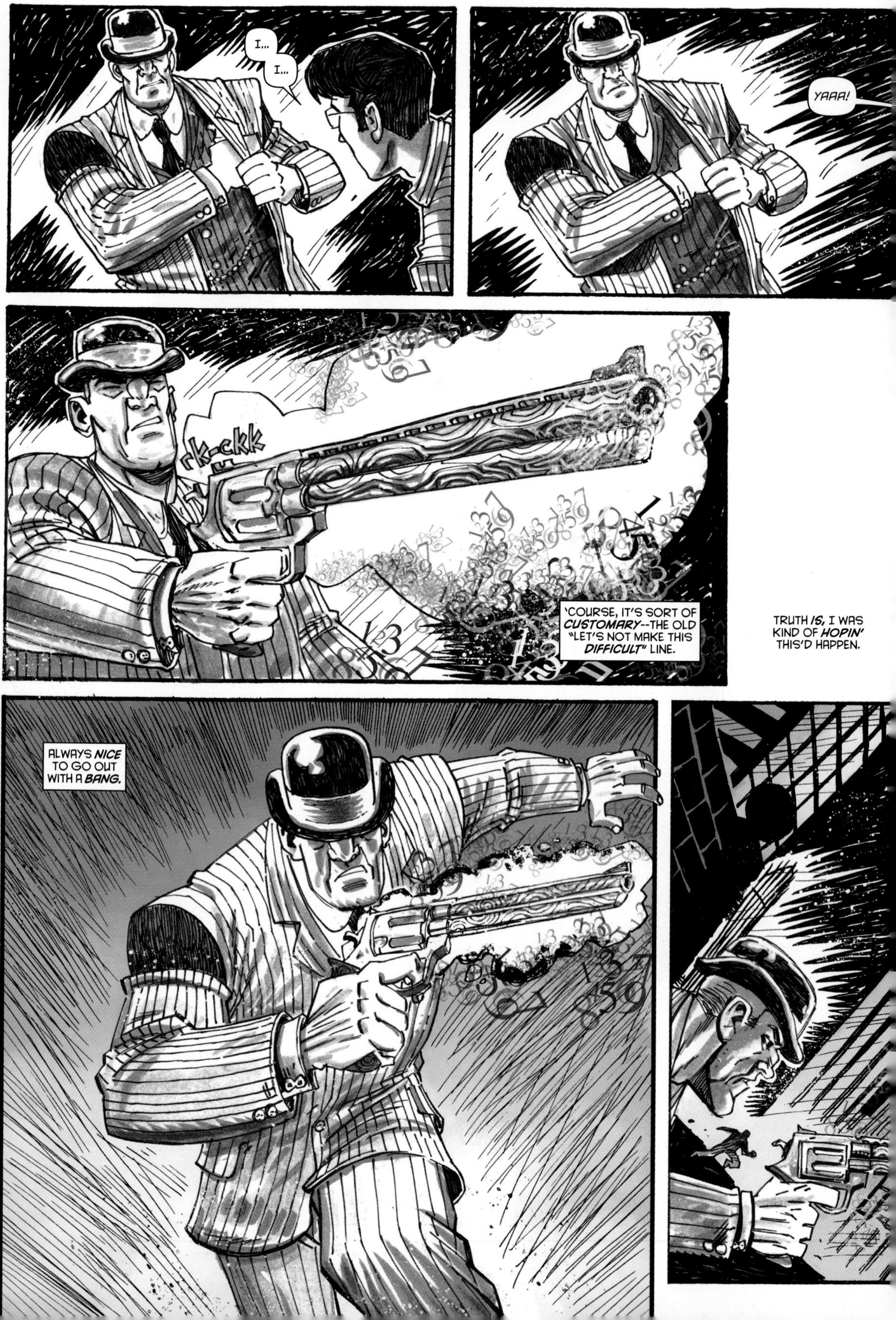
I...
I...
YAAA!
rk-ckk
'COURSE, IT'S SORT OF CUSTOMARY--THE OLD "LET'S NOT MAKE THIS DIFFICULT" LINE.
TRUTH IS, I WAS KIND OF HOPIN' THIS'D HAPPEN.
ALWAYS NICE TO GO OUT WITH A BANG.

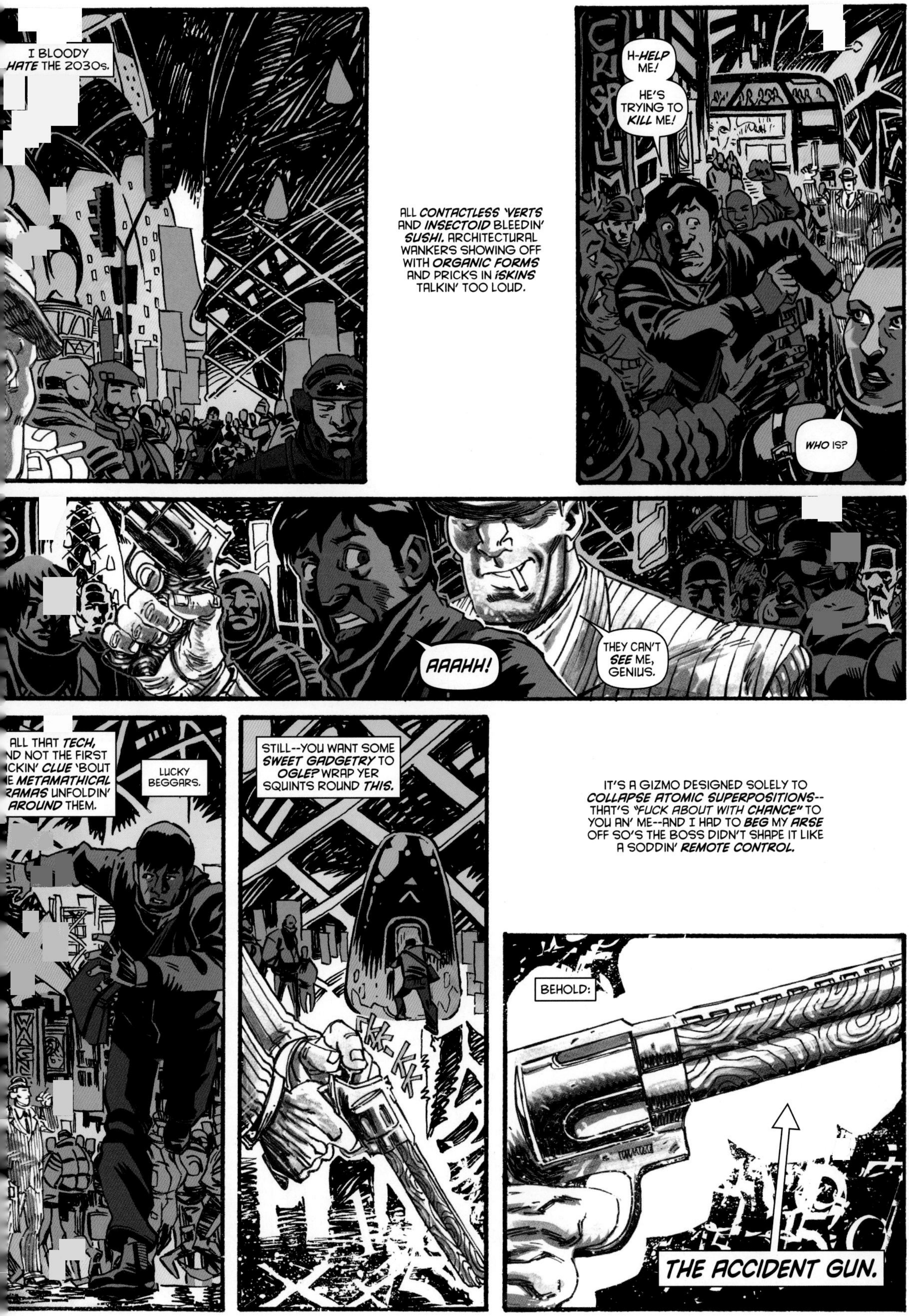
I BLOODY HATE THE 2030s.
ALL CONTACTLESS 'VERTS AND INSECTOID BLEEDIN' SUSHI. ARCHITECTURAL WANKERS SHOWING OFF WITH ORGANIC FORMS AND PRICKS IN iSKINS TALKIN' TOO LOUD.
H-HELP ME!
HE'S TRYING TO KILL ME!
WHO IS?
AAAHH!
THEY CAN'T SEE ME, GENIUS.
ALL THAT TECH, ND NOT THE FIRST CKIN' CLUE 'BOUT E METAMATHICAL RAMAS UNFOLDIN' AROUND THEM.
LUCKY BEGGARS.
STILL--YOU WANT SOME SWEET GADGETRY TO OGLE? WRAP YER SQUINTS ROUND THIS.
CLIK-KK
IT'S A GIZMO DESIGNED SOLELY TO COLLAPSE ATOMIC SUPERPOSITIONS-- THAT'S "FUCK ABOUT WITH CHANCE" TO YOU AN' ME--AND I HAD TO BEG MY ARSE OFF SO'S THE BOSS DIDN'T SHAPE IT LIKE A SODDIN' REMOTE CONTROL.
BEHOLD:
THE ACCIDENT GUN.

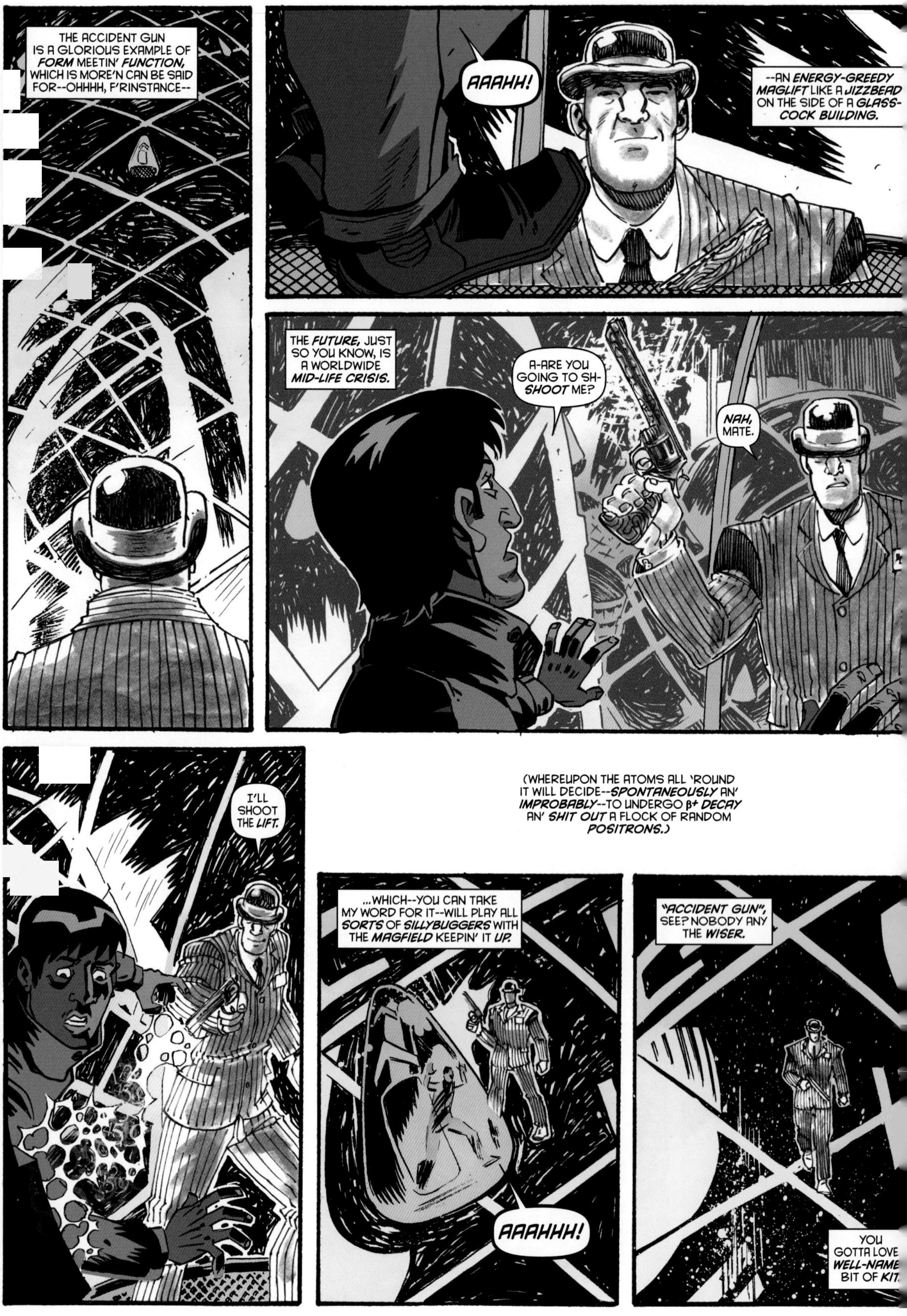
THE ACCIDENT GUN IS A GLORIOUS EXAMPLE OF FORM MEETIN' FUNCTION, WHICH IS MORE'N CAN BE SAID FOR--OHHHH, F'RINSTANCE--
AAAHH!
--AN ENERGY-GREEDY MAGLIFT LIKE A JIZZBEAD ON THE SIDE OF A GLASS-COCK BUILDING.
THE FUTURE, JUST SO YOU KNOW, IS A WORLDWIDE MID-LIFE CRISIS.
A-ARE YOU GOING TO SH-SHOOT ME?
NAH, MATE.
I'LL SHOOT THE LIFT.
(WHEREUPON THE ATOMS ALL 'ROUND IT WILL DECIDE--SPONTANEOUSLY AN' IMPROBABLY--TO UNDERGO β+ DECAY AN' SHIT OUT A FLOCK OF RANDOM POSITRONS.)
...WHICH--YOU CAN TAKE MY WORD FOR IT--WILL PLAY ALL SORTS OF SILLYBUGGERS WITH THE MAGFIELD KEEPIN' IT UP.
AAAHHH!
"ACCIDENT GUN", SEE? NOBODY ANY THE WISER.
YOU GOTTA LOVE WELL-NAME BIT OF KIT

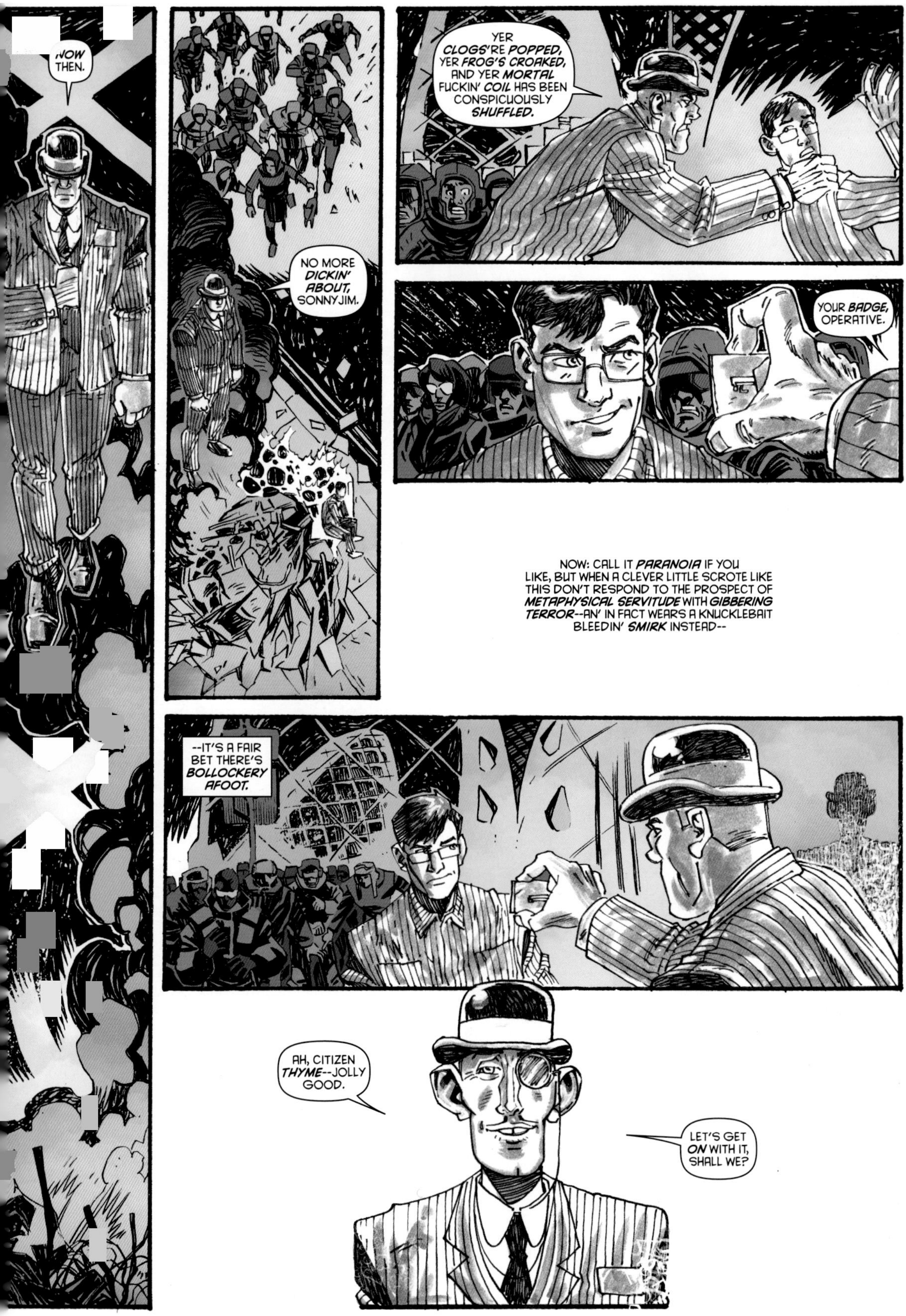
NOW THEN.
NO MORE DICKIN' ABOUT, SONNYJIM.
YER CLOGS'RE POPPED, YER FROG'S CROAKED, AND YER MORTAL FUCKIN' COIL HAS BEEN CONSPICUOUSLY SHUFFLED.
YOUR BADGE, OPERATIVE.
NOW: CALL IT PARANOIA IF YOU LIKE, BUT WHEN A CLEVER LITTLE SCROTE LIKE THIS DON'T RESPOND TO THE PROSPECT OF METAPHYSICAL SERVITUDE WITH GIBBERING TERROR--AN' IN FACT WEARS A KNUCKLEBAIT BLEEDIN' SMIRK INSTEAD--
--IT'S A FAIR BET THERE'S BOLLOCKERY AFOOT.
AH, CITIZEN THYME--JOLLY GOOD.
LET'S GET ON WITH IT, SHALL WE?

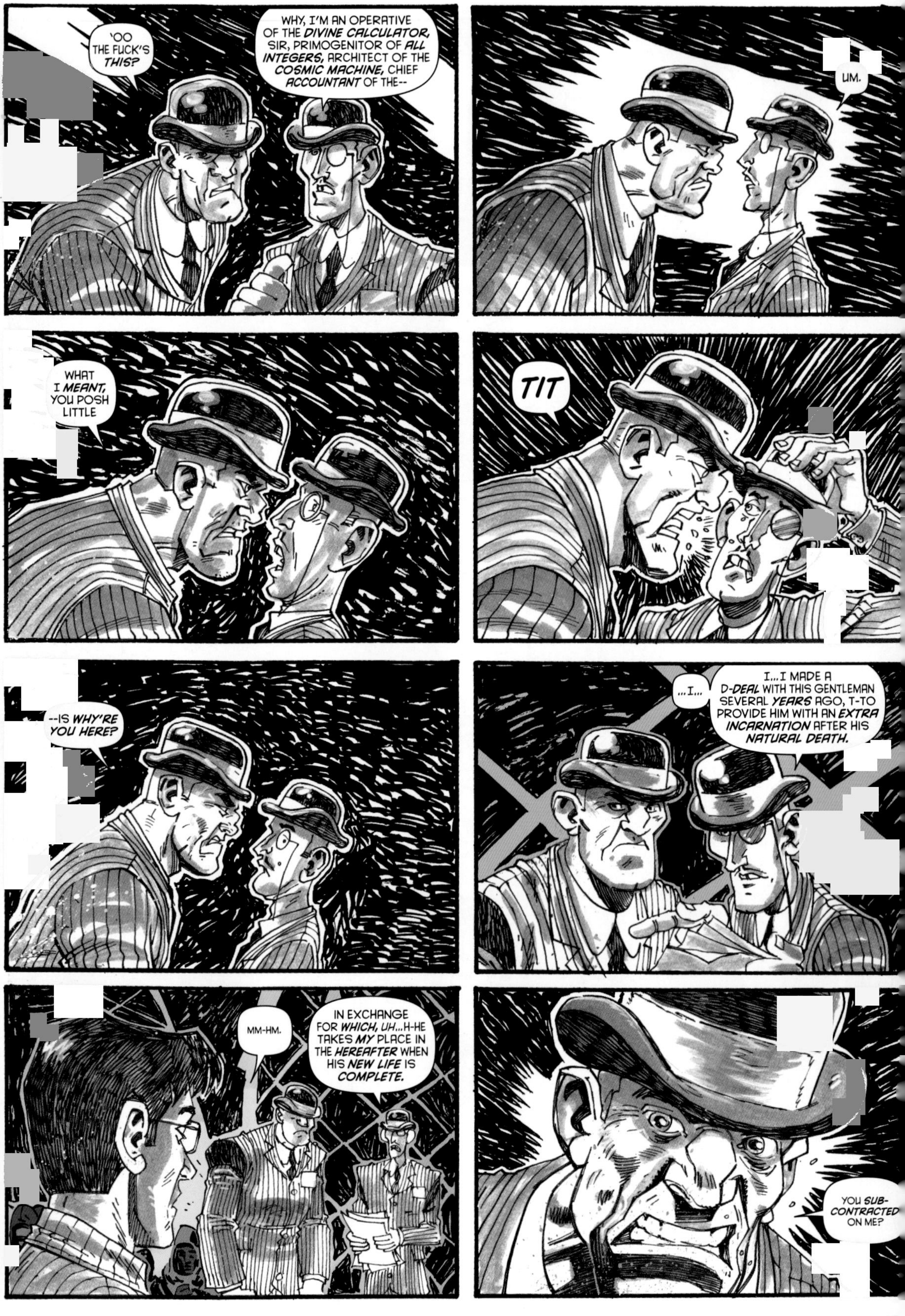
'OO THE FUCK'S THIS?
WHY, I'M AN OPERATIVE OF THE DIVINE CALCULATOR, SIR, PRIMOGENITOR OF ALL INTEGERS, ARCHITECT OF THE COSMIC MACHINE, CHIEF ACCOUNTANT OF THE--
UM.
WHAT I MEANT, YOU POSH LITTLE
TIT
--IS WHY'RE YOU HERE?
...I...
I...I MADE A D-DEAL WITH THIS GENTLEMAN SEVERAL YEARS AGO, T-TO PROVIDE HIM WITH AN EXTRA INCARNATION AFTER HIS NATURAL DEATH.
MM-HM.
IN EXCHANGE FOR WHICH, UH...H-HE TAKES MY PLACE IN THE HEREAFTER WHEN HIS NEW LIFE IS COMPLETE.
YOU SUB-CONTRACTED ON ME?

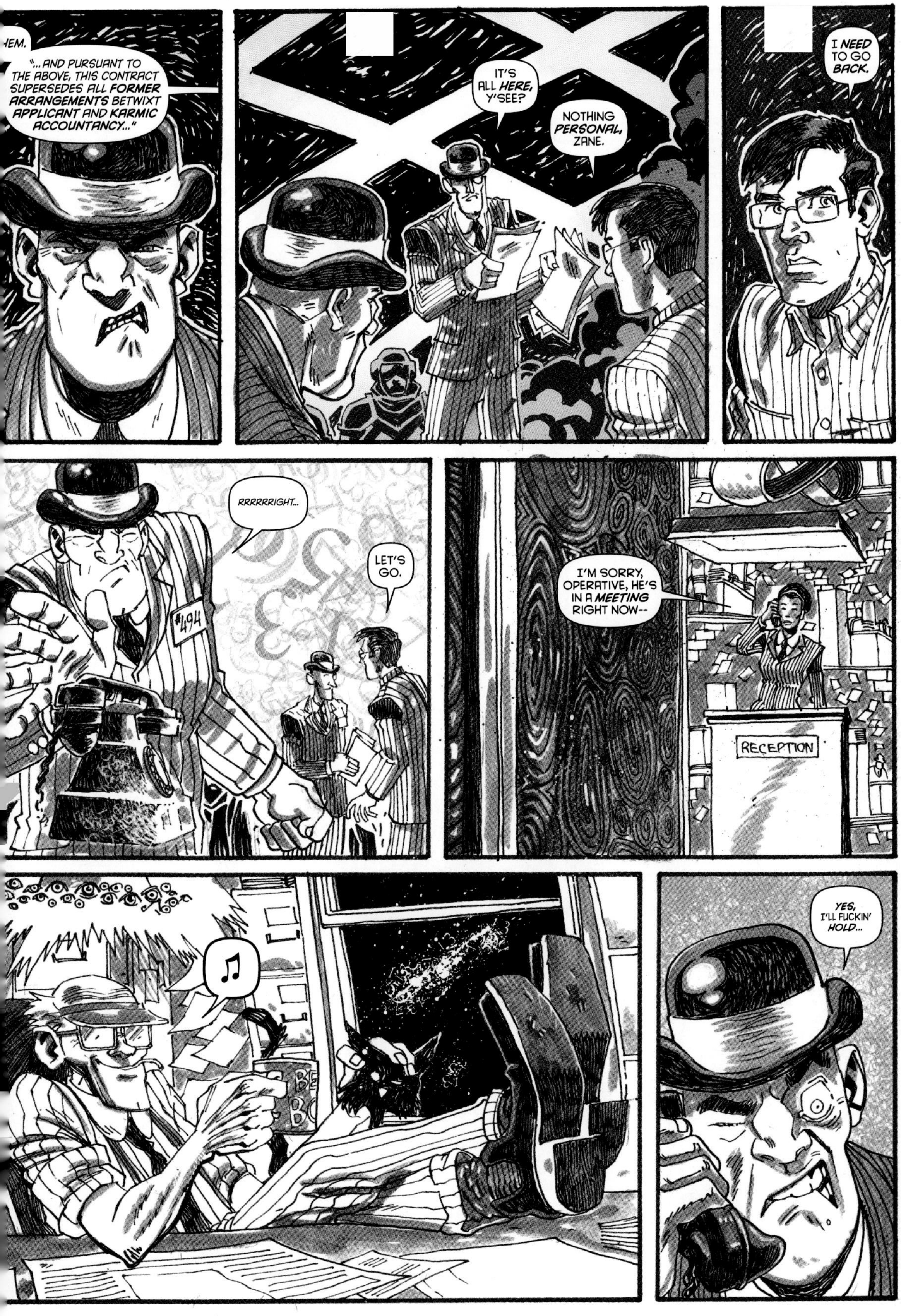
HEM.
"...AND PURSUANT TO THE ABOVE, THIS CONTRACT SUPERSEDES ALL FORMER ARRANGEMENTS BETWIXT APPLICANT AND KARMIC ACCOUNTANCY..."
IT'S ALL HERE, Y'SEE?
NOTHING PERSONAL, ZANE.
I NEED TO GO BACK.
RRRRRRIGHT...
#494
LET'S GO.
I'M SORRY, OPERATIVE, HE'S IN A MEETING RIGHT NOW--
RECEPTION
♫
YES, I'LL FUCKIN' HOLD...

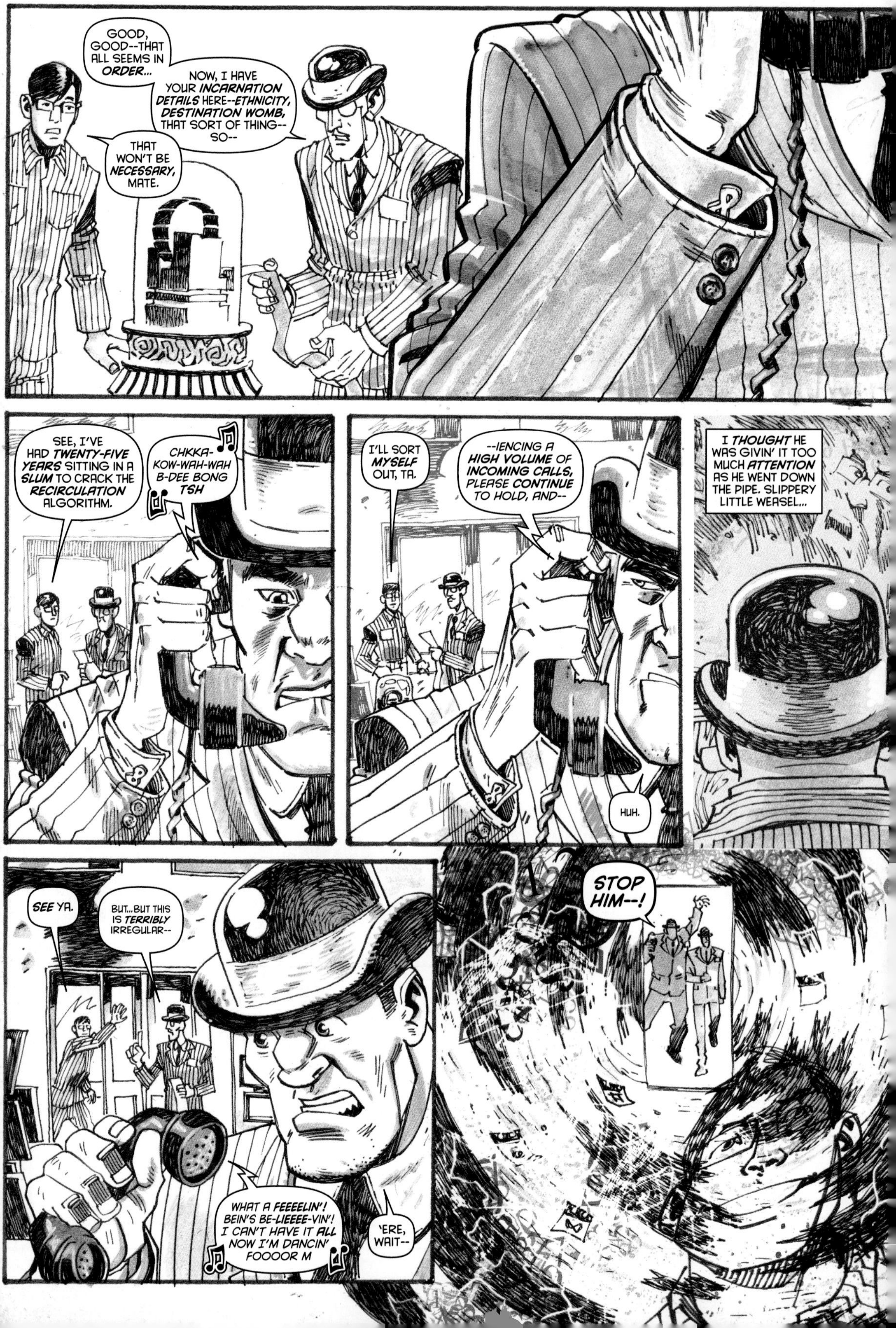
GOOD, GOOD--THAT ALL SEEMS IN ORDER...
NOW, I HAVE YOUR INCARNATION DETAILS HERE--ETHNICITY, DESTINATION WOMB, THAT SORT OF THING-- SO--
THAT WON'T BE NECESSARY, MATE.
SEE, I'VE HAD TWENTY-FIVE YEARS SITTING IN A SLUM TO CRACK THE RECIRCULATION ALGORITHM.
CHKKA-KOW-WAH-WAH B-DEE BONG TSH
I'LL SORT MYSELF OUT, TA.
--IENCING A HIGH VOLUME OF INCOMING CALLS, PLEASE CONTINUE TO HOLD, AND--
HUH.
I THOUGHT HE WAS GIVIN' IT TOO MUCH ATTENTION AS HE WENT DOWN THE PIPE. SLIPPERY LITTLE WEASEL...
SEE YA.
BUT...BUT THIS IS TERRIBLY IRREGULAR--
WHAT A FEEEELIN'! BEIN'S BE-LIEEEE-VIN'! I CAN'T HAVE IT ALL NOW I'M DANCIN' FOOOOR M
'ERE, WAIT--
STOP HIM--!

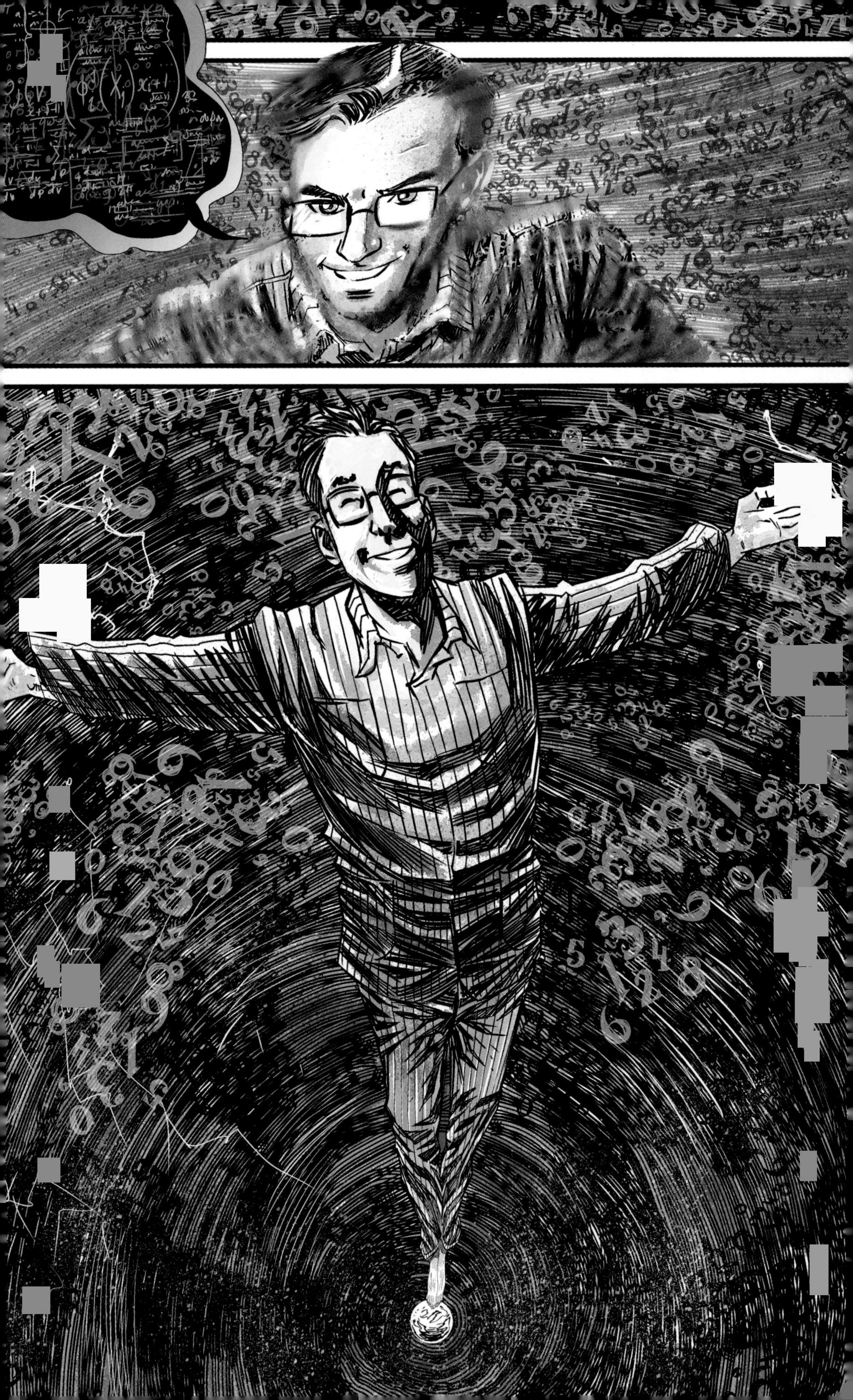

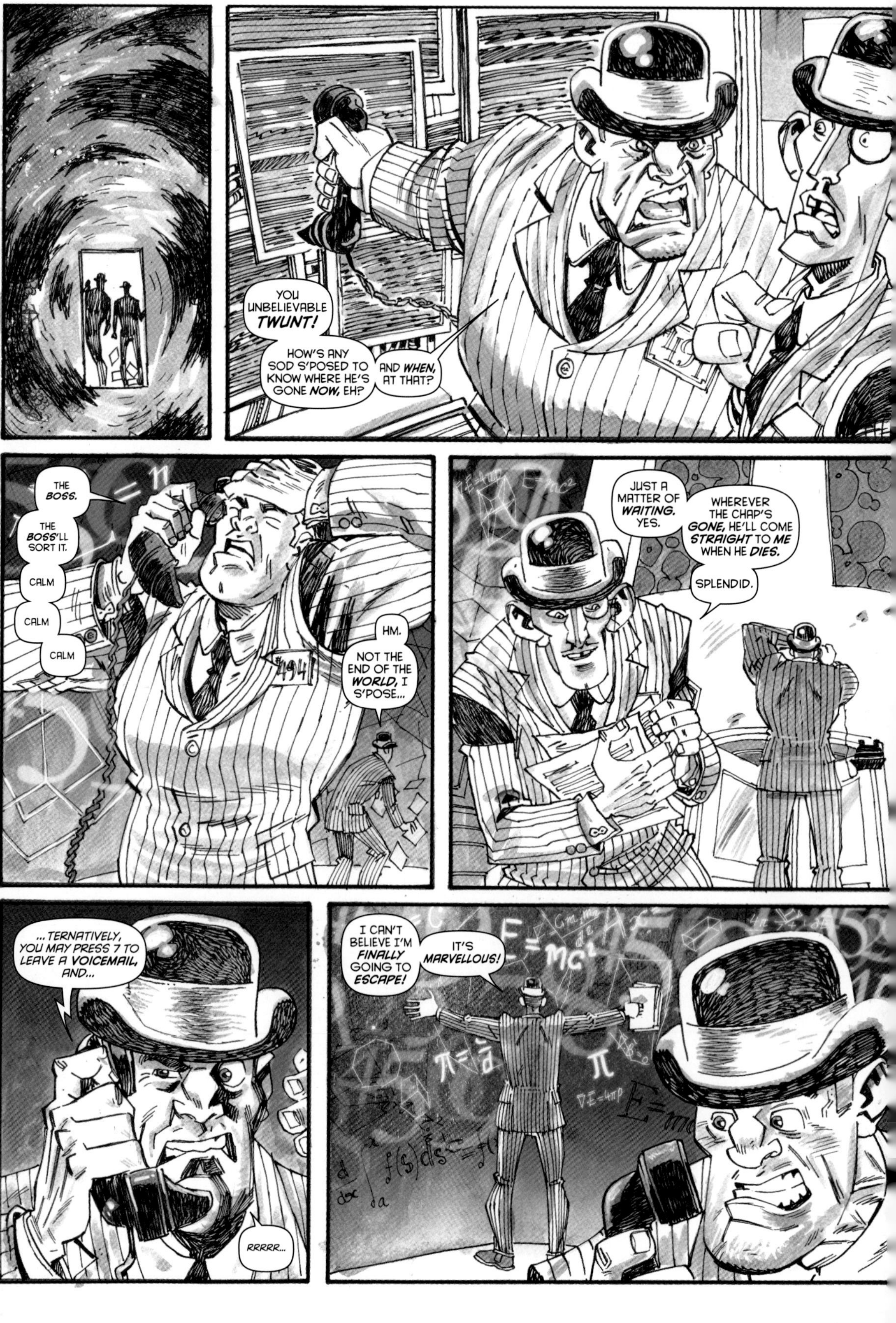

YOU UNBELIEVABLE TWUNT!
HOW'S ANY SOD S'POSED TO KNOW WHERE HE'S GONE NOW, EH?
AND WHEN, AT THAT?
THE BOSS.
THE BOSS'LL SORT IT.
CALM
CALM
CALM
HM.
NOT THE END OF THE WORLD, I S'POSE...
JUST A MATTER OF WAITING. YES.
WHEREVER THE CHAP'S GONE, HE'LL COME STRAIGHT TO ME WHEN HE DIES.
SPLENDID.
...TERNATIVELY, YOU MAY PRESS 7 TO LEAVE A VOICEMAIL, AND...
RRRRR...
I CAN'T BELIEVE I'M FINALLY GOING TO ESCAPE!
IT'S MARVELLOUS!

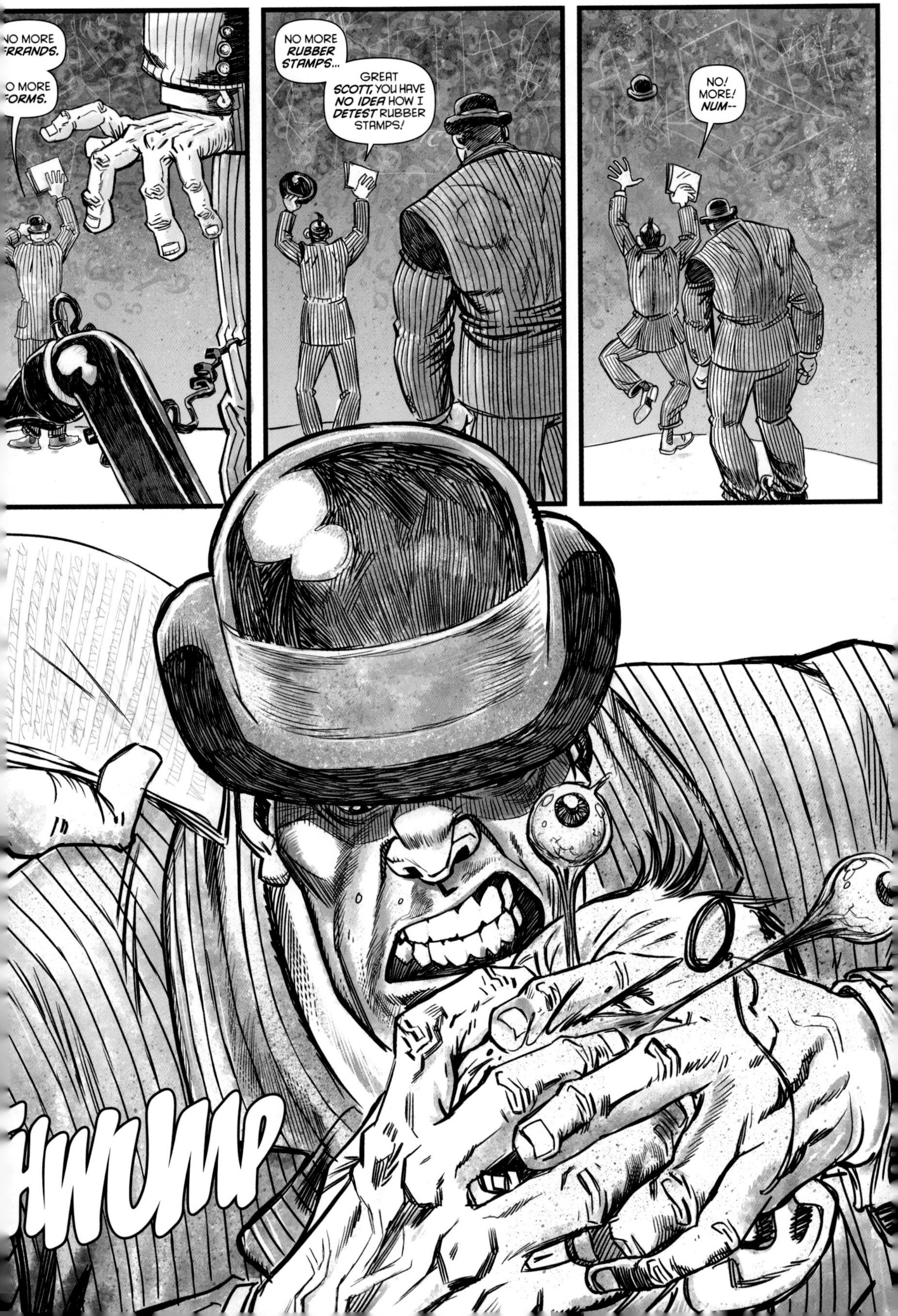

NO MORE ERRANDS.
NO MORE FORMS.
NO MORE RUBBER STAMPS...
GREAT SCOTT, YOU HAVE NO IDEA HOW I DETEST RUBBER STAMPS!
NO! MORE! NUM--
HWUMP

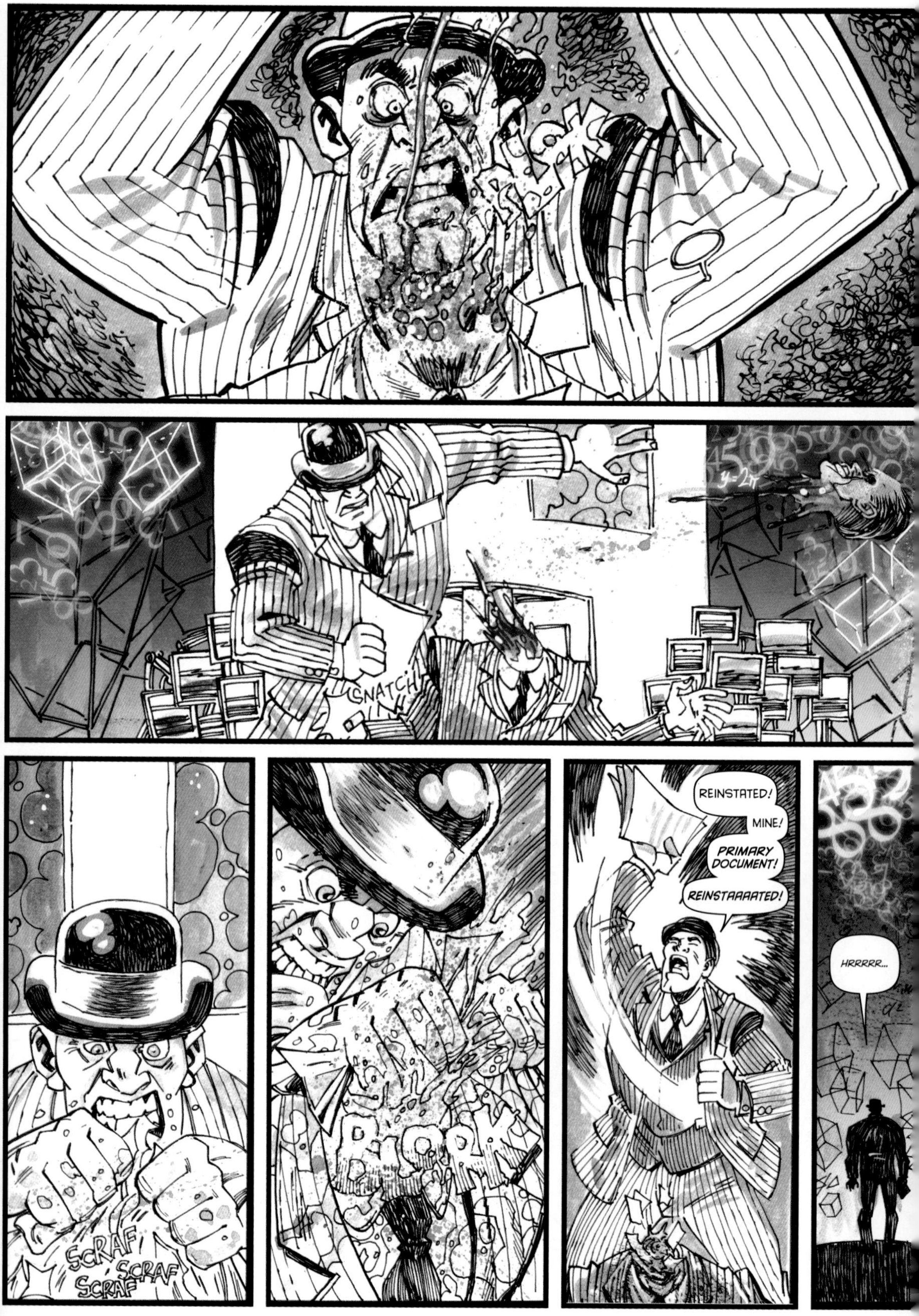
SNATCH
SCRAF
SCRAF
SCRAF
REINSTATED!
MINE!
PRIMARY DOCUMENT!
REINSTAAAATED!
HRRRRR...

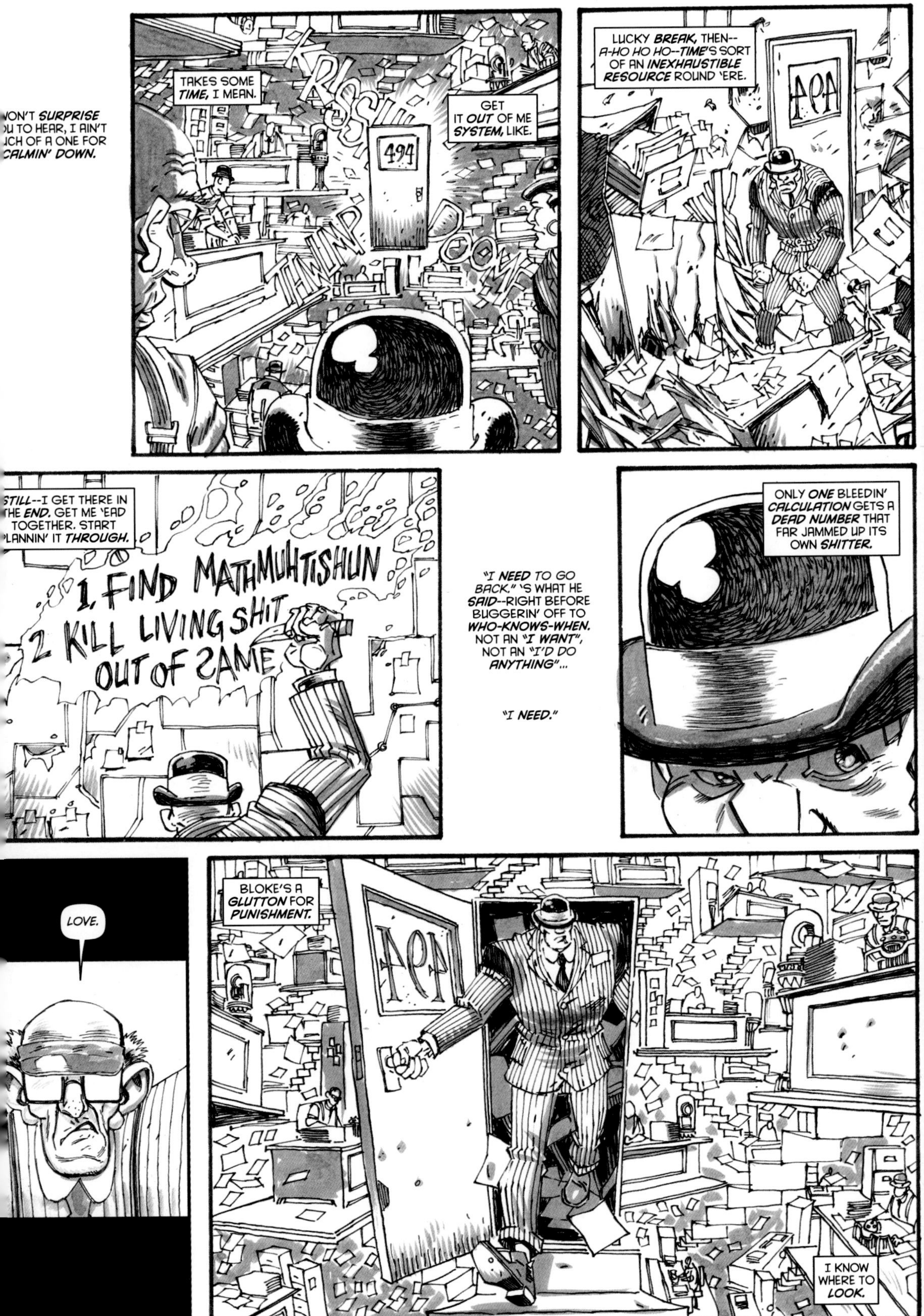
WON'T SURPRISE
OU TO HEAR, I AIN'T
UCH OF A ONE FOR
CALMIN' DOWN.
TAKES SOME TIME, I MEAN.
KRISS
THWUMP
DOOM
494
GET IT OUT OF ME SYSTEM, LIKE.
LUCKY BREAK, THEN-- A-HO HO HO--TIME'S SORT OF AN INEXHAUSTIBLE RESOURCE ROUND 'ERE.
STILL--I GET THERE IN THE END. GET ME 'EAD TOGETHER. START PLANNIN' IT THROUGH.
1. FIND MATHMUHTISHUN
2 KILL LIVING SHIT OUT OF SAME
"I NEED TO GO BACK." 'S WHAT HE SAID--RIGHT BEFORE BUGGERIN' OFF TO WHO-KNOWS-WHEN. NOT AN "I WANT", NOT AN "I'D DO ANYTHING"...
"I NEED."
ONLY ONE BLEEDIN' CALCULATION GETS A DEAD NUMBER THAT FAR JAMMED UP ITS OWN SHITTER.
LOVE.
BLOKE'S A GLUTTON FOR PUNISHMENT.
I KNOW WHERE TO LOOK.

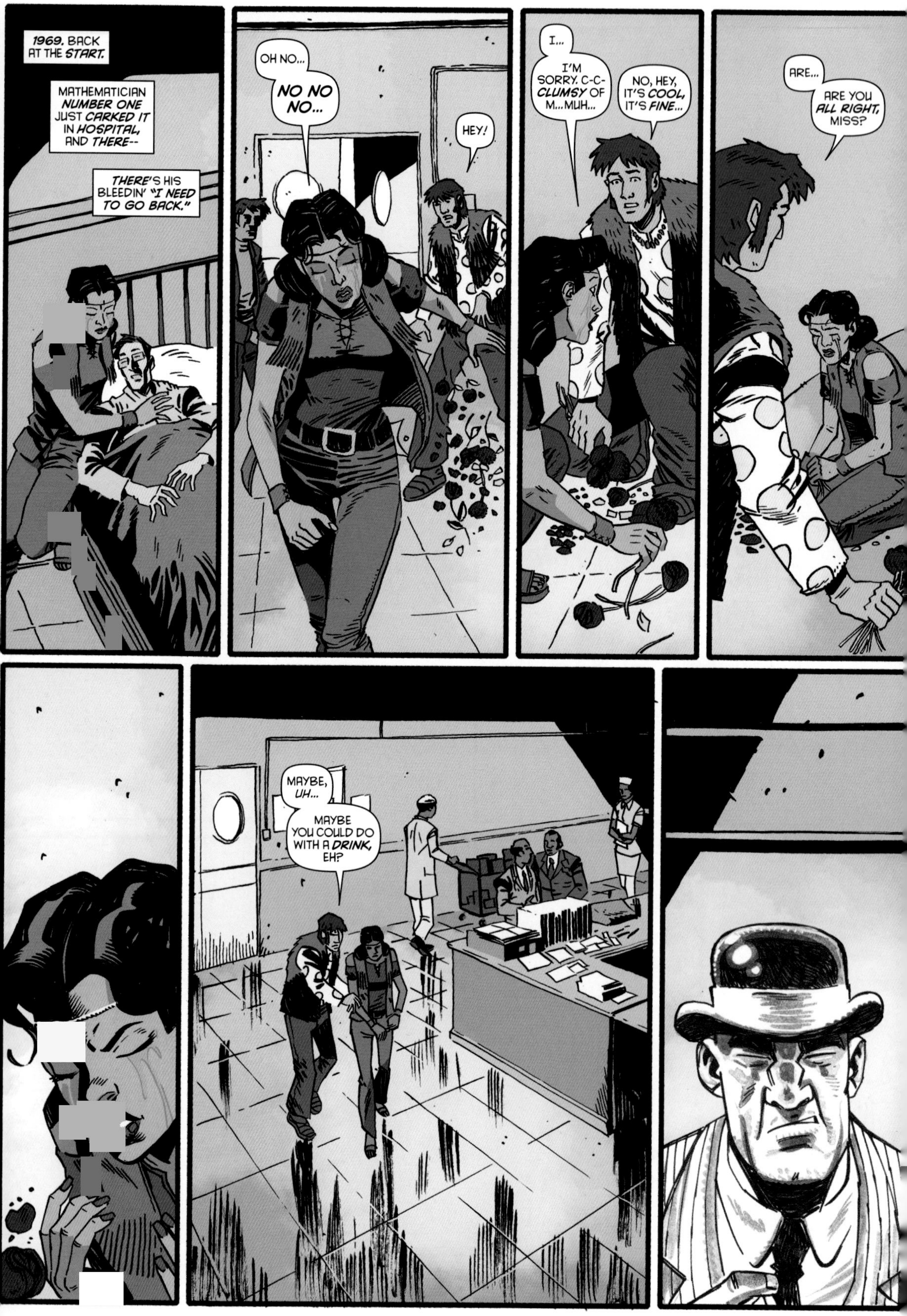
1969. BACK AT THE START.
MATHEMATICIAN NUMBER ONE JUST CARKED IT IN HOSPITAL, AND THERE--
THERE'S HIS BLEEDIN' "I NEED TO GO BACK."
OH NO...
NO NO NO...
HEY!
I...
I'M SORRY. C-C-CLUMSY OF M...MUH...
NO, HEY, IT'S COOL, IT'S FINE...
ARE...
ARE YOU ALL RIGHT, MISS?
MAYBE, UH...
MAYBE YOU COULD DO WITH A DRINK, EH?

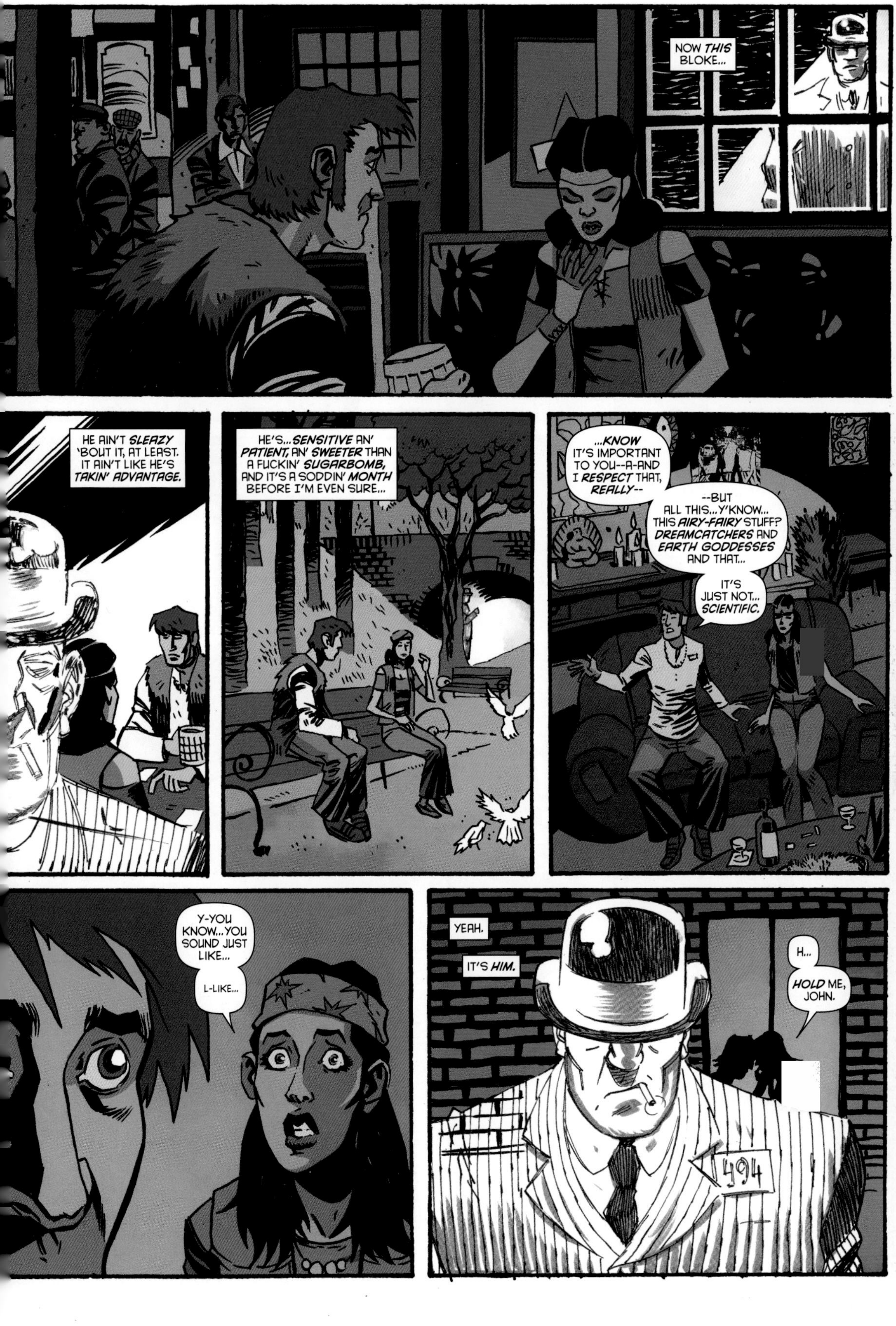
NOW THIS BLOKE...
HE AIN'T SLEAZY 'BOUT IT, AT LEAST. IT AIN'T LIKE HE'S TAKIN' ADVANTAGE.
HE'S...SENSITIVE AN' PATIENT, AN' SWEETER THAN A FUCKIN' SUGARBOMB, AND IT'S A SODDIN' MONTH BEFORE I'M EVEN SURE...
...KNOW IT'S IMPORTANT TO YOU--A-AND I RESPECT THAT, REALLY--
--BUT ALL THIS...Y'KNOW... THIS AIRY-FAIRY STUFF? DREAMCATCHERS AND EARTH GODDESSES AND THAT...
IT'S JUST NOT... SCIENTIFIC.
Y-YOU KNOW...YOU SOUND JUST LIKE...
L-LIKE...
YEAH.
IT'S HIM.
H...
HOLD ME, JOHN.
494

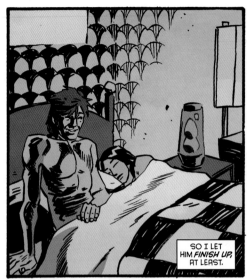

HE'S PLAYED IT JUST *RIGHT,* CLEVER PRICK. GOT HIMSELF *BORN* TWENTY YEARS BACK, SO HE'S INNA RIGHT *TIME 'N PLACE* TO *PICK UP* WHERE #1 *LEFT OFF.*

IT'S *IMPRESSIVE.* REALLY.

SO I LET HIM *FINISH UP,* AT LEAST.

I AIN'T A *COMPLETE* SHIT, AFTER ALL.

AAAHH!

J...JOHN?

JOHN, WHERE ARE YOU G--

C'MON, MATE.

AAAHH!

'AVEN'T WE BEEN *THROUGH* ALL THIS?

YOU'RE A *SMART* GEEZER...

ALL THIS *RUNNIN' AWAY* BOLLOCKS--

AJ ELECTRICS

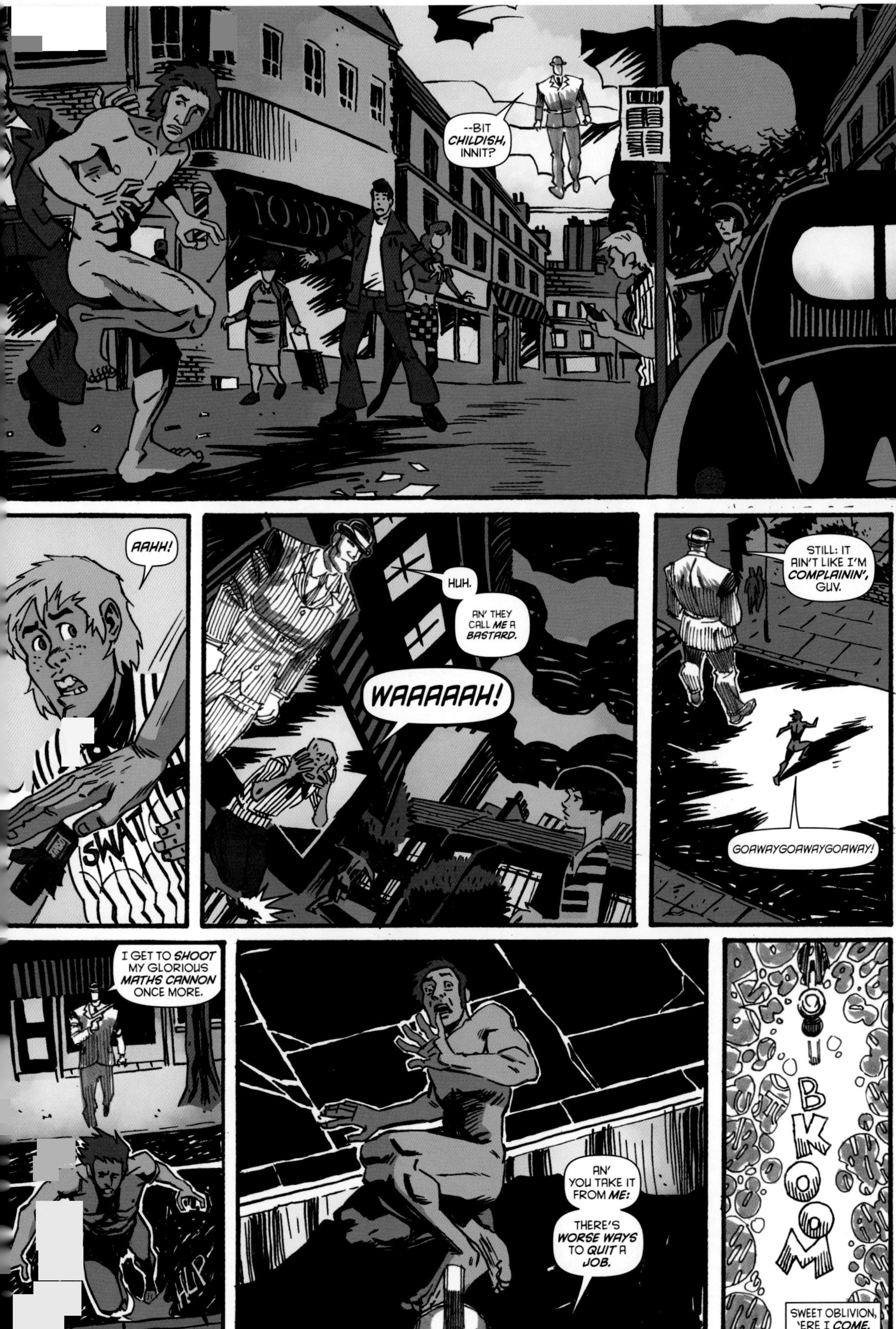
--BIT CHILDISH, INNIT?
AAHH!
SWAT
HUH.
AN' THEY CALL ME A BASTARD.
WAAAAAH!
STILL: IT AIN'T LIKE I'M COMPLAININ', GUV.
GOAWAYGOAWAYGOAWAY!
I GET TO SHOOT MY GLORIOUS MATHS CANNON ONCE MORE.
AN' YOU TAKE IT FROM ME:
THERE'S WORSE WAYS TO QUIT A JOB.
BKOOOM
SWEET OBLIVION, 'ERE I COME.

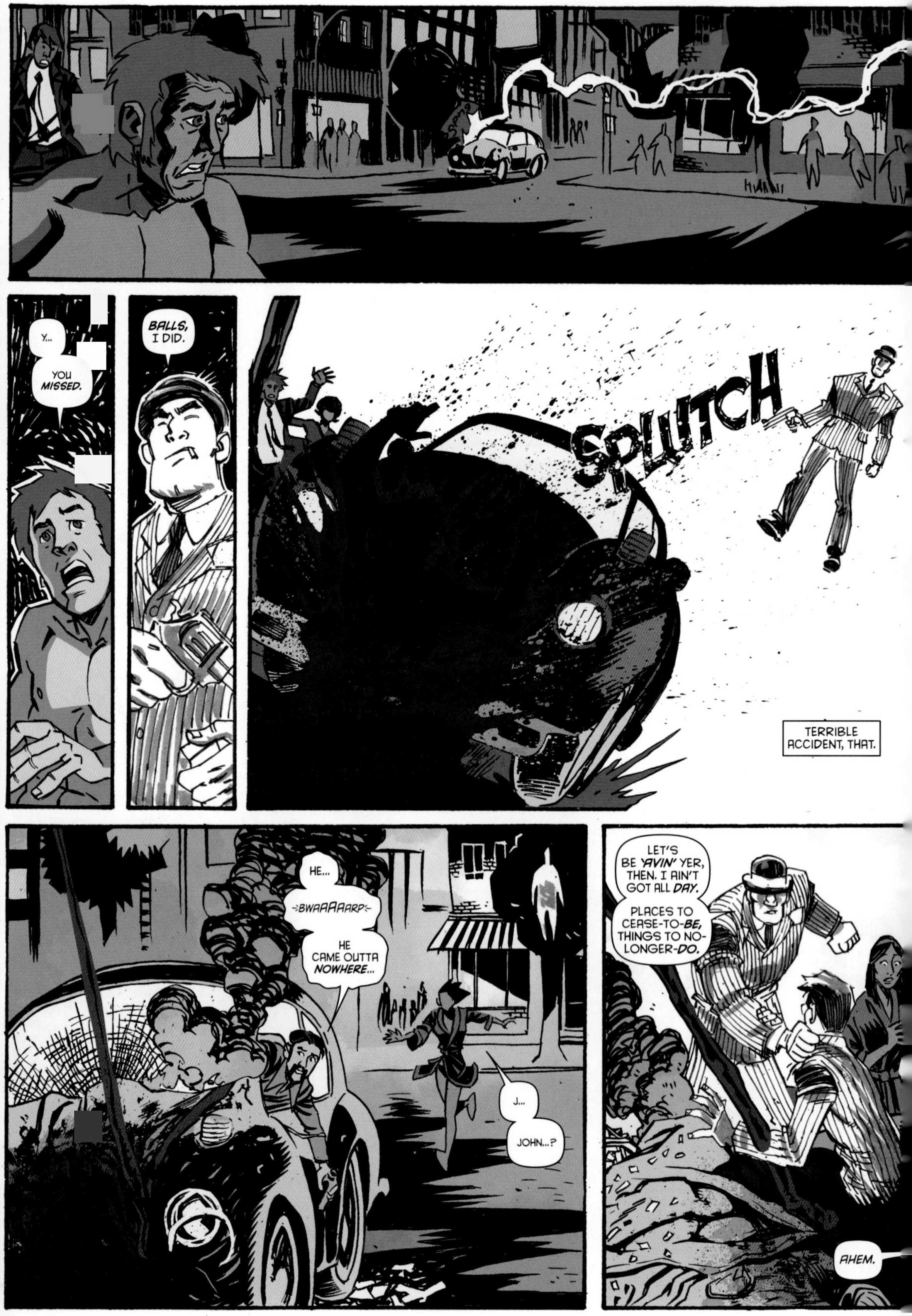
Y...
YOU *MISSED.*
BALLS, I DID.
SPLUTCH
TERRIBLE ACCIDENT, THAT.
HE...
~BWAAAAAARP~
HE CAME OUTTA *NOWHERE...*
J...
JOHN...?
LET'S BE *'AVIN'* YER, THEN. I AIN'T GOT ALL *DAY.*
PLACES TO CEASE-TO-*BE,* THINGS TO NO-LONGER-*DO.*
AHEM.

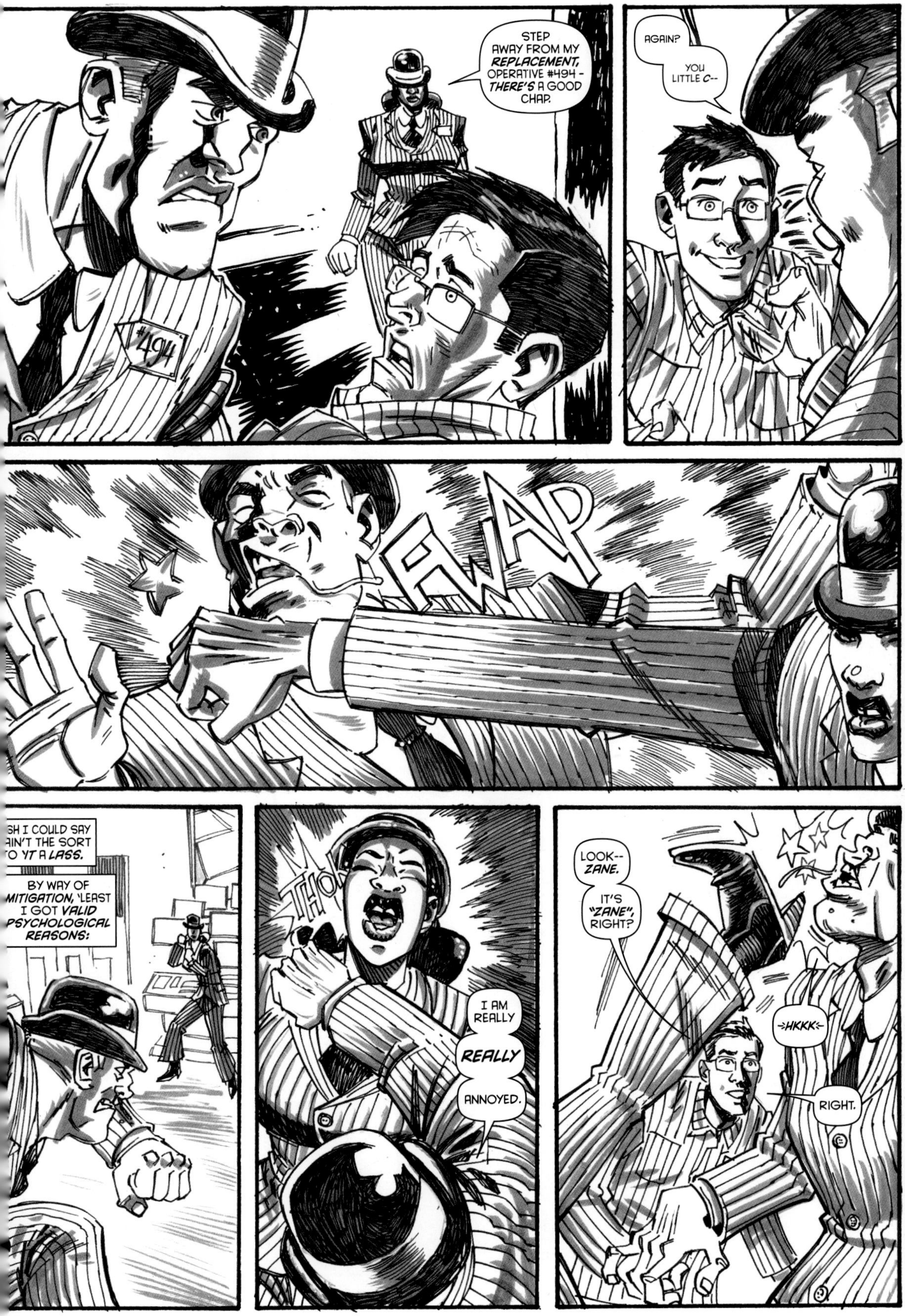

STEP AWAY FROM MY *REPLACEMENT*, OPERATIVE #494 - *THERE'S* A GOOD CHAP.
#494
AGAIN?
YOU LITTLE *C*--
FWAP
SH I COULD SAY AIN'T THE SORT TO *YT* A *LASS.*
BY WAY OF *MITIGATION*, 'LEAST I GOT *VALID PSYCHOLOGICAL REASONS:*
I AM REALLY
REALLY
ANNOYED.
LOOK-- *ZANE.*
IT'S *"ZANE"*, RIGHT?
HKKK
RIGHT.

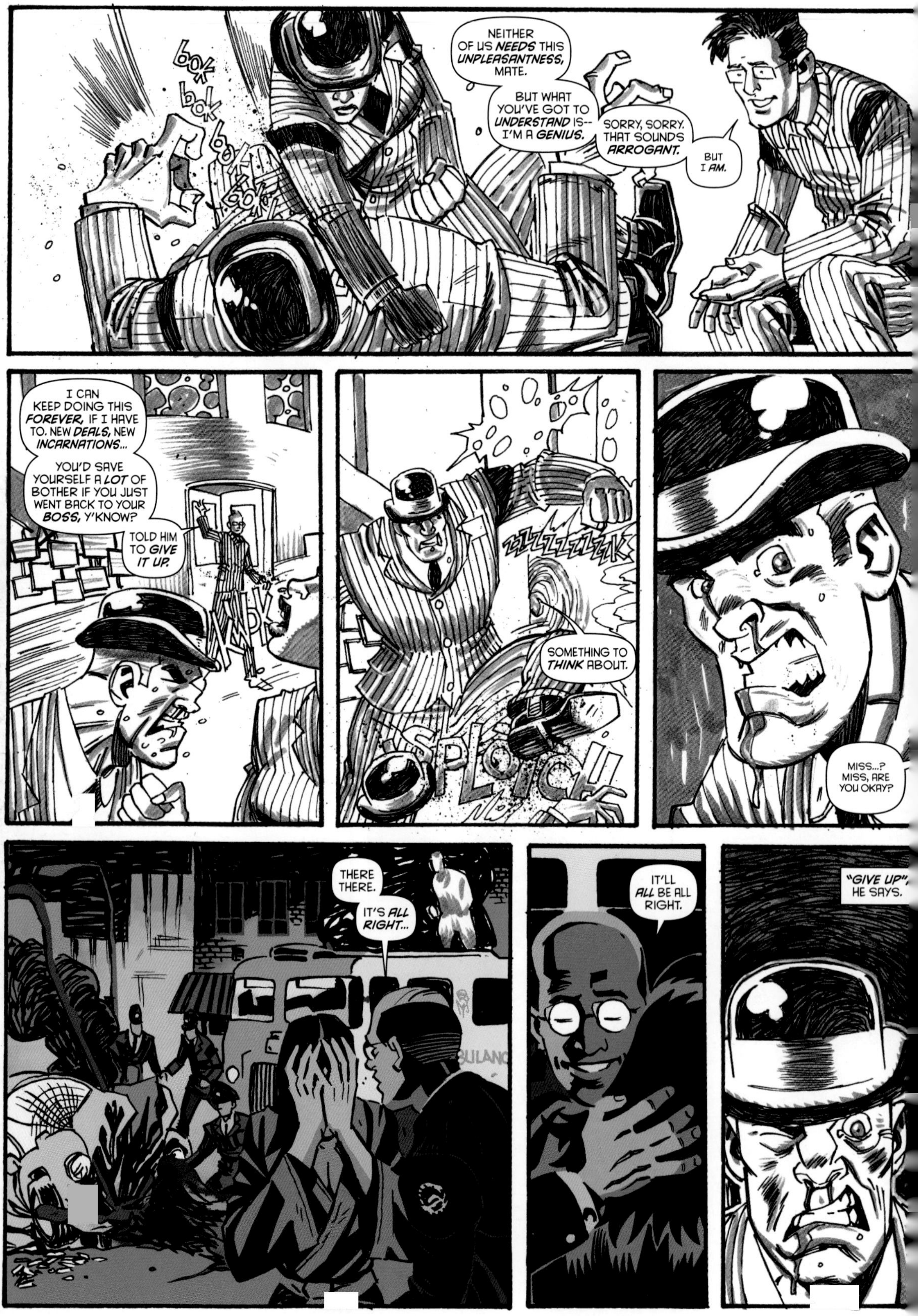
bok
bok
bok
bok
NEITHER OF US NEEDS THIS UNPLEASANTNESS, MATE.
BUT WHAT YOU'VE GOT TO UNDERSTAND IS-- I'M A GENIUS.
SORRY, SORRY. THAT SOUNDS ARROGANT.
BUT I AM.
I CAN KEEP DOING THIS FOREVER, IF I HAVE TO. NEW DEALS, NEW INCARNATIONS...
YOU'D SAVE YOURSELF A LOT OF BOTHER IF YOU JUST WENT BACK TO YOUR BOSS, Y'KNOW?
TOLD HIM TO GIVE IT UP.
ZZZZZZZZK
SOMETHING TO THINK ABOUT.
SPLOTCH!!
MISS...? MISS, ARE YOU OKAY?
THERE THERE.
IT'S ALL RIGHT...
IT'LL ALL BE ALL RIGHT.
"GIVE UP", HE SAYS.

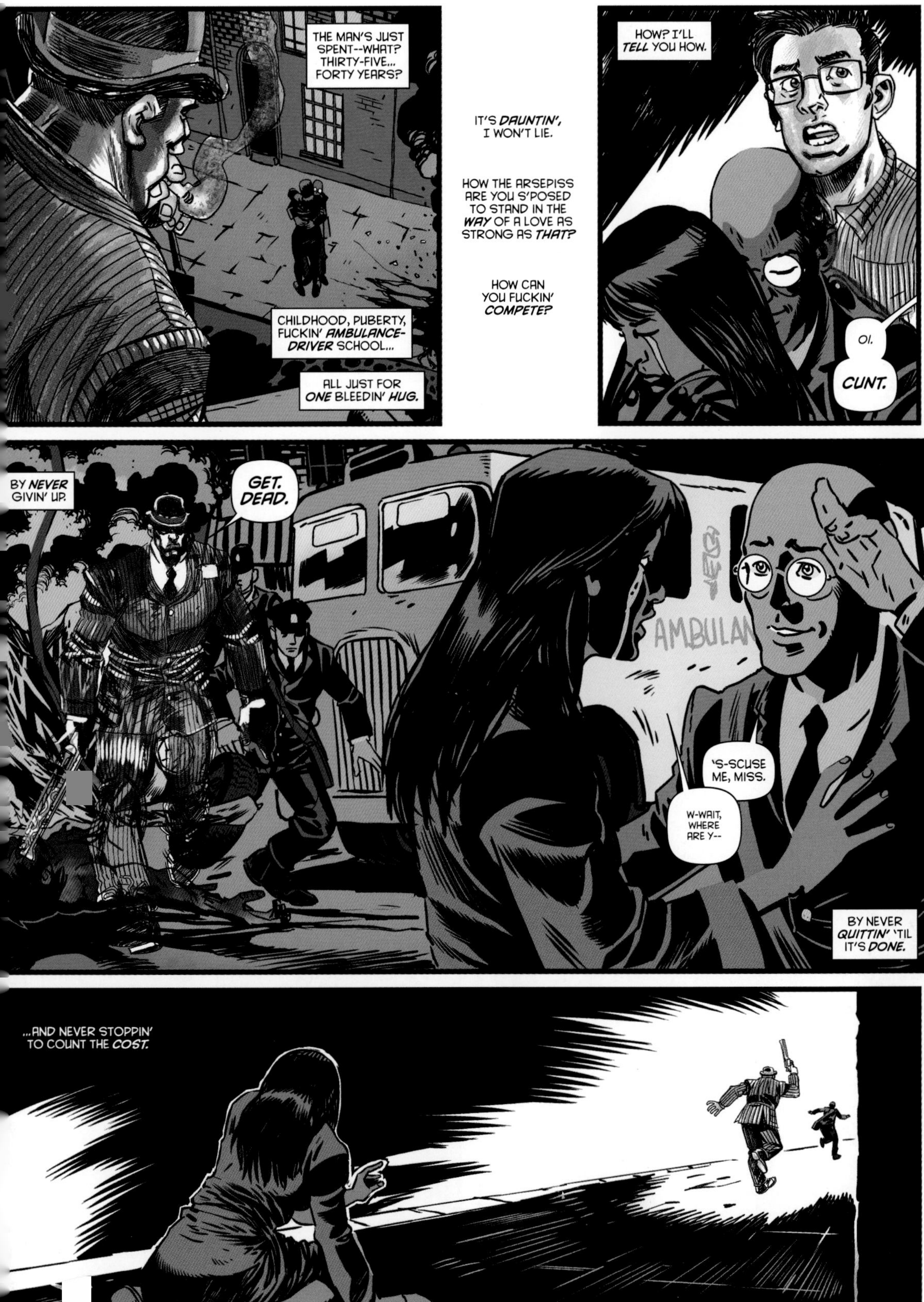
THE MAN'S JUST SPENT--WHAT? THIRTY-FIVE... FORTY YEARS?
CHILDHOOD, PUBERTY, FUCKIN' AMBULANCE-DRIVER SCHOOL...
ALL JUST FOR ONE BLEEDIN' HUG.
IT'S DAUNTIN', I WON'T LIE.
HOW THE ARSEPISS ARE YOU S'POSED TO STAND IN THE WAY OF A LOVE AS STRONG AS THAT?
HOW CAN YOU FUCKIN' COMPETE?
HOW? I'LL TELL YOU HOW.
OI.
CUNT.
BY NEVER GIVIN' UP.
GET. DEAD.
AMBULAN
'S-SCUSE ME, MISS.
W-WAIT, WHERE ARE Y--
BY NEVER QUITTIN' 'TIL IT'S DONE.
...AND NEVER STOPPIN' TO COUNT THE COST.

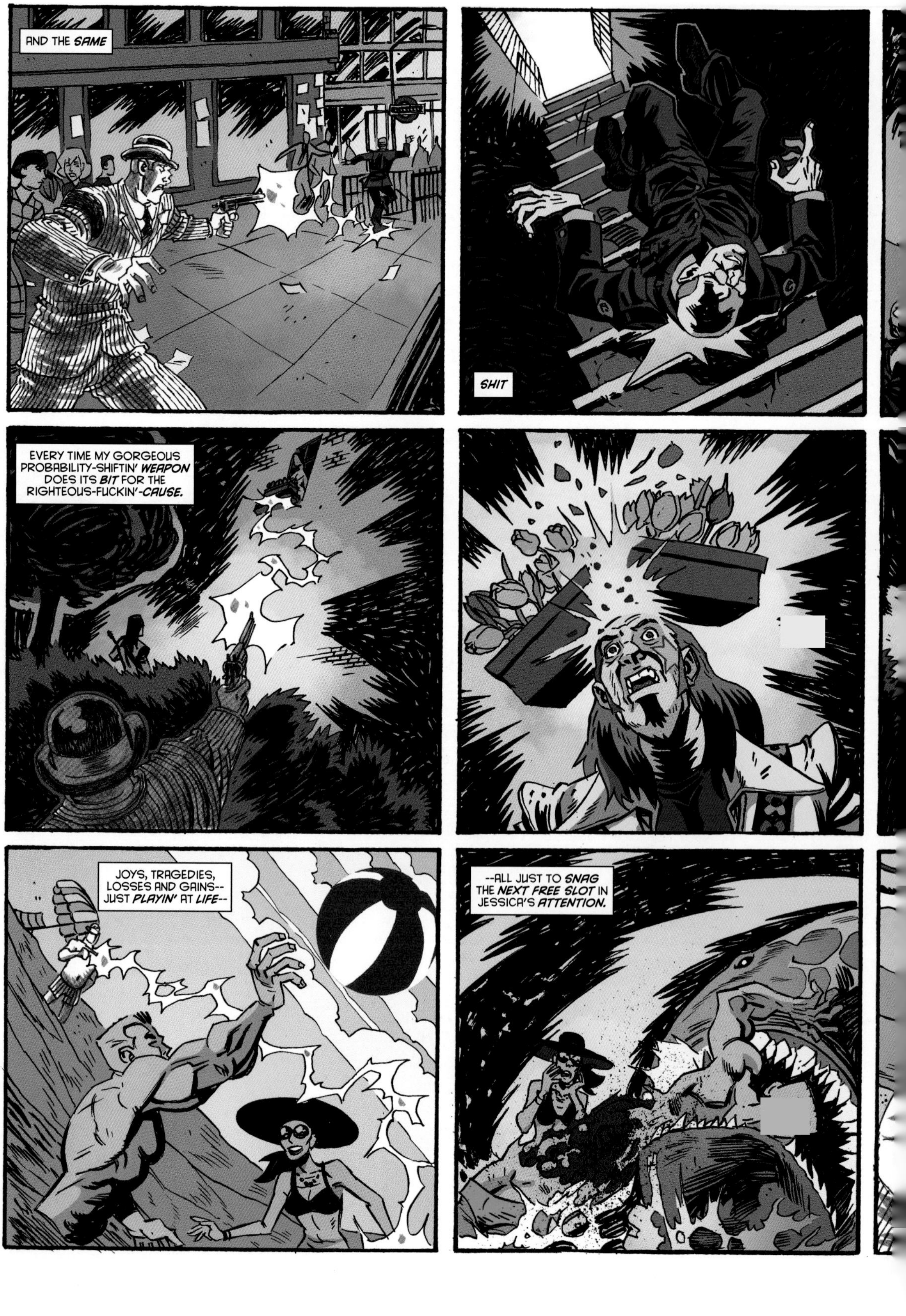
AND THE SAME
SHIT
EVERY TIME MY GORGEOUS PROBABILITY-SHIFTIN' WEAPON DOES ITS BIT FOR THE RIGHTEOUS-FUCKIN'-CAUSE.
JOYS, TRAGEDIES, LOSSES AND GAINS-- JUST PLAYIN' AT LIFE--
--ALL JUST TO SNAG THE NEXT FREE SLOT IN JESSICA'S ATTENTION.

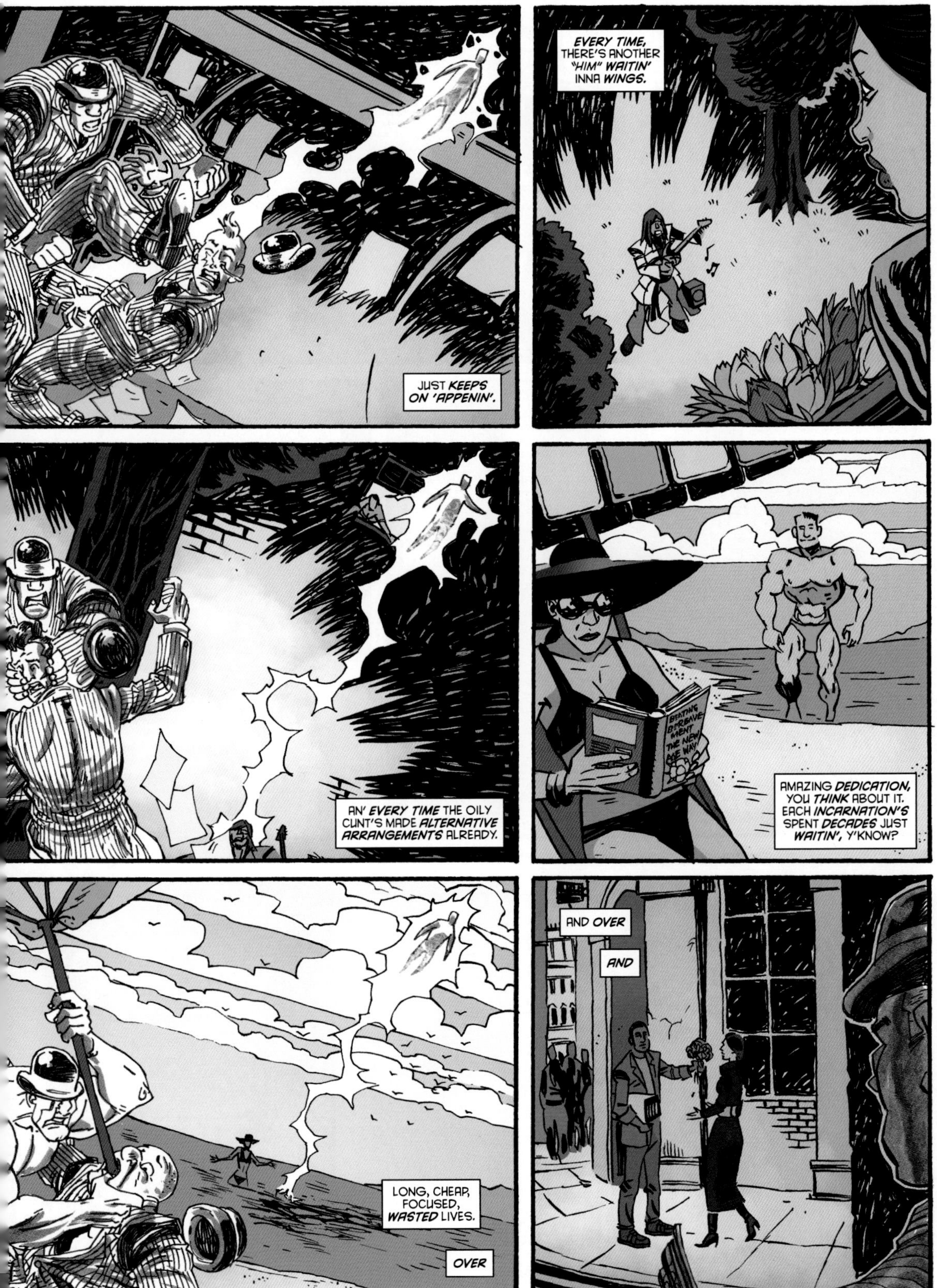

JUST KEEPS ON 'APPENIN'.
EVERY TIME, THERE'S ANOTHER "HIM" WAITIN' INNA WINGS.
AN' EVERY TIME THE OILY CUNT'S MADE ALTERNATIVE ARRANGEMENTS ALREADY.
AMAZING DEDICATION, YOU THINK ABOUT IT. EACH INCARNATION'S SPENT DECADES JUST WAITIN', Y'KNOW?
LONG, CHEAP, FOCUSED, WASTED LIVES.
OVER
AND OVER
AND

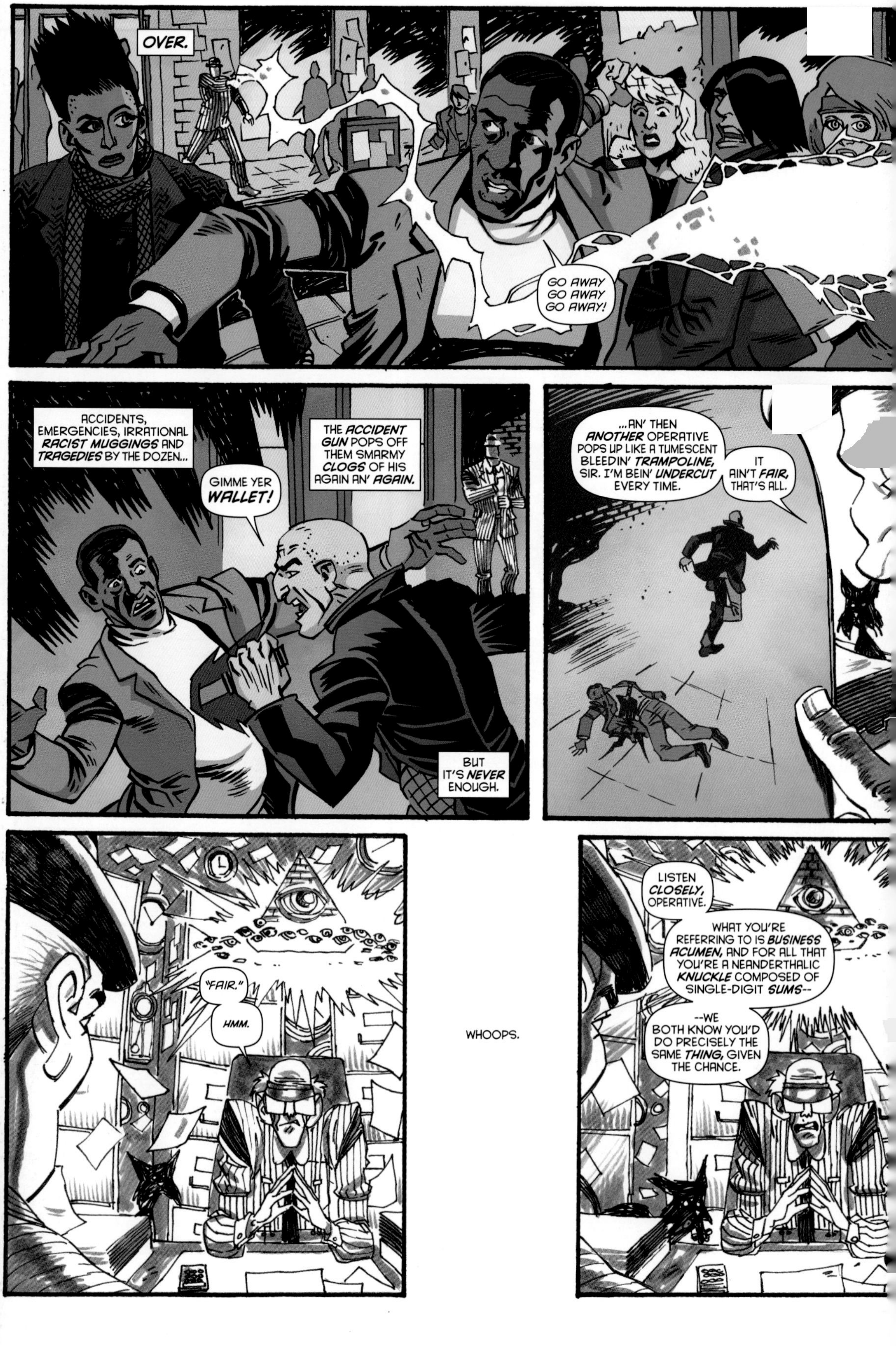
OVER.
GO AWAY
GO AWAY
GO AWAY!
ACCIDENTS, EMERGENCIES, IRRATIONAL RACIST MUGGINGS AND TRAGEDIES BY THE DOZEN...
GIMME YER WALLET!
THE ACCIDENT GUN POPS OFF THEM SMARMY CLOGS OF HIS AGAIN AN' AGAIN.
BUT IT'S NEVER ENOUGH.
...AN' THEN ANOTHER OPERATIVE POPS UP LIKE A TUMESCENT BLEEDIN' TRAMPOLINE, SIR. I'M BEIN' UNDERCUT EVERY TIME.
IT AIN'T FAIR, THAT'S ALL.
"FAIR."
HMM.
WHOOPS.
LISTEN CLOSELY, OPERATIVE.
WHAT YOU'RE REFERRING TO IS BUSINESS ACUMEN, AND FOR ALL THAT YOU'RE A NEANDERTHALIC KNUCKLE COMPOSED OF SINGLE-DIGIT SUMS--
--WE BOTH KNOW YOU'D DO PRECISELY THE SAME THING, GIVEN THE CHANCE.

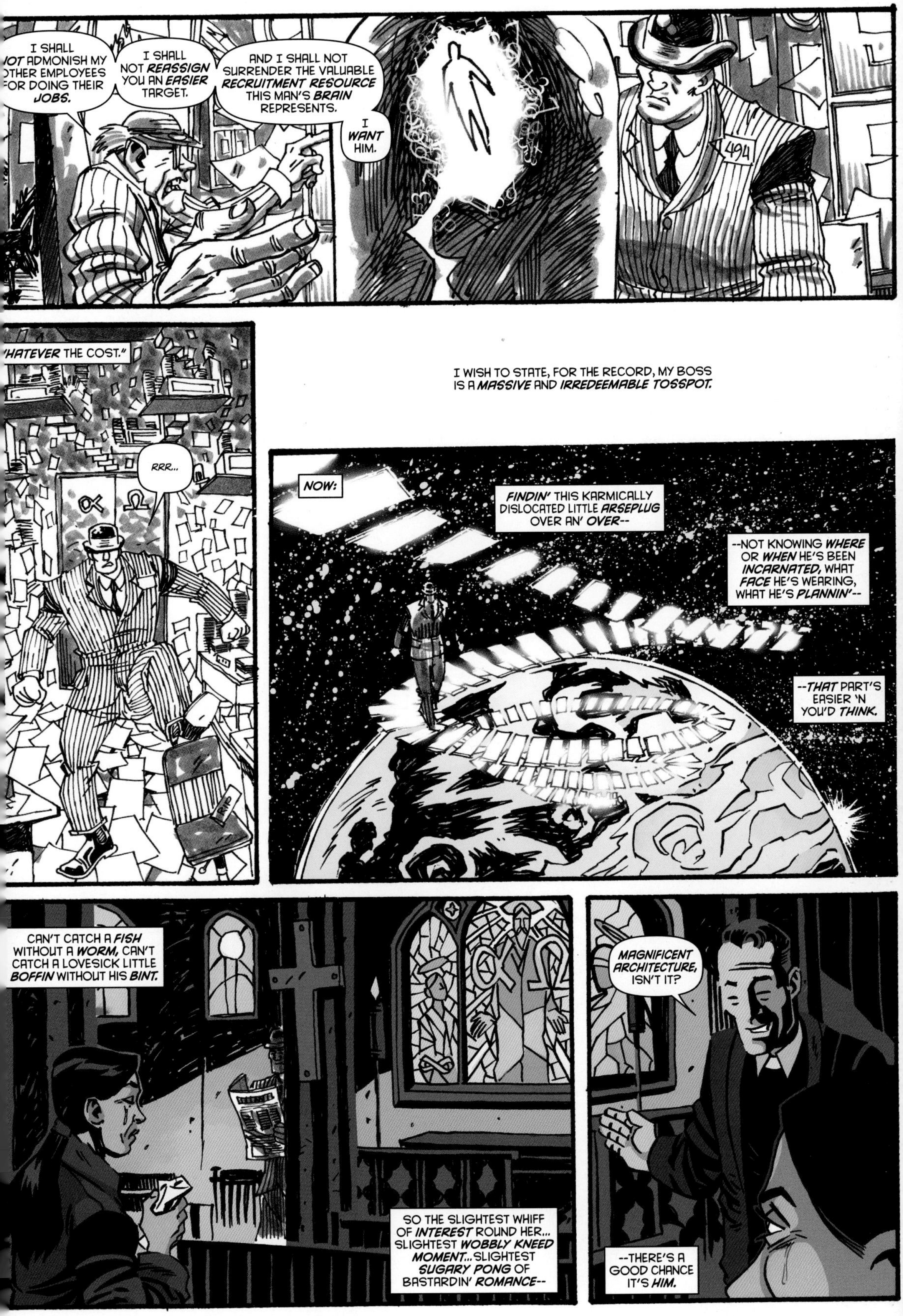

I SHALL NOT ADMONISH MY OTHER EMPLOYEES FOR DOING THEIR JOBS.
I SHALL NOT REASSIGN YOU AN EASIER TARGET.
AND I SHALL NOT SURRENDER THE VALUABLE RECRUITMENT RESOURCE THIS MAN'S BRAIN REPRESENTS.
I WANT HIM.
494
"WHATEVER THE COST."
RRR...
I WISH TO STATE, FOR THE RECORD, MY BOSS IS A MASSIVE AND IRREDEEMABLE TOSSPOT.
NOW:
FINDIN' THIS KARMICALLY DISLOCATED LITTLE ARSEPLUG OVER AN' OVER--
--NOT KNOWING WHERE OR WHEN HE'S BEEN INCARNATED, WHAT FACE HE'S WEARING, WHAT HE'S PLANNIN'--
--THAT PART'S EASIER 'N YOU'D THINK.
CAN'T CATCH A FISH WITHOUT A WORM, CAN'T CATCH A LOVESICK LITTLE BOFFIN WITHOUT HIS BINT.
SO THE SLIGHTEST WHIFF OF INTEREST ROUND HER... SLIGHTEST WOBBLY KNEED MOMENT... SLIGHTEST SUGARY PONG OF BASTARDIN' ROMANCE--
MAGNIFICENT ARCHITECTURE, ISN'T IT?
--THERE'S A GOOD CHANCE IT'S HIM.

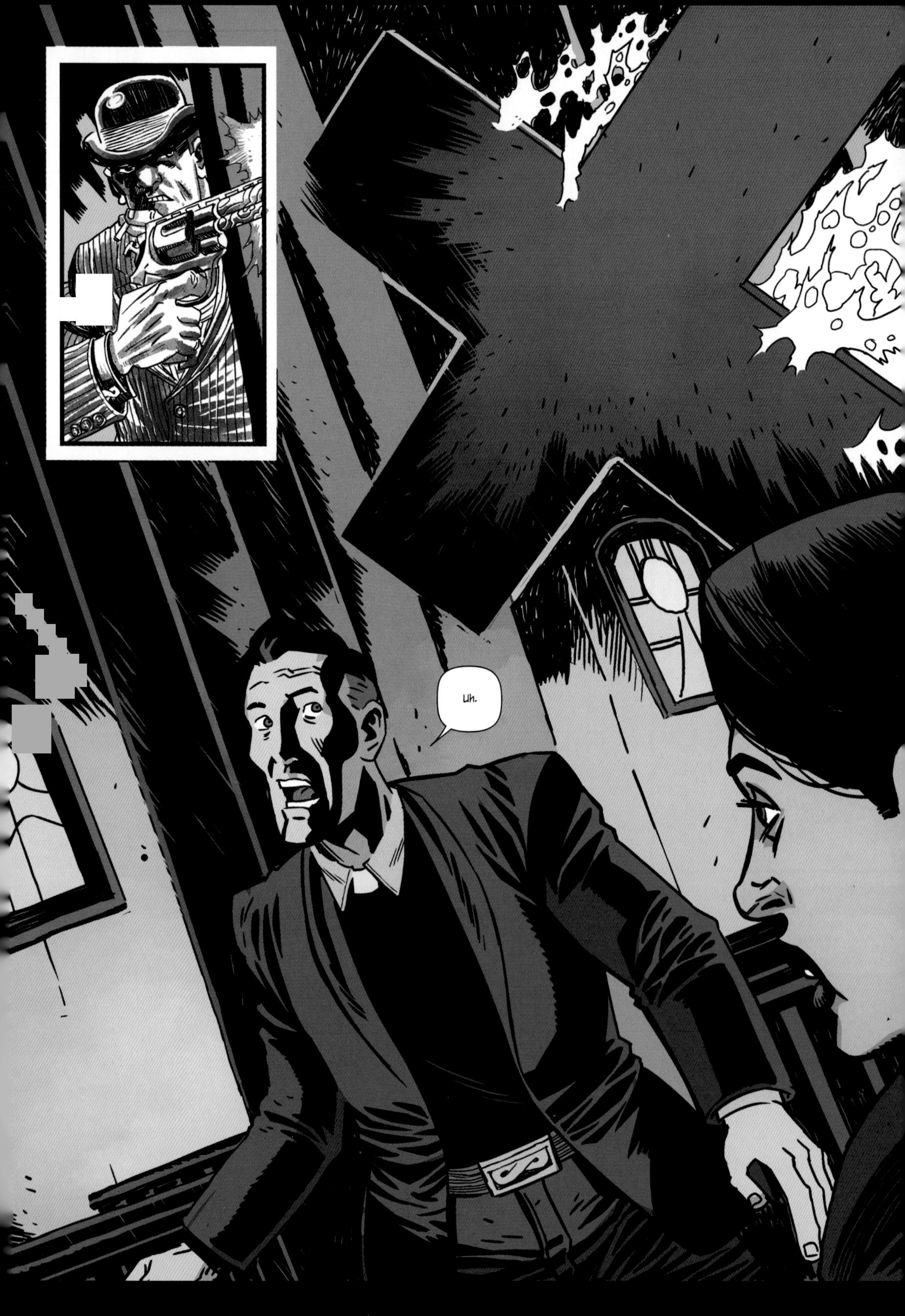
Uh.

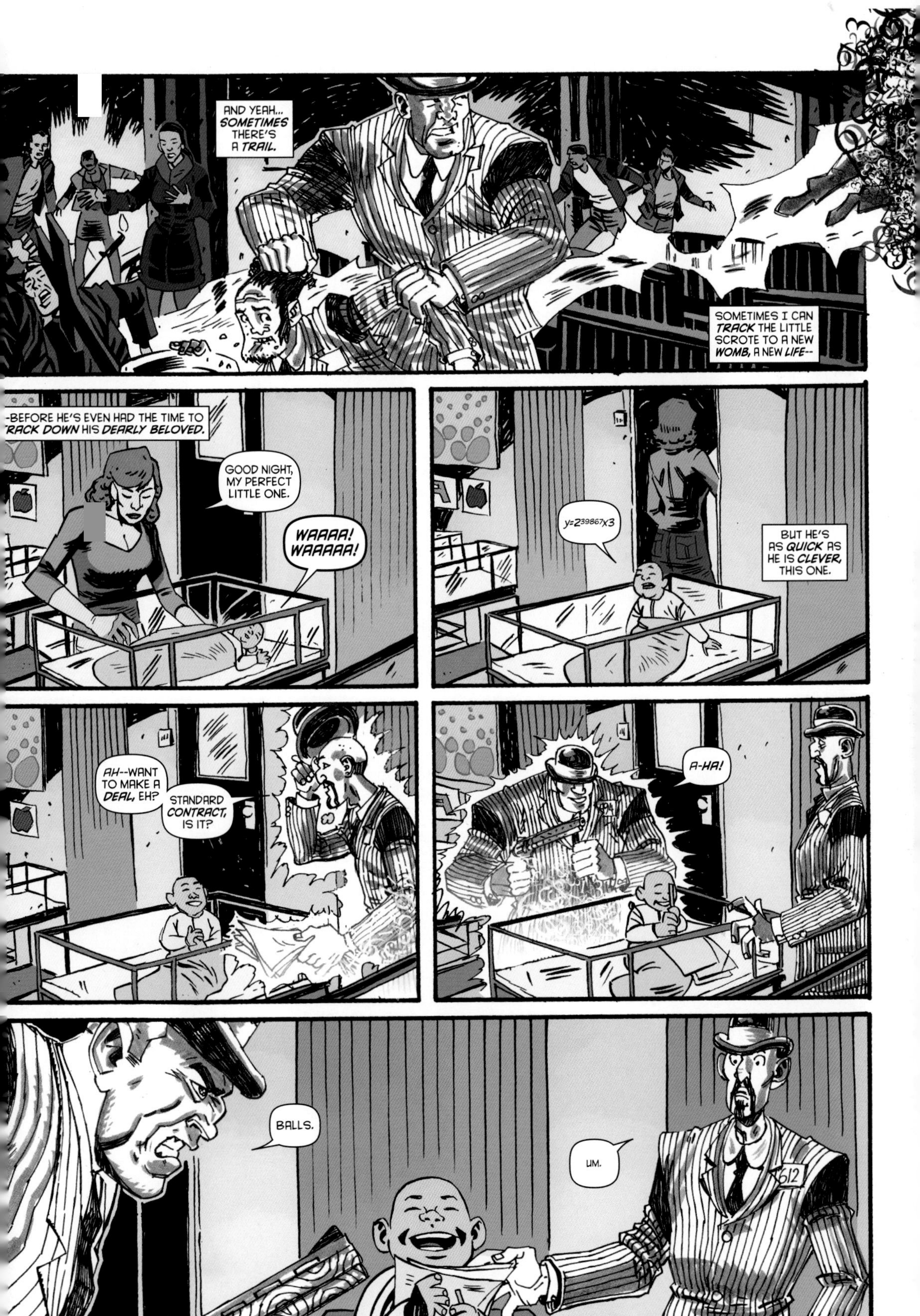
AND YEAH... SOMETIMES THERE'S A TRAIL.
SOMETIMES I CAN TRACK THE LITTLE SCROTE TO A NEW WOMB, A NEW LIFE--
--BEFORE HE'S EVEN HAD THE TIME TO TRACK DOWN HIS DEARLY BELOVED.
GOOD NIGHT, MY PERFECT LITTLE ONE.
WAAAAA! WAAAAAA!
$y=z^{39867}x3$
BUT HE'S AS QUICK AS HE IS CLEVER, THIS ONE.
AH--WANT TO MAKE A DEAL, EH?
STANDARD CONTRACT, IS IT?
A-HA!
BALLS.
UM.
612

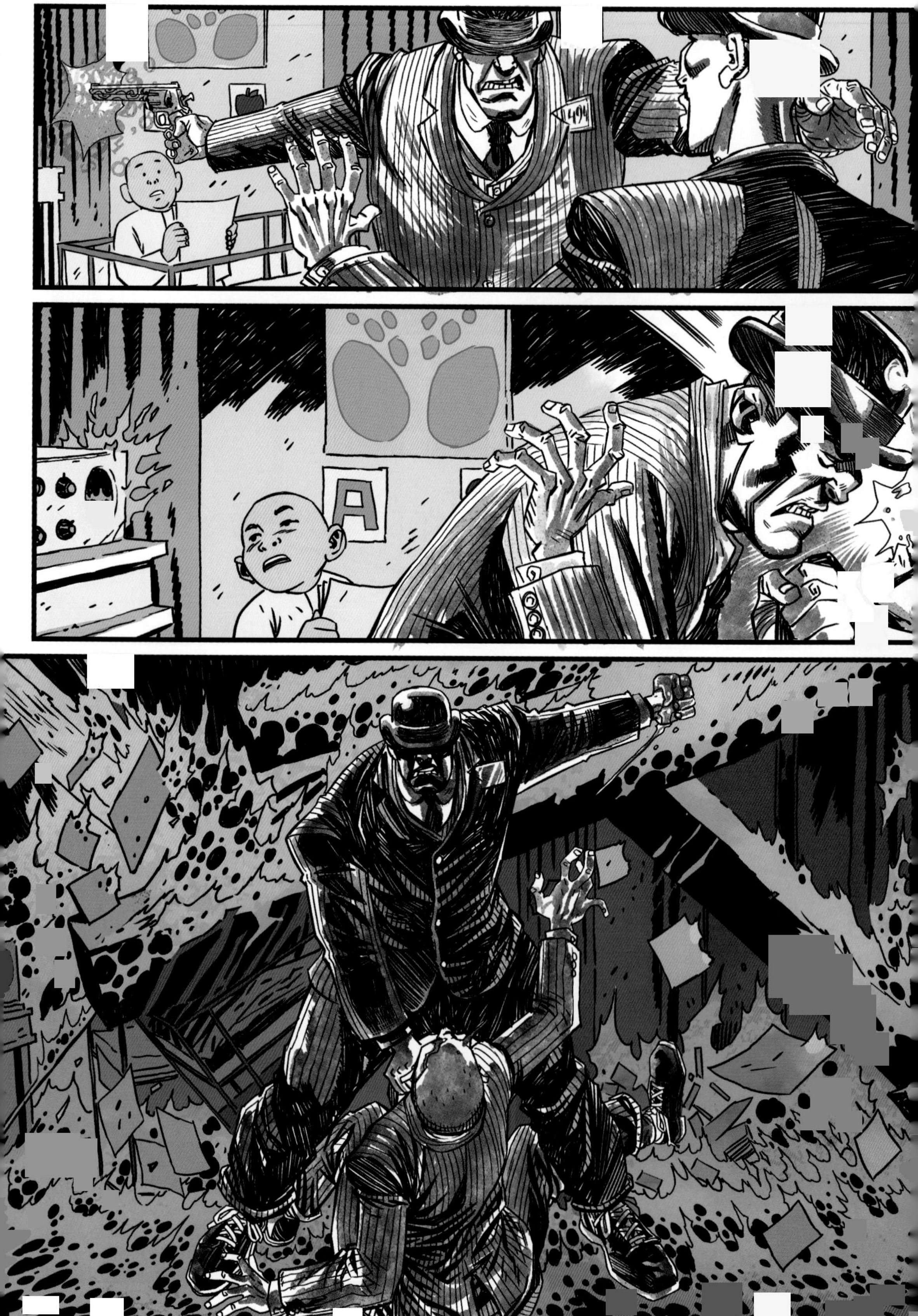

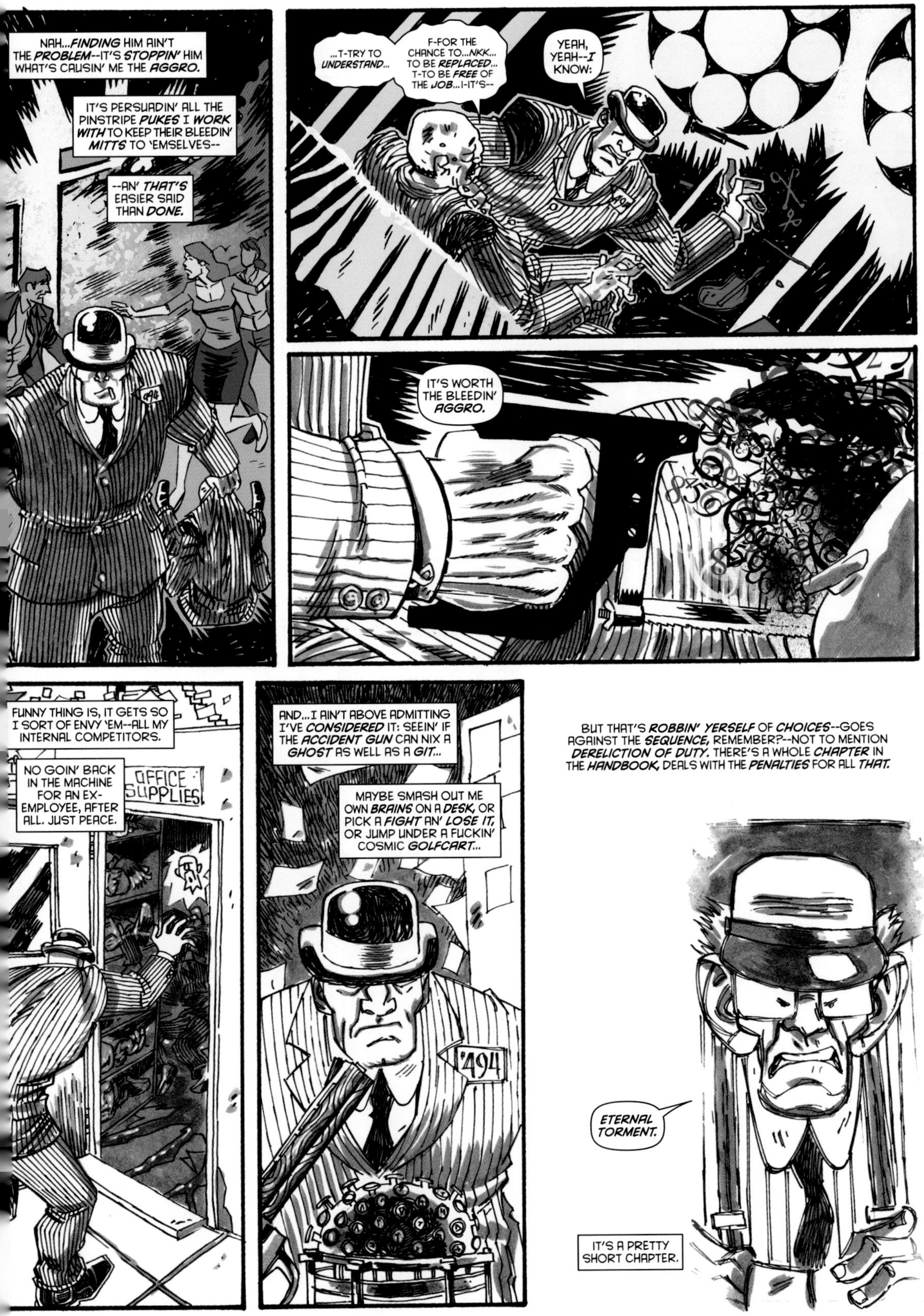
NAH...FINDING HIM AIN'T THE PROBLEM--IT'S STOPPIN' HIM WHAT'S CAUSIN' ME THE AGGRO.
IT'S PERSUADIN' ALL THE PINSTRIPE PUKES I WORK WITH TO KEEP THEIR BLEEDIN' MITTS TO 'EMSELVES--
--AN' THAT'S EASIER SAID THAN DONE.
...T-TRY TO UNDERSTAND...
F-FOR THE CHANCE TO...NKK... TO BE REPLACED... T-TO BE FREE OF THE JOB...I-IT'S--
YEAH, YEAH--I KNOW:
IT'S WORTH THE BLEEDIN' AGGRO.
FUNNY THING IS, IT GETS SO I SORT OF ENVY 'EM--ALL MY INTERNAL COMPETITORS.
NO GOIN' BACK IN THE MACHINE FOR AN EX-EMPLOYEE, AFTER ALL. JUST PEACE.
OFFICE SUPPLIES
AND...I AIN'T ABOVE ADMITTING I'VE CONSIDERED IT: SEEIN' IF THE ACCIDENT GUN CAN NIX A GHOST AS WELL AS A GIT...
MAYBE SMASH OUT ME OWN BRAINS ON A DESK, OR PICK A FIGHT AN' LOSE IT, OR JUMP UNDER A FUCKIN' COSMIC GOLFCART...
494
BUT THAT'S ROBBIN' YERSELF OF CHOICES--GOES AGAINST THE SEQUENCE, REMEMBER?--NOT TO MENTION DERELICTION OF DUTY. THERE'S A WHOLE CHAPTER IN THE HANDBOOK, DEALS WITH THE PENALTIES FOR ALL THAT.
ETERNAL TORMENT.
IT'S A PRETTY SHORT CHAPTER.

SO THE MATHEMATICIAN KEEPS ON GETTIN' THROUGH TO *JESS*-- YEARS TICKIN' ON *BY*--

--AN' *I* KEEP ON PLAYING THE *KILLJOY*, LURKIN' ROUND HER LIKE A BAD BLEEDIN' *SMELL*.

HE AIN'T JUST ABOUT *LUSTIN'* FOR THE *FLESH*, MIND.

FIRST IT'S THE *LOVE LETTERS*, INNIT? THEN *TEXT MESSAGES*, DIRECT *TWEETS*, POD-TO-POD BLOODY *E-RUTTING*...

HE'S *BRIGHTER'N* ME AND HE *FUCKIN' KNOWS* IT--

--SO BEFORE YOU CAN SAY "*SMUG LITTLE TIT*" HE'S STARTED TARGETING *ME* 'N ALL.

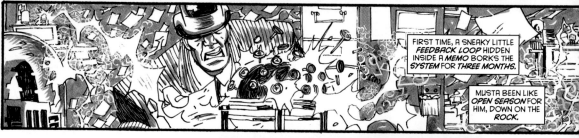

FIRST TIME, A SNEAKY LITTLE *FEEDBACK LOOP* HIDDEN INSIDE A *MEMO* BORKS THE *SYSTEM* FOR *THREE MONTHS*.

MUSTA BEEN LIKE *OPEN SEASON* FOR HIM, DOWN ON THE *ROCK*.

ANOTHER TIME HE MAKES A *FRACTAL SHIELD* TO WEAR UNDER HIS *JACKET*. TAKES A *MONTH* TO *RETUNE* ME *ASTRAL BULLETS*, FOR THAT.

ONE TIME HE LAYS A *PARADOX TRAP* IN THE BRAIN OF A *COMATOSE INCARNATION*, AN' I'M SQUEEZIN' *MANDELBROTS* OUT ME *ARSE* FOR A BLEEDIN' *YEAR*.

HELL, ONE TIME HE USES A FUCKIN' *LUCKY CHARM* TO KEEP ME OUT--

(WHICH IS PROOF HE'S EITHER *GETTIN' DESPERATE* OR TURNIN' JUST AS HIPPYSHIT *MENTAL* AS HIS *MISSUS*)

--BUT IT STILL BLEEDIN' *WORKS*.

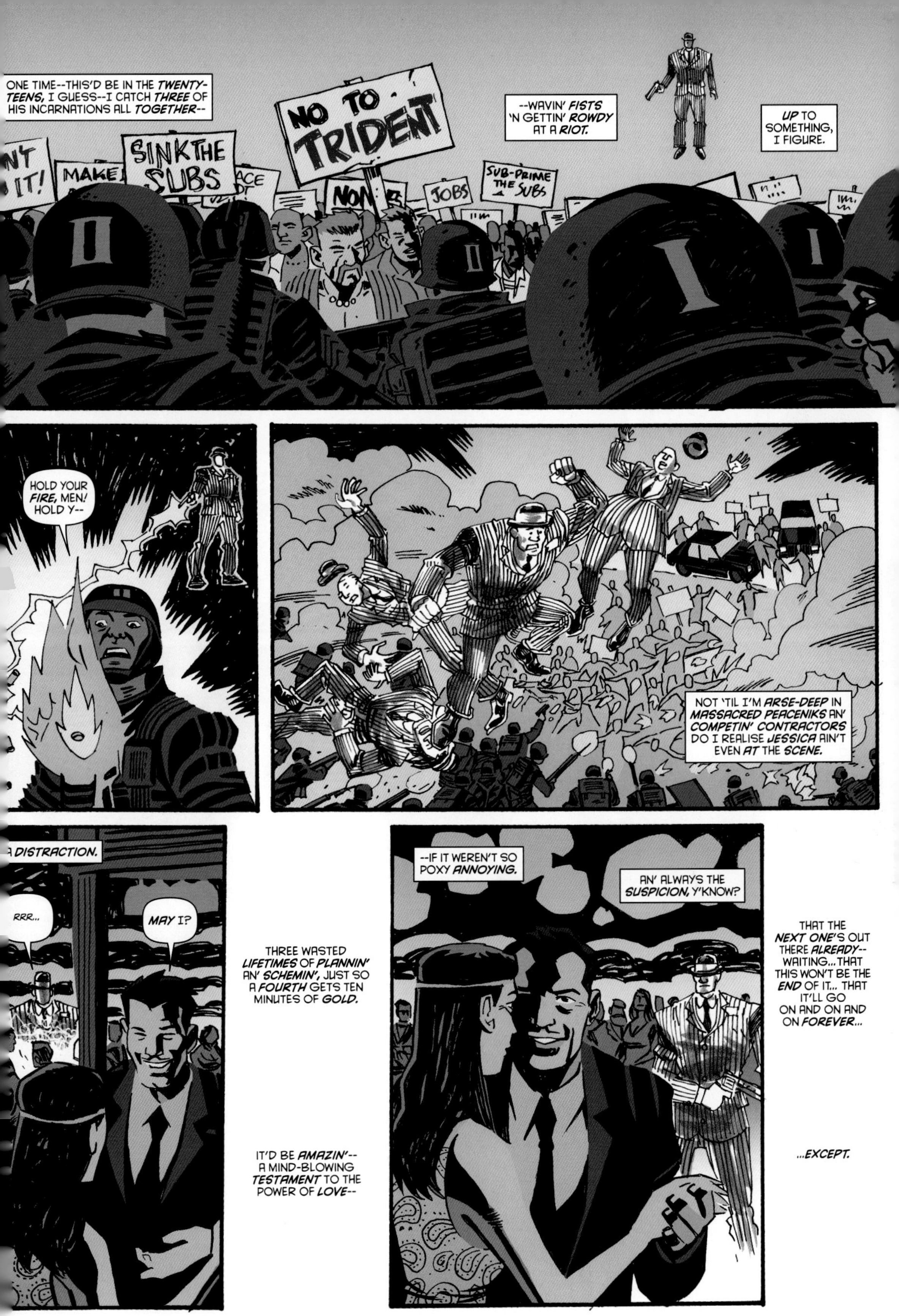
ONE TIME--THIS'D BE IN THE TWENTY-TEENS, I GUESS--I CATCH THREE OF HIS INCARNATIONS ALL TOGETHER--
NO TO TRIDENT
SINK THE SUBS
SUB-PRIME THE SUBS
JOBS
--WAVIN' FISTS 'N GETTIN' ROWDY AT A RIOT.
UP TO SOMETHING, I FIGURE.
HOLD YOUR FIRE, MEN! HOLD Y--
NOT 'TIL I'M ARSE-DEEP IN MASSACRED PEACENIKS AN' COMPETIN' CONTRACTORS DO I REALISE JESSICA AIN'T EVEN AT THE SCENE.
A DISTRACTION.
RRR...
MAY I?
THREE WASTED LIFETIMES OF PLANNIN' AN' SCHEMIN', JUST SO A FOURTH GETS TEN MINUTES OF GOLD.
IT'D BE AMAZIN'--A MIND-BLOWING TESTAMENT TO THE POWER OF LOVE--
--IF IT WEREN'T SO POXY ANNOYING.
AN' ALWAYS THE SUSPICION, Y'KNOW?
THAT THE NEXT ONE'S OUT THERE ALREADY--WAITING... THAT THIS WON'T BE THE END OF IT... THAT IT'LL GO ON AND ON AND ON FOREVER...
...EXCEPT.

EXCEPT THAT IN AMIDST IT ALL--
THE FIDDLIN' AND FIXIN' AND FANNYIN'
ABOUT WITH *REALITY*--THERE'S *ONE*
RESOURCE YOU'D CALL
CONSPICUOUSLY BLOODY *FINITE.*

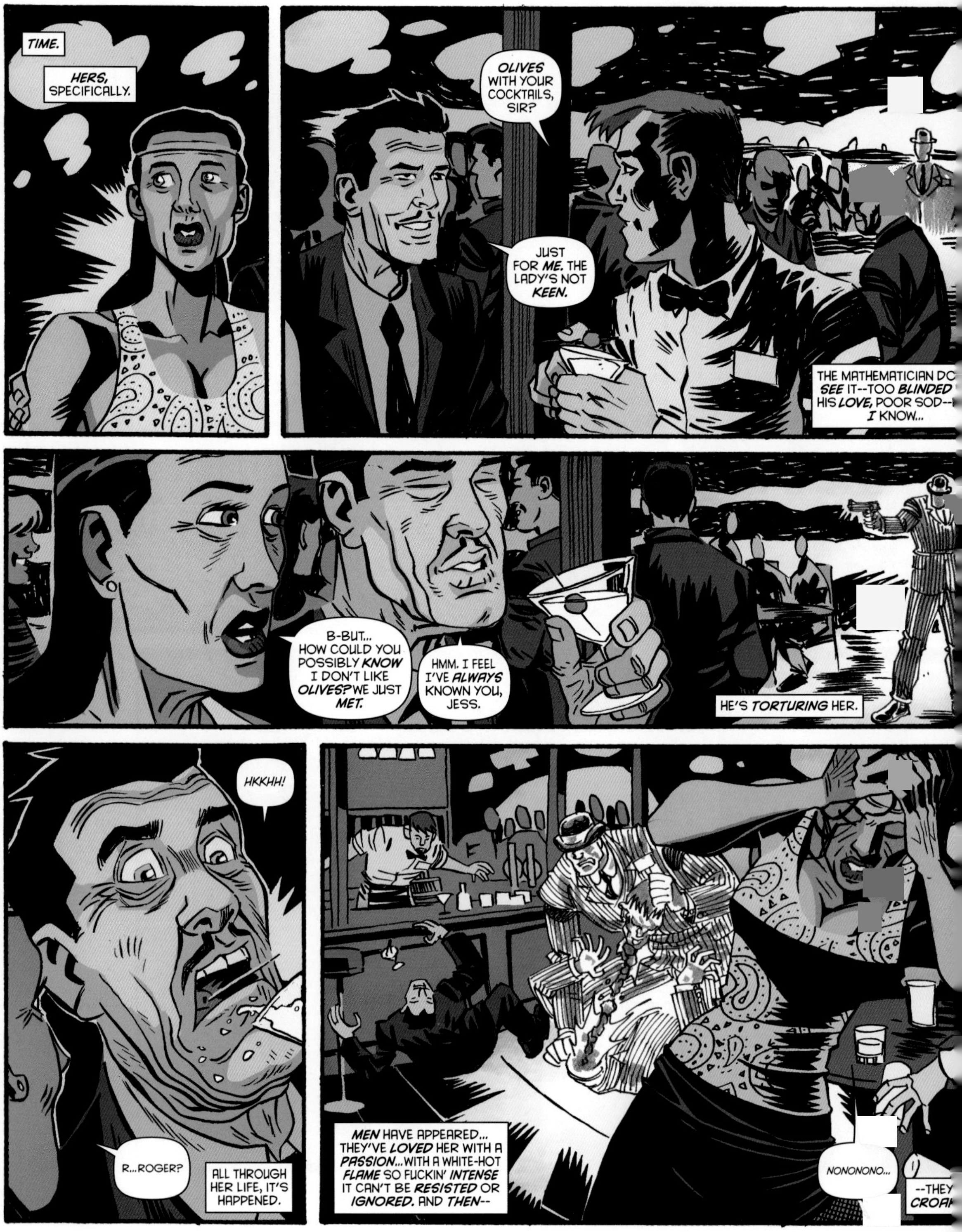
TIME.
HERS, SPECIFICALLY.
OLIVES WITH YOUR COCKTAILS, SIR?
JUST FOR ME. THE LADY'S NOT KEEN.
THE MATHEMATICIAN DC SEE IT--TOO BLINDED HIS LOVE, POOR SOD-- I KNOW...
B-BUT... HOW COULD YOU POSSIBLY KNOW I DON'T LIKE OLIVES? WE JUST MET.
HMM. I FEEL I'VE ALWAYS KNOWN YOU, JESS.
HE'S TORTURING HER.
HKKHH!
R...ROGER?
ALL THROUGH HER LIFE, IT'S HAPPENED.
MEN HAVE APPEARED... THEY'VE LOVED HER WITH A PASSION... WITH A WHITE-HOT FLAME SO FUCKIN' INTENSE IT CAN'T BE RESISTED OR IGNORED. AND THEN--
NONONONO...
--THEY CROA

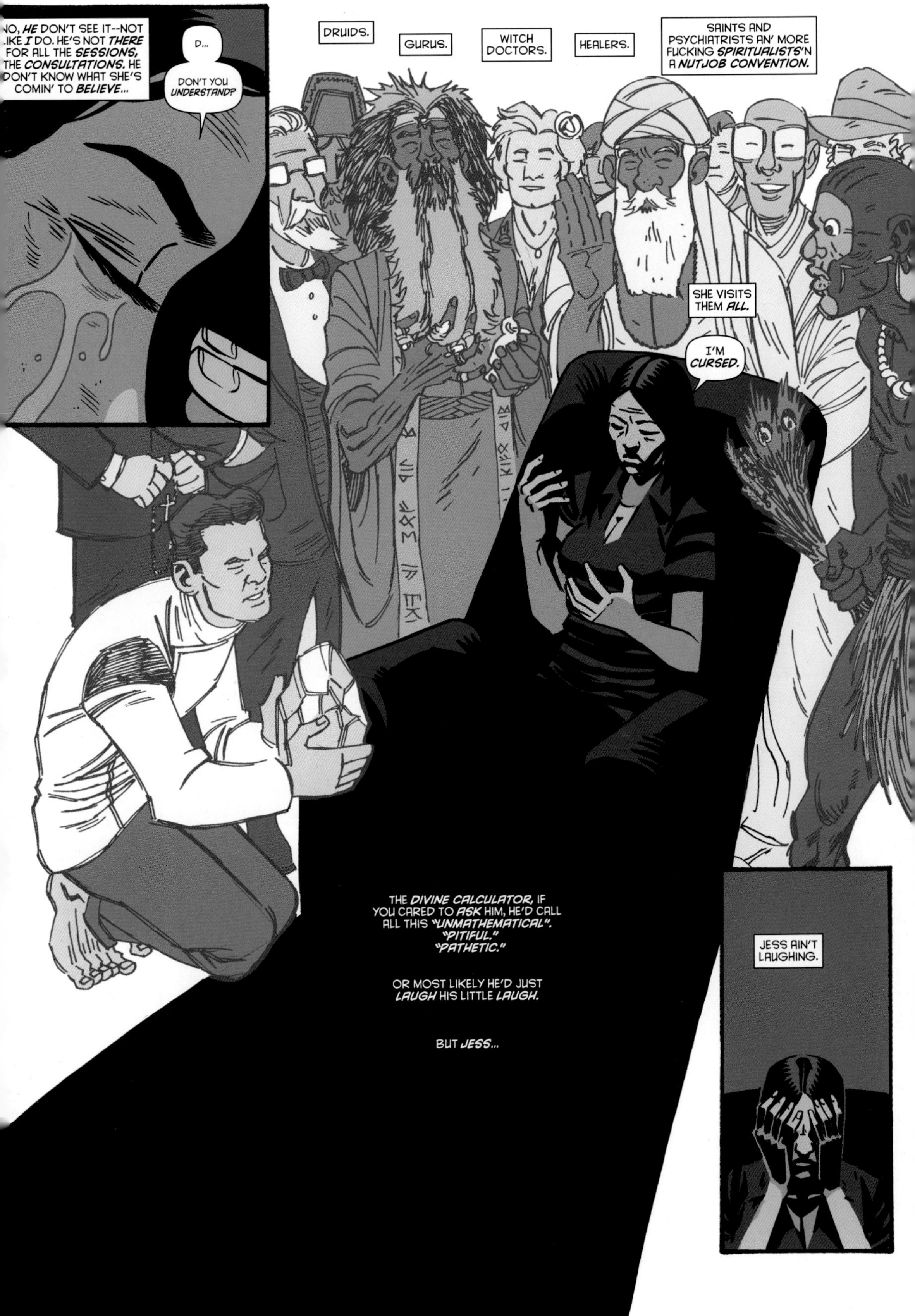

NO, HE DON'T SEE IT--NOT LIKE I DO. HE'S NOT THERE FOR ALL THE SESSIONS, THE CONSULTATIONS. HE DON'T KNOW WHAT SHE'S COMIN' TO BELIEVE...
D...
DON'T YOU UNDERSTAND?
DRUIDS.
GURUS.
WITCH DOCTORS.
HEALERS.
SAINTS AND PSYCHIATRISTS AN' MORE FUCKING SPIRITUALISTS'N A NUTJOB CONVENTION.
SHE VISITS THEM ALL.
I'M CURSED.
THE DIVINE CALCULATOR, IF YOU CARED TO ASK HIM, HE'D CALL ALL THIS "UNMATHEMATICAL". "PITIFUL." "PATHETIC."
OR MOST LIKELY HE'D JUST LAUGH HIS LITTLE LAUGH.
BUT JESS...
JESS AIN'T LAUGHING.

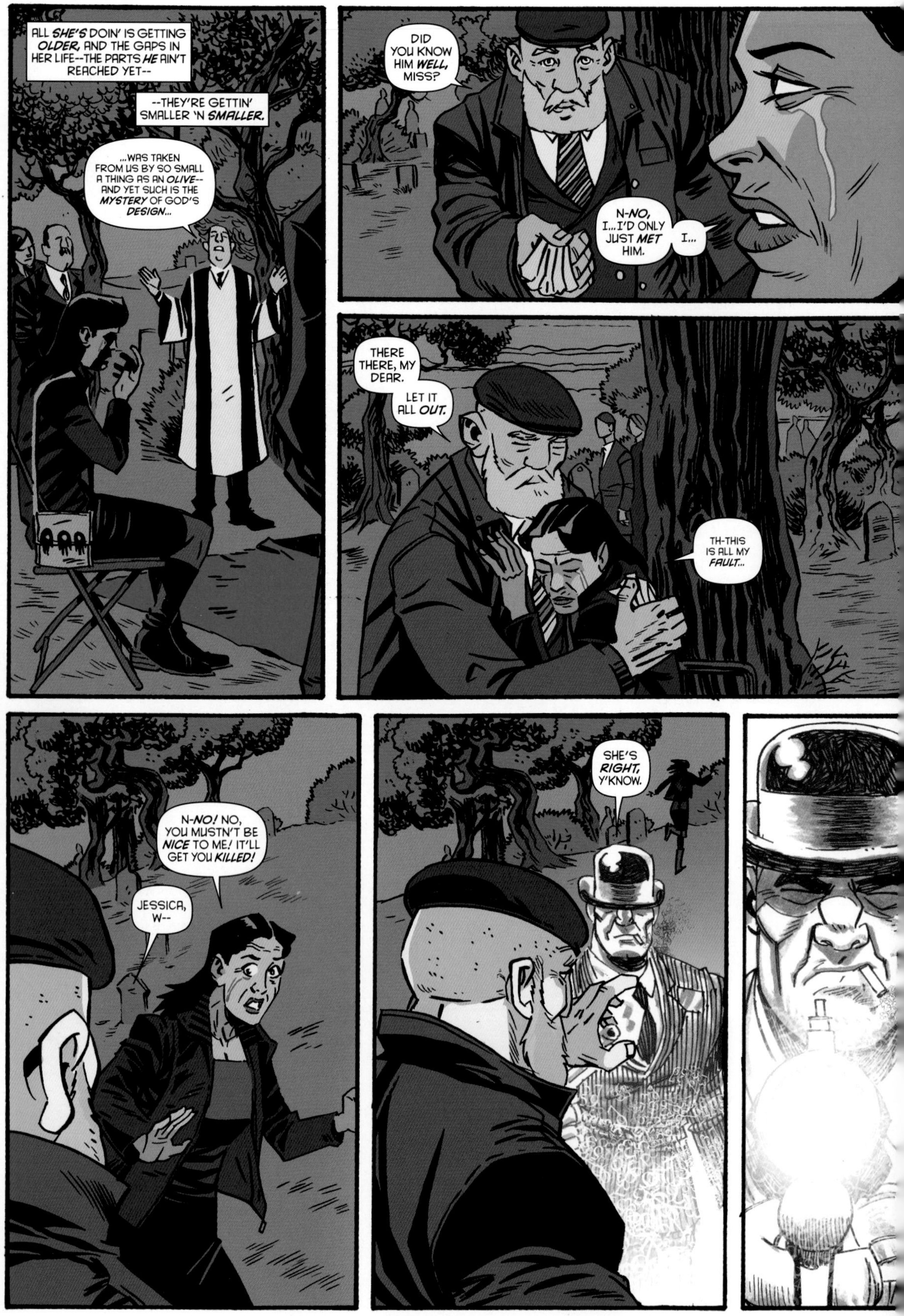
ALL SHE'S DOIN' IS GETTING OLDER, AND THE GAPS IN HER LIFE--THE PARTS HE AIN'T REACHED YET--
--THEY'RE GETTIN' SMALLER 'N SMALLER.
...WAS TAKEN FROM US BY SO SMALL A THING AS AN OLIVE-- AND YET SUCH IS THE MYSTERY OF GOD'S DESIGN...
DID YOU KNOW HIM WELL, MISS?
N-NO, I...I'D ONLY JUST MET HIM.
I...
THERE THERE, MY DEAR.
LET IT ALL OUT.
TH-THIS IS ALL MY FAULT...
N-NO! NO, YOU MUSTN'T BE NICE TO ME! IT'LL GET YOU KILLED!
JESSICA, W--
SHE'S RIGHT, Y'KNOW.

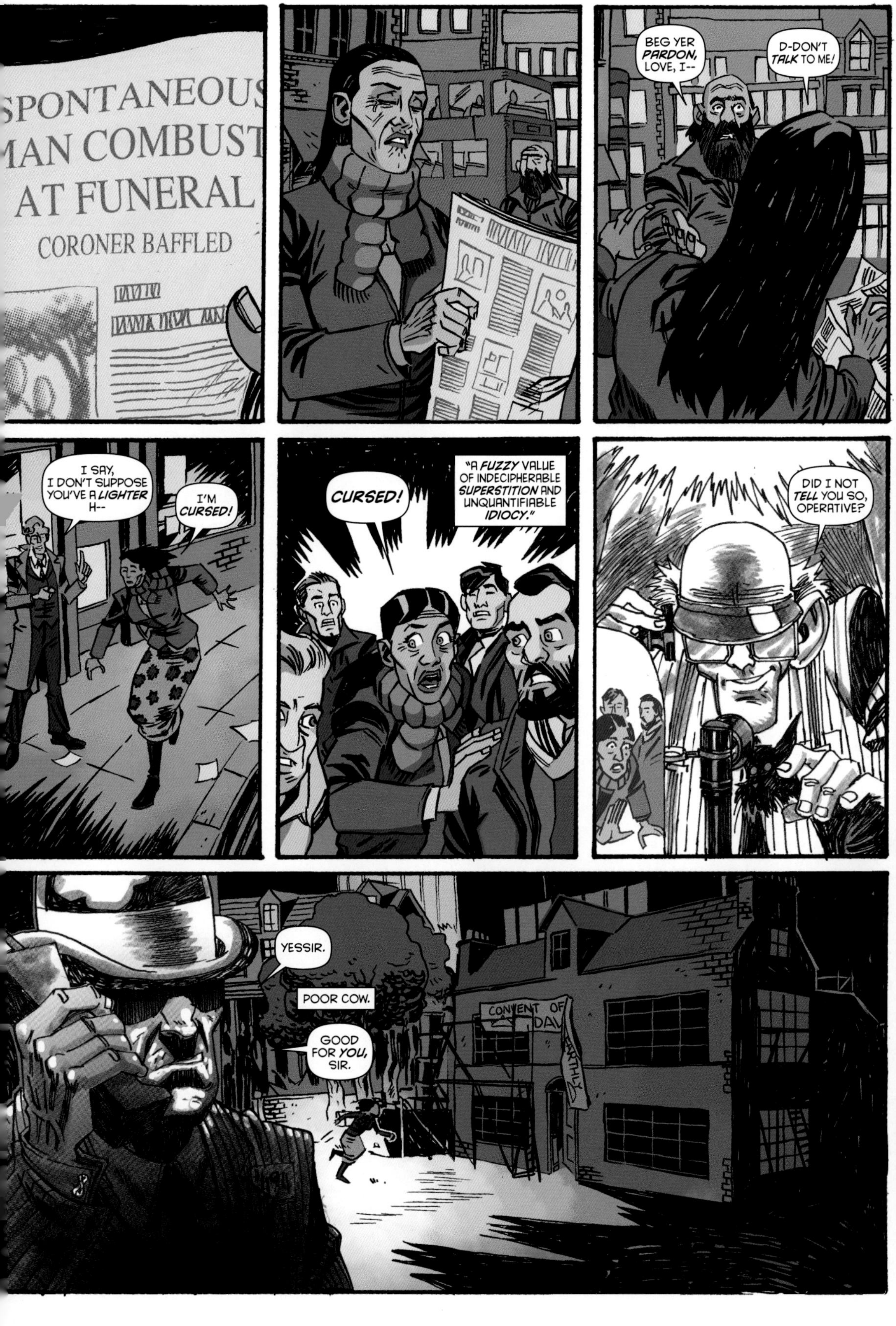
SPONTANEOUS
MAN COMBUST
AT FUNERAL
CORONER BAFFLED
BEG YER PARDON, LOVE, I--
D-DON'T TALK TO ME!
I SAY, I DON'T SUPPOSE YOU'VE A LIGHTER H--
I'M CURSED!
CURSED!
"A FUZZY VALUE OF INDECIPHERABLE SUPERSTITION AND UNQUANTIFIABLE IDIOCY."
DID I NOT TELL YOU SO, OPERATIVE?
YESSIR.
POOR COW.
GOOD FOR YOU, SIR.
CONVENT OF

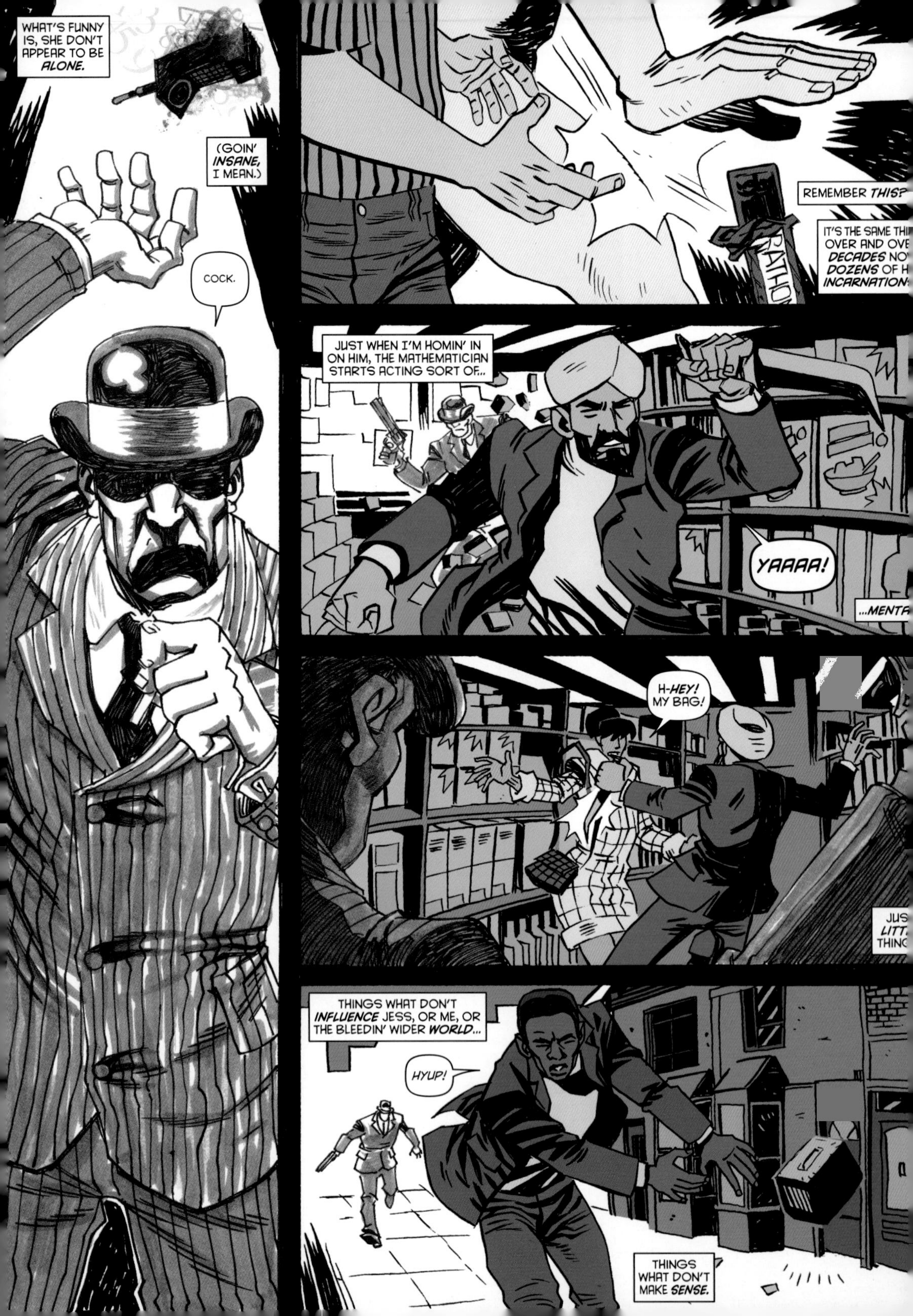
WHAT'S FUNNY IS, SHE DON'T APPEAR TO BE *ALONE.*
(GOIN' *INSANE,* I MEAN.)
COCK.
REMEMBER *THIS?*
IT'S THE SAME THI OVER AND OVE *DECADES* NO *DOZENS* OF H *INCARNATION*
JUST WHEN I'M HOMIN' IN ON HIM, THE MATHEMATICIAN STARTS ACTING SORT OF...
YAAAA!
...MENTA
H-*HEY!* MY BAG!
JUS *LITT* THING
THINGS WHAT DON'T *INFLUENCE* JESS, OR ME, OR THE BLEEDIN' WIDER *WORLD*...
HYUP!
THINGS WHAT DON'T MAKE *SENSE.*

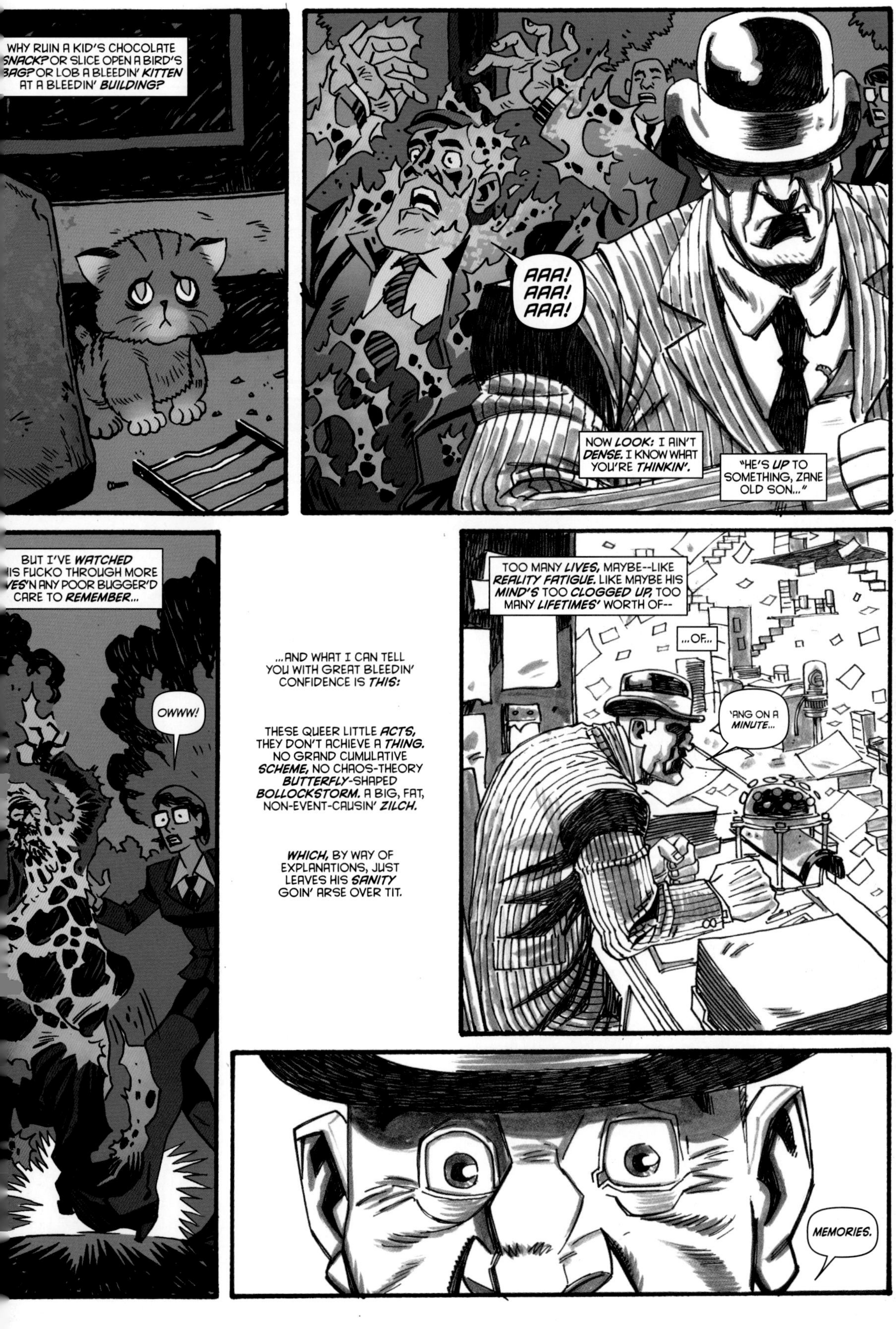

WHY RUIN A KID'S CHOCOLATE SNACK? OR SLICE OPEN A BIRD'S BAG? OR LOB A BLEEDIN' KITTEN AT A BLEEDIN' BUILDING?
AAA! AAA! AAA!
NOW LOOK: I AIN'T DENSE. I KNOW WHAT YOU'RE THINKIN'.
"HE'S UP TO SOMETHING, ZANE OLD SON..."
BUT I'VE WATCHED IS FUCKO THROUGH MORE VES'N ANY POOR BUGGER'D CARE TO REMEMBER...
OWWW!
...AND WHAT I CAN TELL YOU WITH GREAT BLEEDIN' CONFIDENCE IS THIS:
THESE QUEER LITTLE ACTS, THEY DON'T ACHIEVE A THING. NO GRAND CUMULATIVE SCHEME, NO CHAOS-THEORY BUTTERFLY-SHAPED BOLLOCKSTORM. A BIG, FAT, NON-EVENT-CAUSIN' ZILCH.
WHICH, BY WAY OF EXPLANATIONS, JUST LEAVES HIS SANITY GOIN' ARSE OVER TIT.
TOO MANY LIVES, MAYBE--LIKE REALITY FATIGUE. LIKE MAYBE HIS MIND'S TOO CLOGGED UP, TOO MANY LIFETIMES' WORTH OF--
...OF...
'ANG ON A MINUTE...
MEMORIES.

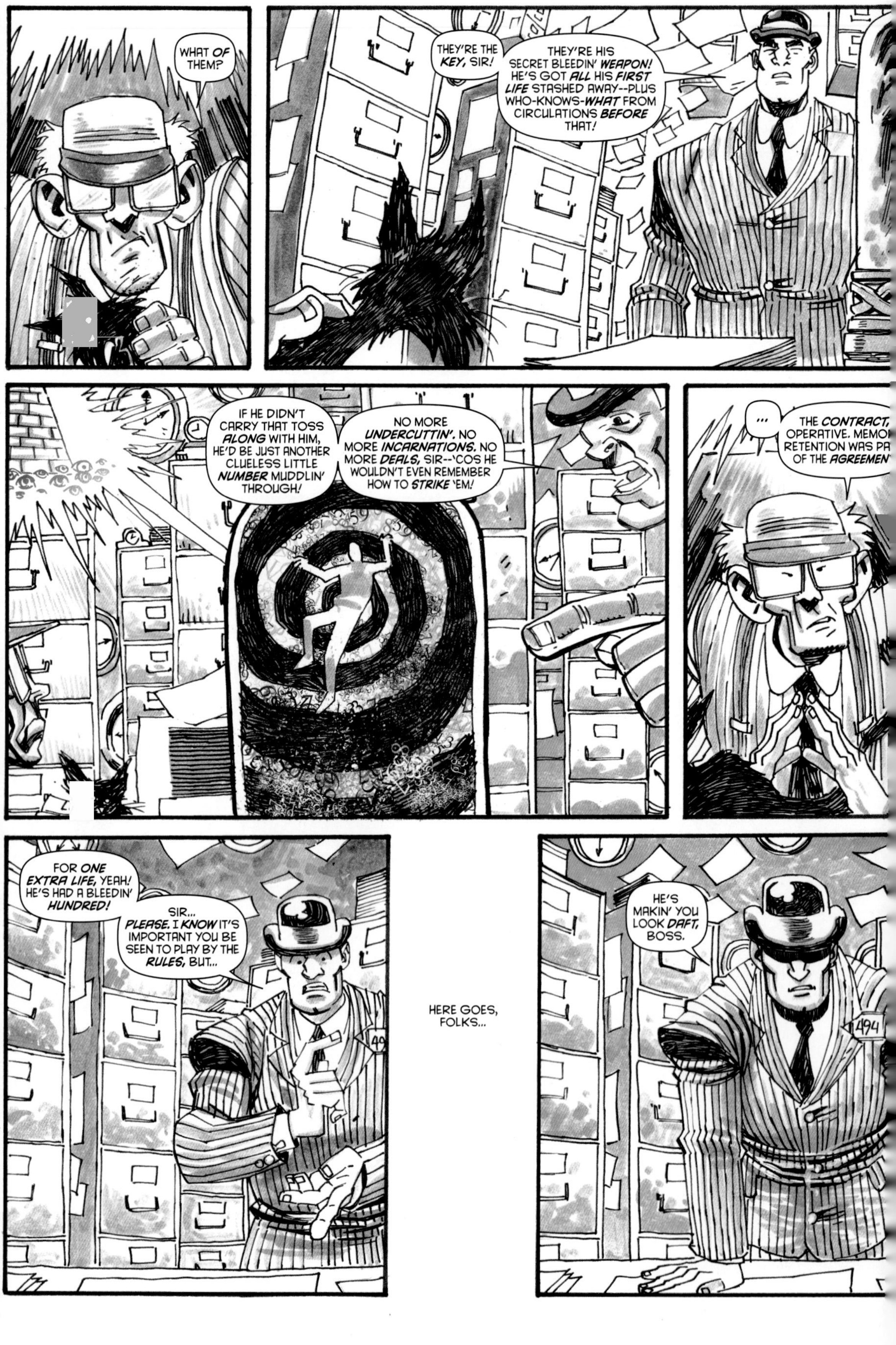
WHAT OF THEM?
THEY'RE THE KEY, SIR!
THEY'RE HIS SECRET BLEEDIN' WEAPON! HE'S GOT ALL HIS FIRST LIFE STASHED AWAY--PLUS WHO-KNOWS-WHAT FROM CIRCULATIONS BEFORE THAT!
IF HE DIDN'T CARRY THAT TOSS ALONG WITH HIM, HE'D BE JUST ANOTHER CLUELESS LITTLE NUMBER MUDDLIN' THROUGH!
NO MORE UNDERCUTTIN'. NO MORE INCARNATIONS. NO MORE DEALS, SIR--'COS HE WOULDN'T EVEN REMEMBER HOW TO STRIKE 'EM!
...
THE CONTRACT, OPERATIVE. MEMOR RETENTION WAS PA OF THE AGREEMEN
FOR ONE EXTRA LIFE, YEAH! HE'S HAD A BLEEDIN' HUNDRED!
SIR... PLEASE. I KNOW IT'S IMPORTANT YOU BE SEEN TO PLAY BY THE RULES, BUT...
HERE GOES, FOLKS...
HE'S MAKIN' YOU LOOK DAFT, BOSS.
494

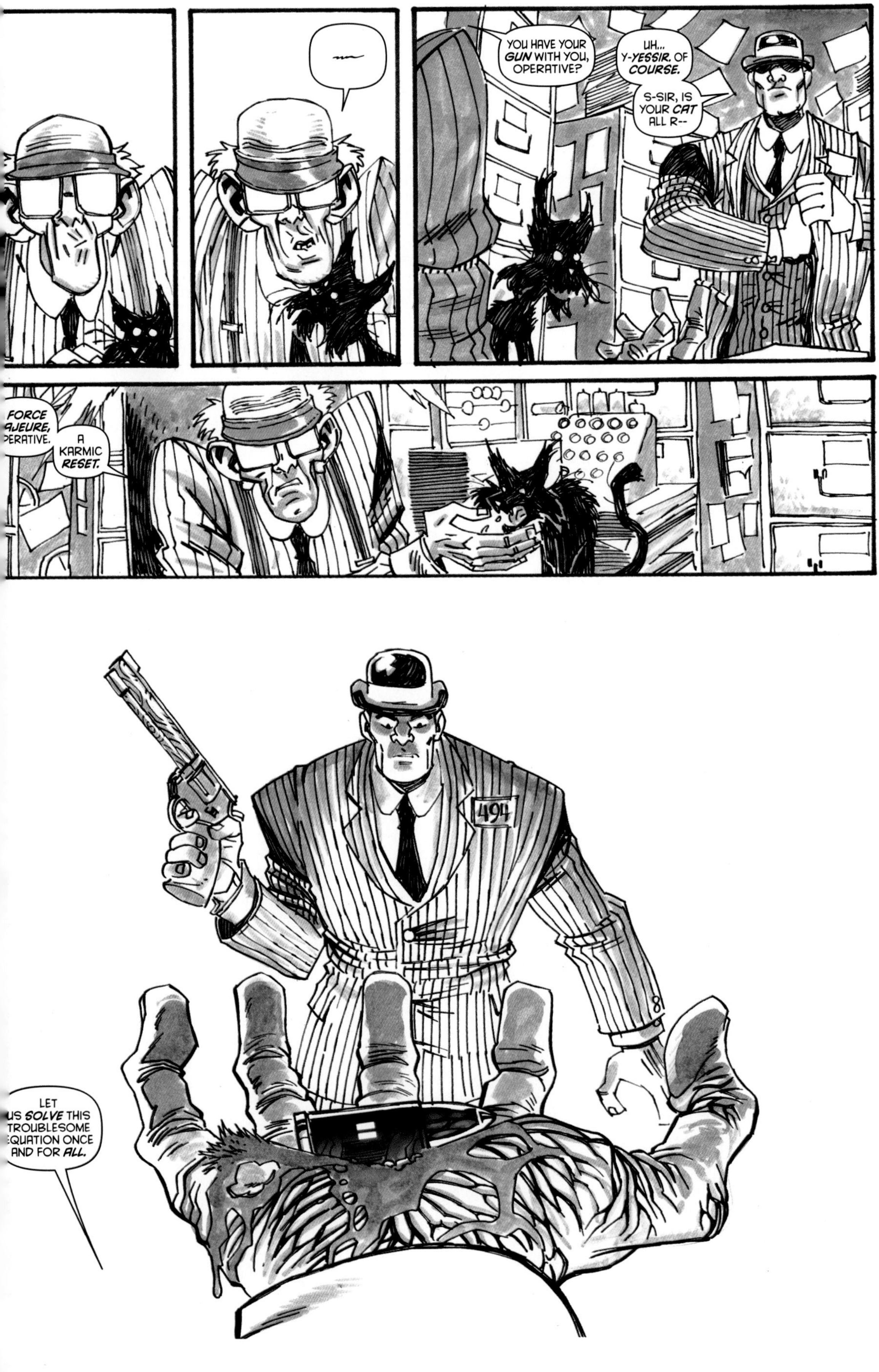
YOU HAVE YOUR GUN WITH YOU, OPERATIVE?
UH... Y-YESSIR. OF COURSE.
S-SIR, IS YOUR CAT ALL R--
FORCE AJEURE, PERATIVE.
A KARMIC RESET.
494
LET US SOLVE THIS TROUBLESOME EQUATION ONCE AND FOR ALL.

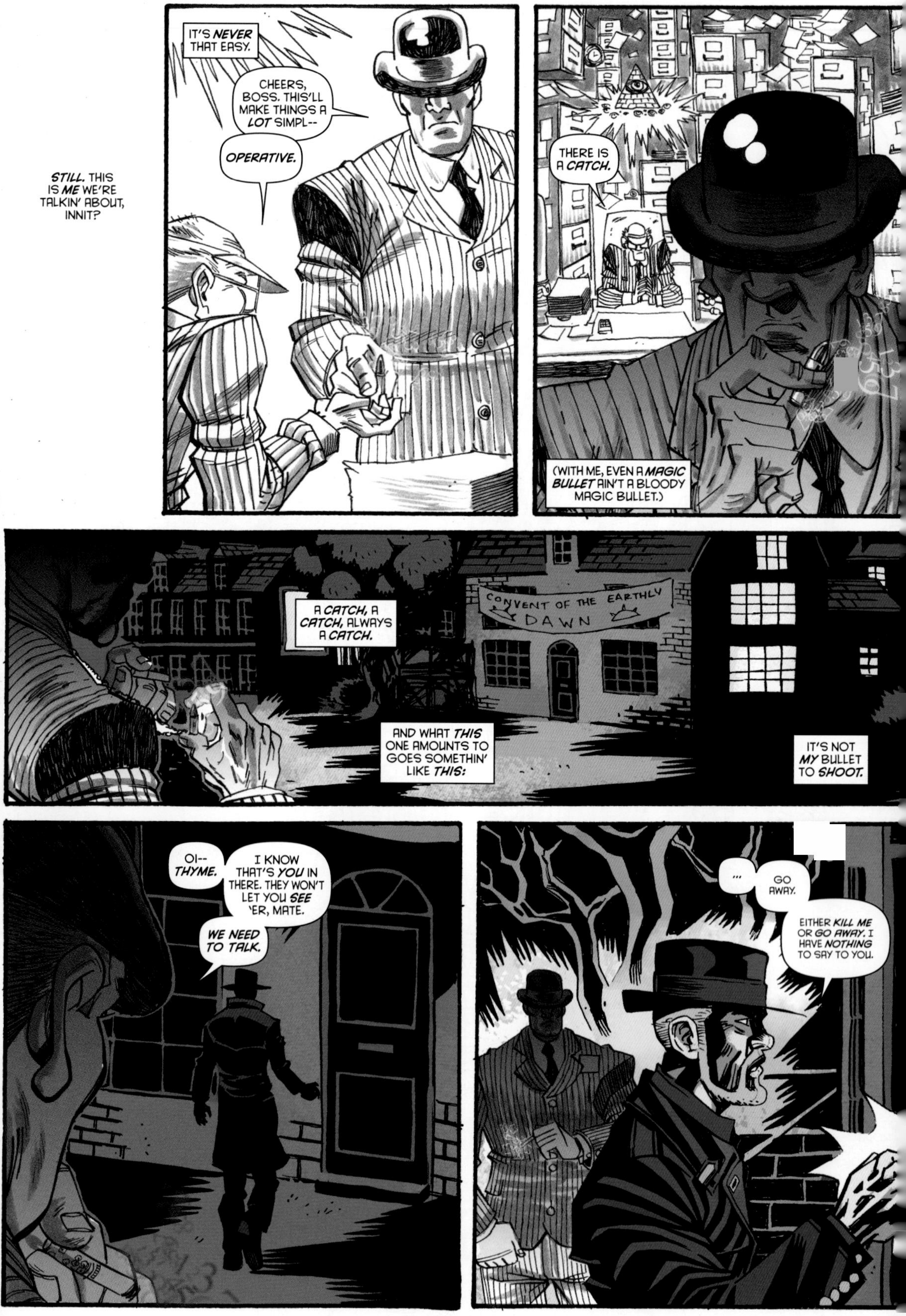
STILL. THIS IS ME WE'RE TALKIN' ABOUT, INNIT?
IT'S NEVER THAT EASY.
CHEERS, BOSS. THIS'LL MAKE THINGS A LOT SIMPL--
OPERATIVE.
THERE IS A CATCH.
(WITH ME, EVEN A MAGIC BULLET AIN'T A BLOODY MAGIC BULLET.)
A CATCH, A CATCH, ALWAYS A CATCH.
CONVENT OF THE EARTHLY DAWN
AND WHAT THIS ONE AMOUNTS TO GOES SOMETHIN' LIKE THIS:
IT'S NOT MY BULLET TO SHOOT.
OI-- THYME.
I KNOW THAT'S YOU IN THERE. THEY WON'T LET YOU SEE 'ER, MATE.
WE NEED TO TALK.
...
GO AWAY.
EITHER KILL ME OR GO AWAY. I HAVE NOTHING TO SAY TO YOU.

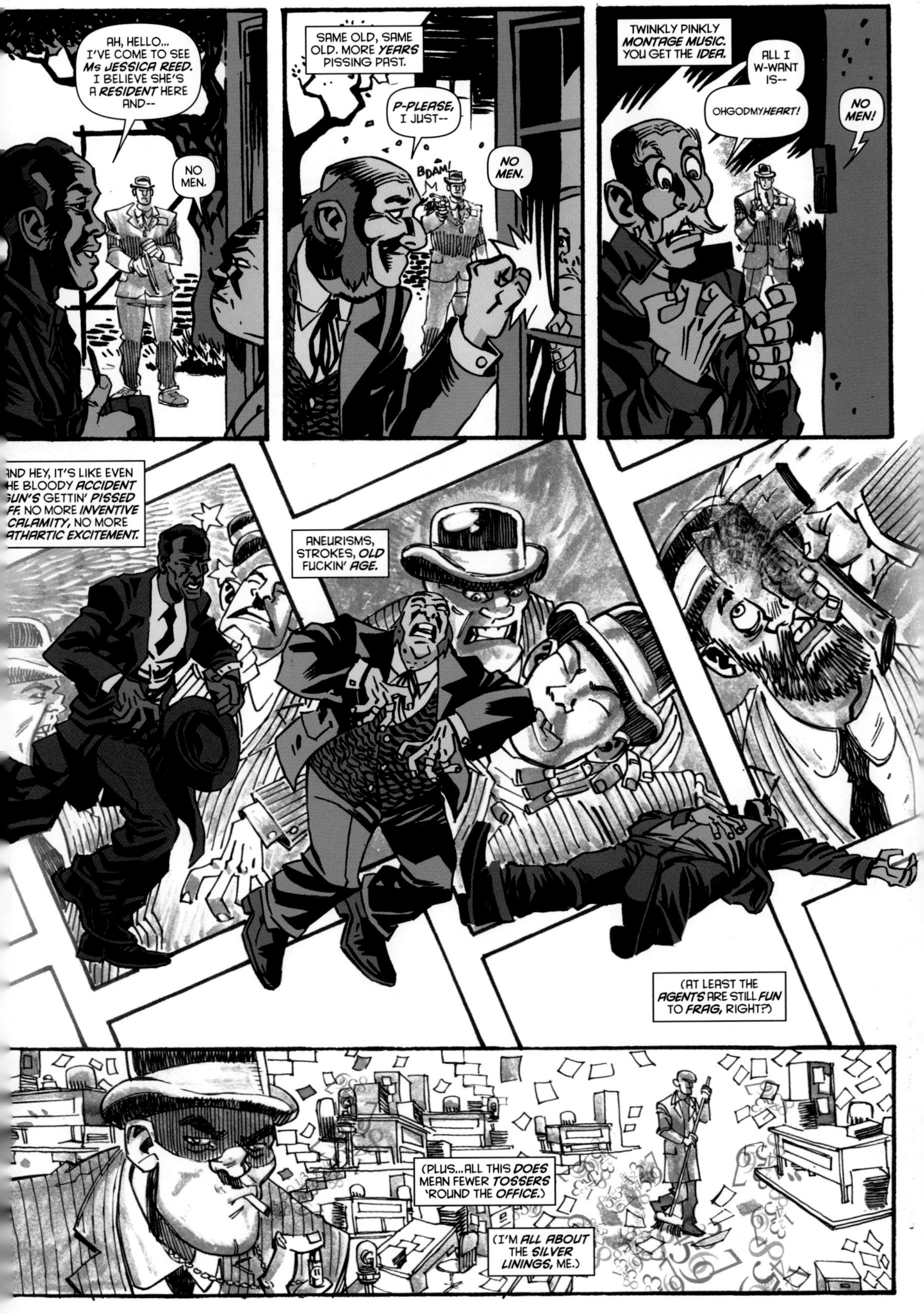
AH, HELLO... I'VE COME TO SEE Ms JESSICA REED. I BELIEVE SHE'S A RESIDENT HERE AND--
NO MEN.
SAME OLD, SAME OLD. MORE YEARS PISSING PAST.
P-PLEASE, I JUST--
BDAM!
NO MEN.
TWINKLY PINKLY MONTAGE MUSIC. YOU GET THE IDEA.
ALL I W-WANT IS--
OHGODMYHEART!
NO MEN!
AND HEY, IT'S LIKE EVEN THE BLOODY ACCIDENT GUN'S GETTIN' PISSED OFF. NO MORE INVENTIVE CALAMITY, NO MORE CATHARTIC EXCITEMENT.
ANEURISMS, STROKES, OLD FUCKIN' AGE.
(AT LEAST THE AGENTS ARE STILL FUN TO FRAG, RIGHT?)
(PLUS...ALL THIS DOES MEAN FEWER TOSSERS 'ROUND THE OFFICE.)
(I'M ALL ABOUT THE SILVER LININGS, ME.)

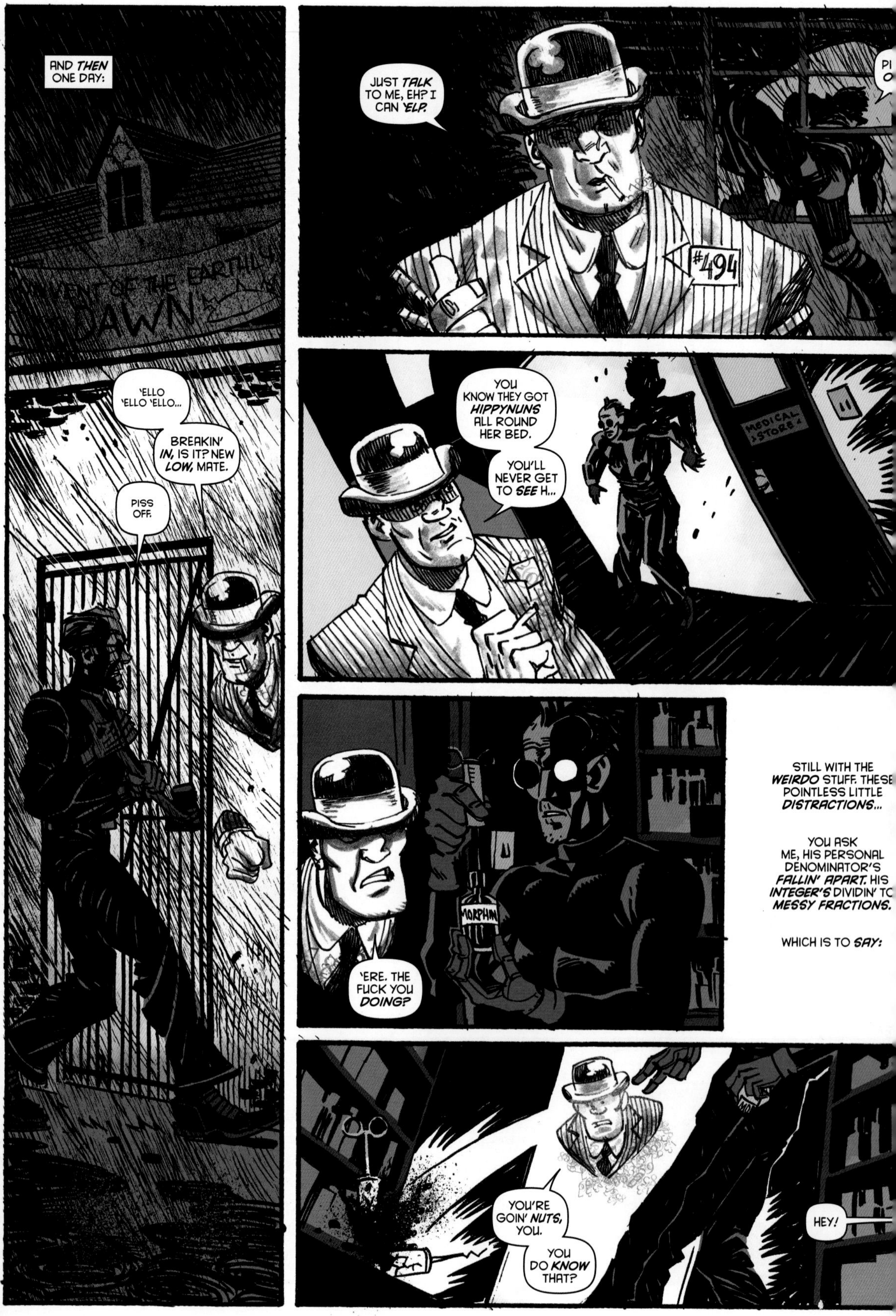
AND *THEN* ONE DAY:
'ELLO 'ELLO 'ELLO...
BREAKIN' *IN,* IS IT? NEW *LOW,* MATE.
PISS OFF.
JUST *TALK* TO ME, EH? I CAN *'ELP.*
#494
YOU KNOW THEY GOT *HIPPYNUNS* ALL ROUND HER BED.
YOU'LL NEVER GET TO *SEE* H...
MEDICAL STORE
'ERE. THE FUCK YOU *DOING?*
MORPHIN
STILL WITH THE *WEIRDO* STUFF. THESE POINTLESS LITTLE *DISTRACTIONS...*
YOU ASK ME, HIS PERSONAL DENOMINATOR'S *FALLIN' APART.* HIS *INTEGER'S* DIVIDIN' TO *MESSY FRACTIONS.*
WHICH IS TO *SAY:*
YOU'RE GOIN' *NUTS,* YOU.
YOU DO *KNOW* THAT?
HEY!

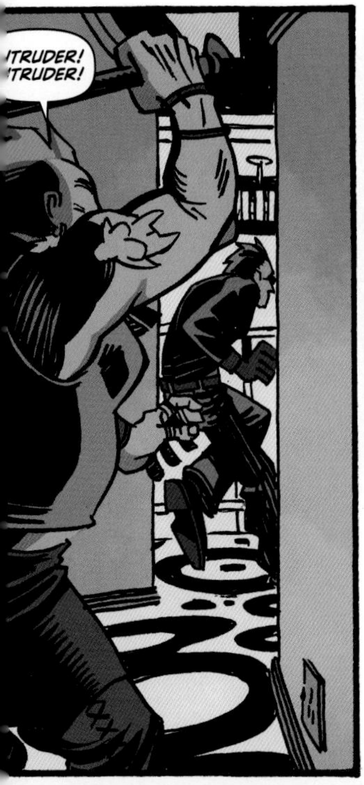
TRUDER!
TRUDER!

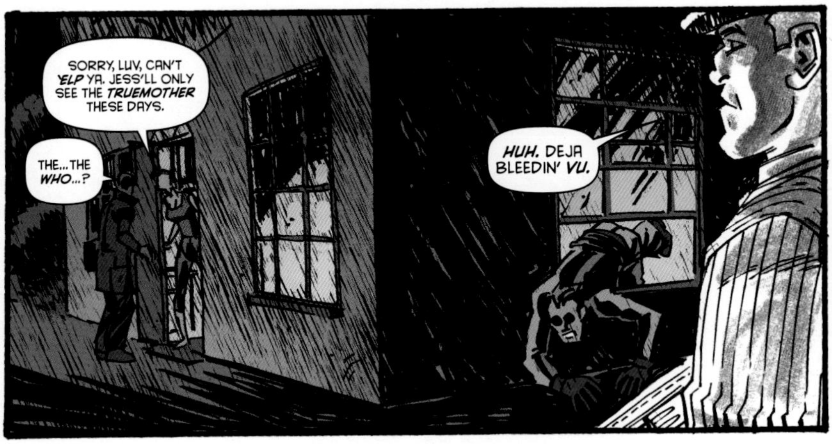
SORRY, LUV, CAN'T 'ELP YA. JESS'LL ONLY SEE THE TRUEMOTHER THESE DAYS.
THE... THE WHO...?
HUH. DEJA BLEEDIN' VU.

'COURSE, FOR THE POOR OLE' ***MATHEMATICIAN*** THAT WAS AN 'UNDRED ***LIFETIMES*** AGO. ***INCARNATION #2,*** BEFORE HIS WHOLE ROMANTIC INFINITY-BOTHERIN' ***MISSION*** WAS BARELY ***BEGUN.***

THAT ***BRAIN*** OF HIS, EH? "SHOOTIN' STRAIGHT AN' TRUE AT ITS ***TARGET.***" I REMEMBER ***THINKIN'*** THAT, EVEN BACK THEN.

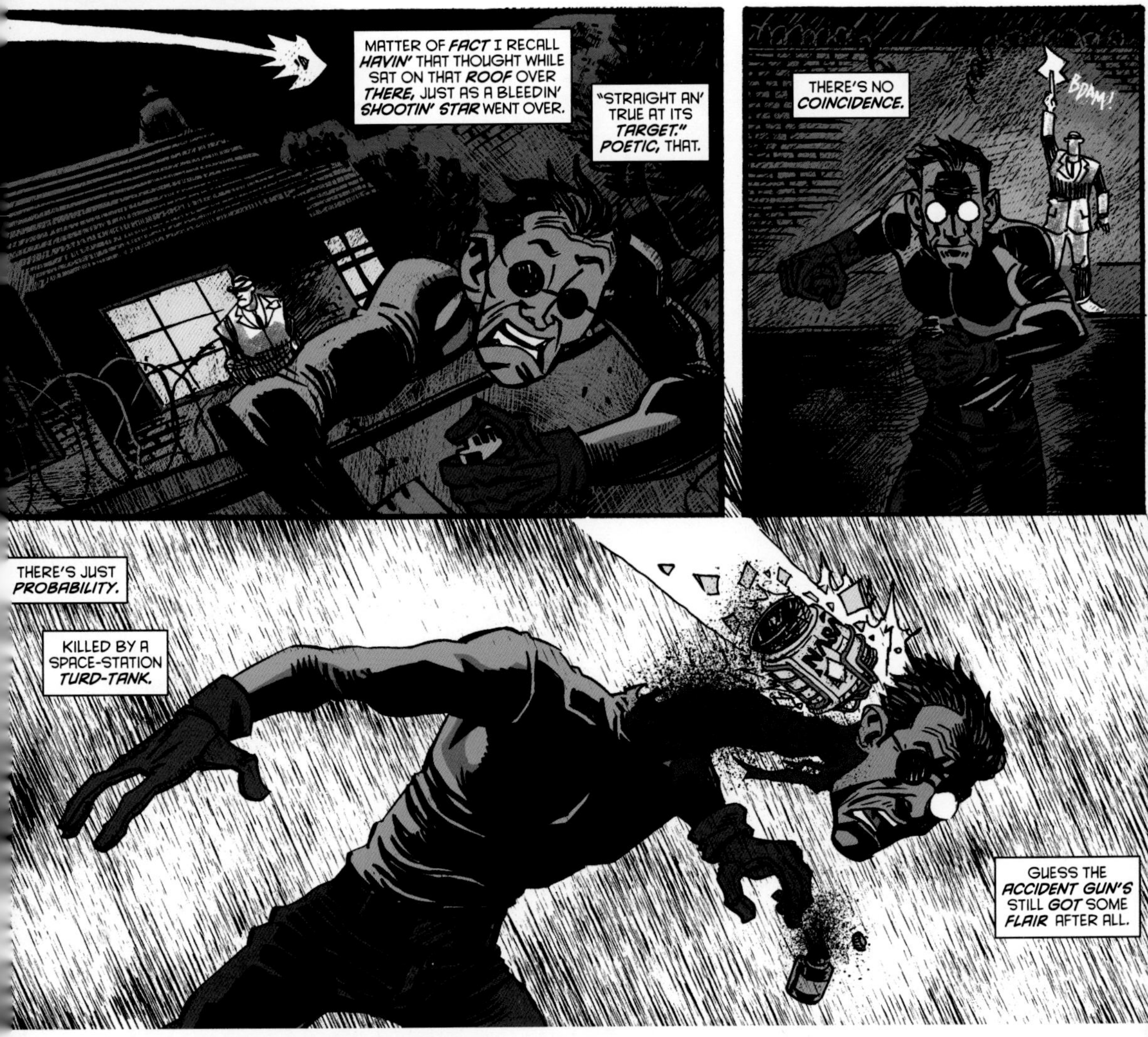
MATTER OF FACT I RECALL HAVIN' THAT THOUGHT WHILE SAT ON THAT ROOF OVER THERE, JUST AS A BLEEDIN' SHOOTIN' STAR WENT OVER.
"STRAIGHT AN' TRUE AT ITS TARGET." POETIC, THAT.
THERE'S NO COINCIDENCE.
BDAM!
THERE'S JUST PROBABILITY.
KILLED BY A SPACE-STATION TURD-TANK.
GUESS THE ACCIDENT GUN'S STILL GOT SOME FLAIR AFTER ALL.

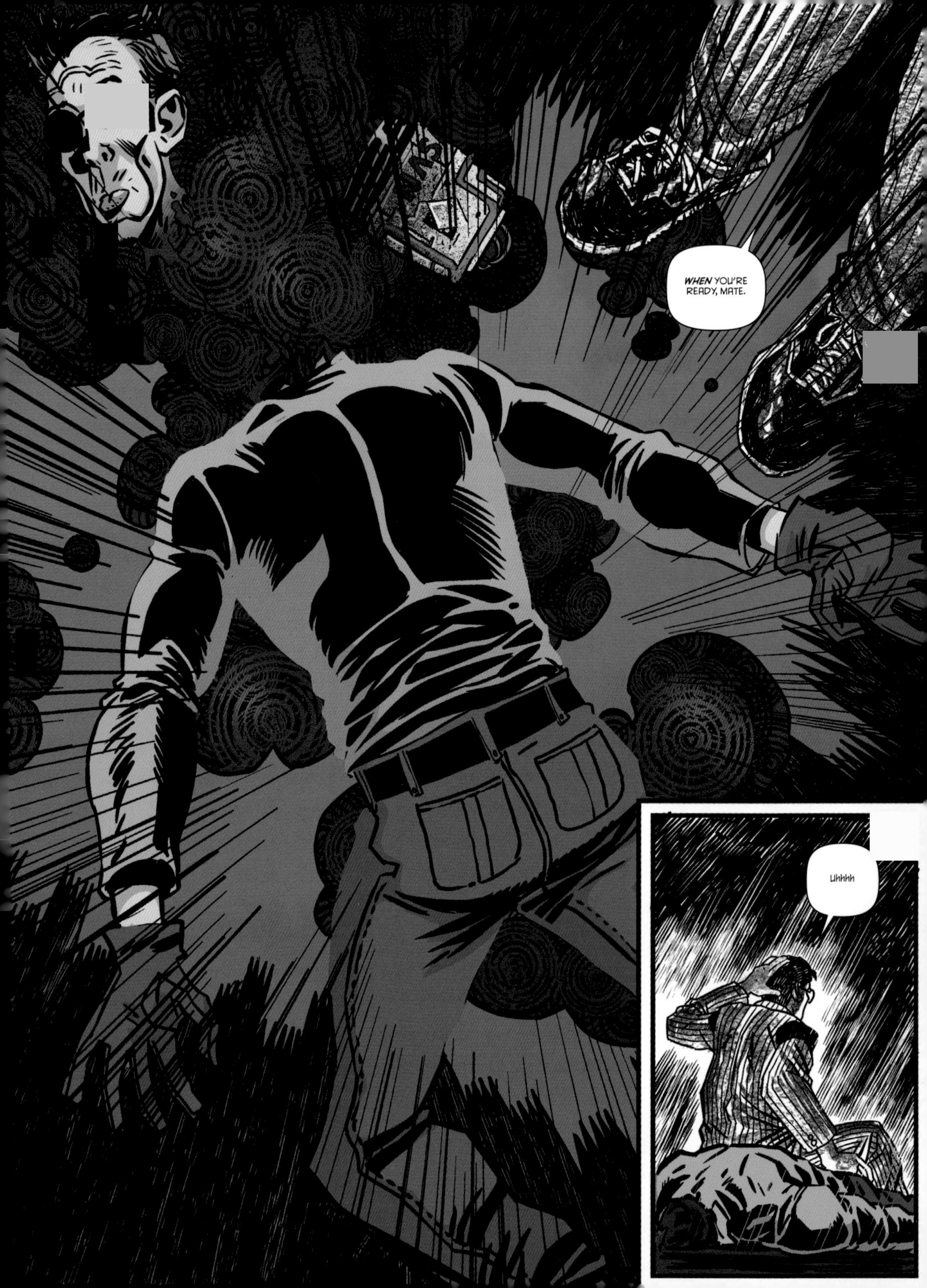
WHEN YOU'RE READY, MATE.
Uhhhh

LAWKS! WHAT A *TERRIBLE* AN' *'LIKELY* ACCIDENT! *CURSE* YOU, OH CALLOUS COSMIC JUNK-DUMPERS!

UUUUH...

ER... *RICHARD THYME?*

CONTRACT FOR YER *NEW LIFE*, GUV.

...THE FUCKIN' *OFFICE CLEANER?*

DESPERATE TIMES.

DESPERATE BLOODY TIMES IS *RIGHT.*

VE...

I'VE RUINED HER WHOLE *LIFE*, HAVEN'T I?

YEP.

I CAN'T STOP *WANTING* HER.

YES, MATE. YOU *CAN.*

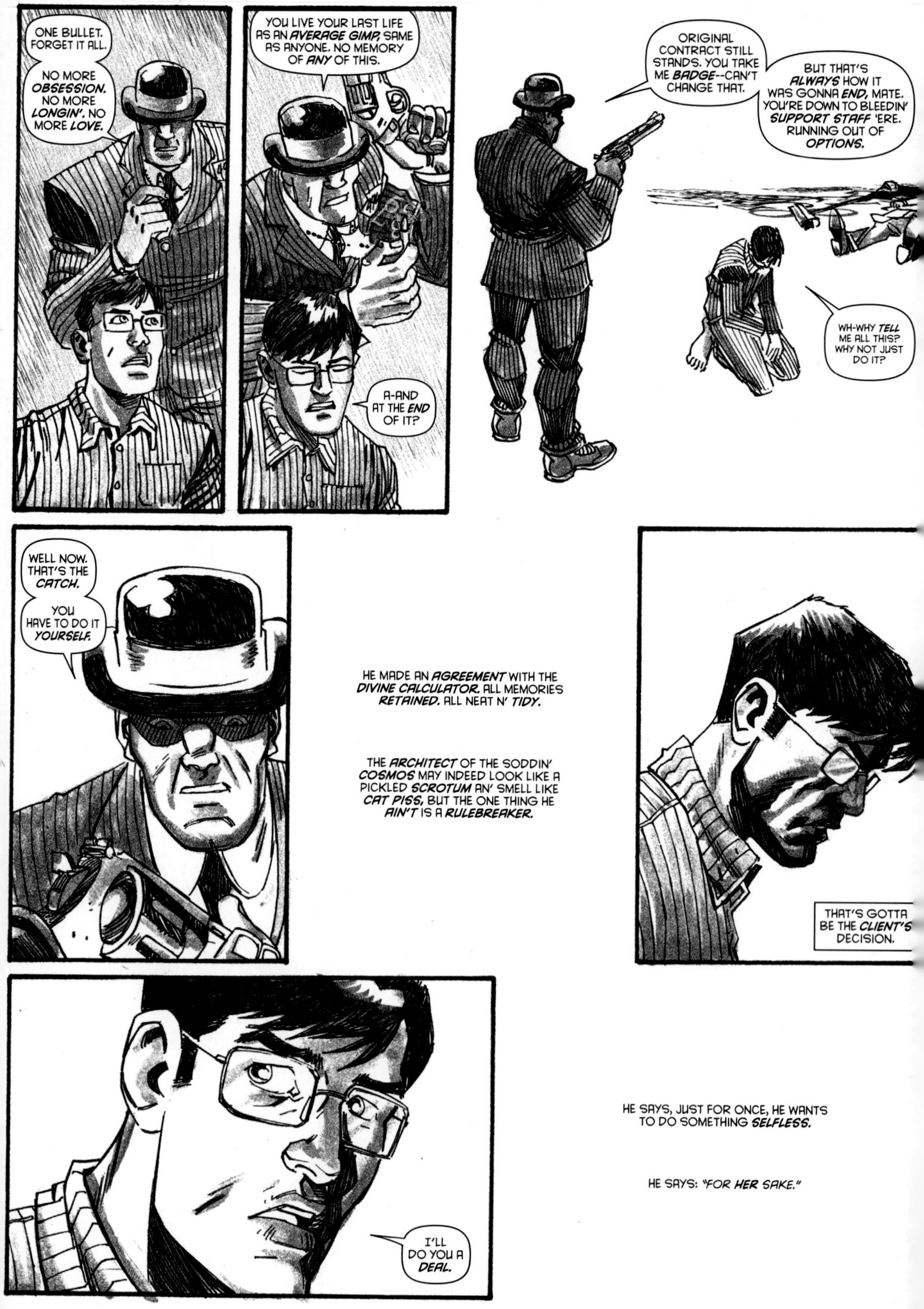
ONE BULLET. FORGET IT ALL.
NO MORE OBSESSION. NO MORE LONGIN'. NO MORE LOVE.
YOU LIVE YOUR LAST LIFE AS AN AVERAGE GIMP, SAME AS ANYONE. NO MEMORY OF ANY OF THIS.
A-AND AT THE END OF IT?
ORIGINAL CONTRACT STILL STANDS. YOU TAKE ME BADGE--CAN'T CHANGE THAT.
BUT THAT'S ALWAYS HOW IT WAS GONNA END, MATE. YOU'RE DOWN TO BLEEDIN' SUPPORT STAFF 'ERE. RUNNING OUT OF OPTIONS.
WH-WHY TELL ME ALL THIS? WHY NOT JUST DO IT?
WELL NOW. THAT'S THE CATCH.
YOU HAVE TO DO IT YOURSELF.
HE MADE AN AGREEMENT WITH THE DIVINE CALCULATOR. ALL MEMORIES RETAINED. ALL NEAT N' TIDY.
THE ARCHITECT OF THE SODDIN' COSMOS MAY INDEED LOOK LIKE A PICKLED SCROTUM AN' SMELL LIKE CAT PISS, BUT THE ONE THING HE AIN'T IS A RULEBREAKER.
THAT'S GOTTA BE THE CLIENT'S DECISION.
I'LL DO YOU A DEAL.
HE SAYS, JUST FOR ONCE, HE WANTS TO DO SOMETHING SELFLESS.
HE SAYS: "FOR HER SAKE."

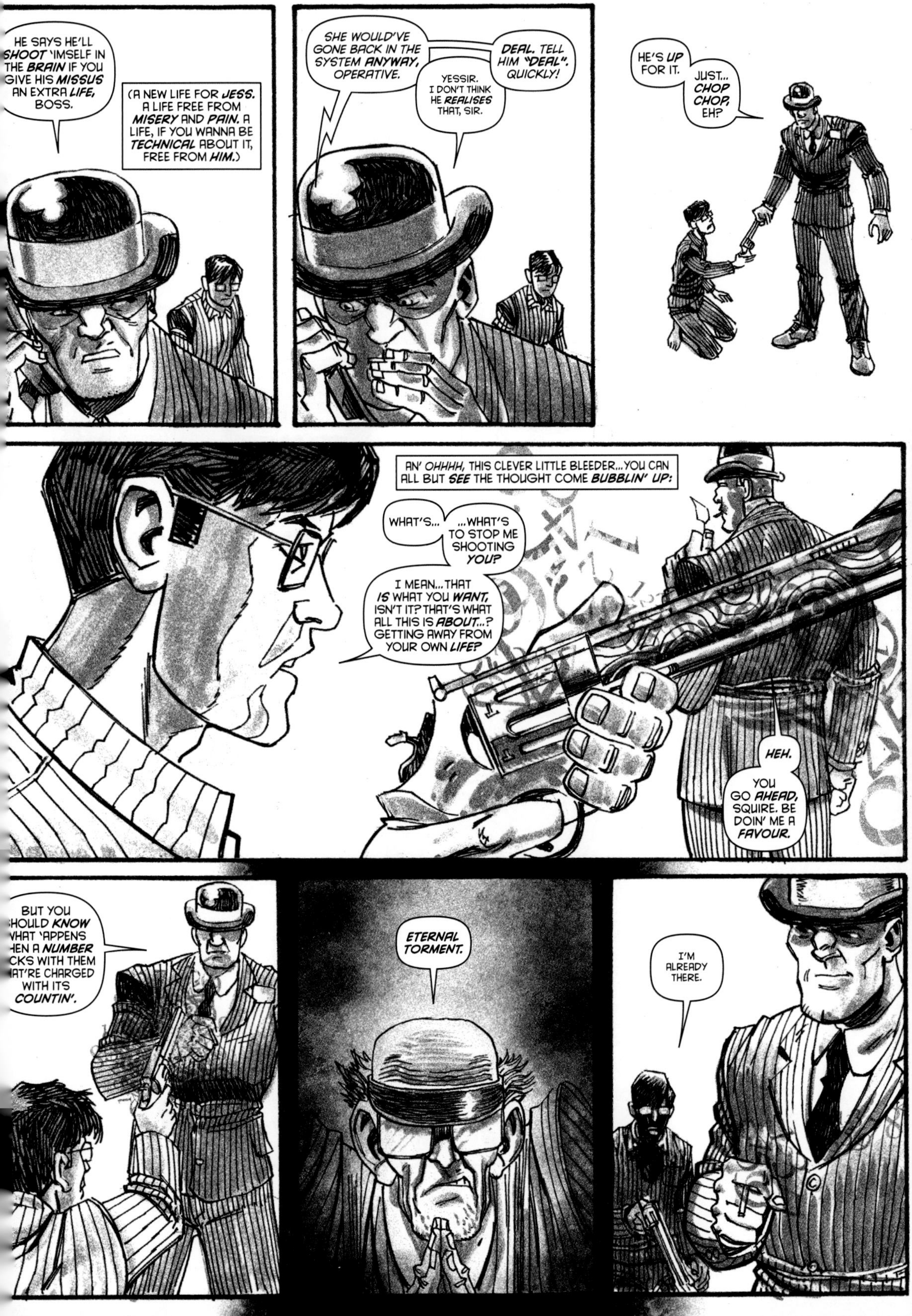
HE SAYS HE'LL SHOOT 'IMSELF IN THE BRAIN IF YOU GIVE HIS MISSUS AN EXTRA LIFE, BOSS.
(A NEW LIFE FOR JESS. A LIFE FREE FROM MISERY AND PAIN. A LIFE, IF YOU WANNA BE TECHNICAL ABOUT IT, FREE FROM HIM.)
SHE WOULD'VE GONE BACK IN THE SYSTEM ANYWAY, OPERATIVE.
YESSIR. I DON'T THINK HE REALISES THAT, SIR.
DEAL. TELL HIM "DEAL". QUICKLY!
HE'S UP FOR IT.
JUST... CHOP CHOP, EH?
AN' OHHHH, THIS CLEVER LITTLE BLEEDER... YOU CAN ALL BUT SEE THE THOUGHT COME BUBBLIN' UP:
WHAT'S...
...WHAT'S TO STOP ME SHOOTING YOU?
I MEAN... THAT IS WHAT YOU WANT, ISN'T IT? THAT'S WHAT ALL THIS IS ABOUT...? GETTING AWAY FROM YOUR OWN LIFE?
HEH.
YOU GO AHEAD, SQUIRE. BE DOIN' ME A FAVOUR.
BUT YOU SHOULD KNOW WHAT 'APPENS HEN A NUMBER CKS WITH THEM AT'RE CHARGED WITH ITS COUNTIN'.
ETERNAL TORMENT.
I'M ALREADY THERE.

SO JUST *END* IT MATE, EH?

FOR THE *BOTH* OF US.

WHAT...UH, WHAT YOU *DOIN'*?

J-JUST...MAKING *ARRANGEMENTS*.

LOOKS LIKE *REINSERTION CALCULUS*. SORTIN OUT YOUR *LAST LIFE*, ARE YA?

WHERE YOU *OFF* TO? ROYAL FAMILY TROPICAL PARADISE?

SECRET.

D-DON'T WANT YOU *HANGING AROUND*, WAITING FOR ME TO *DIE*.

NO *OFFENCE*.

NONE TAKEN.

AND... Y'KNOW...

THANKS.

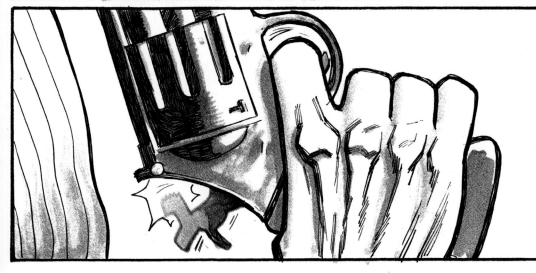

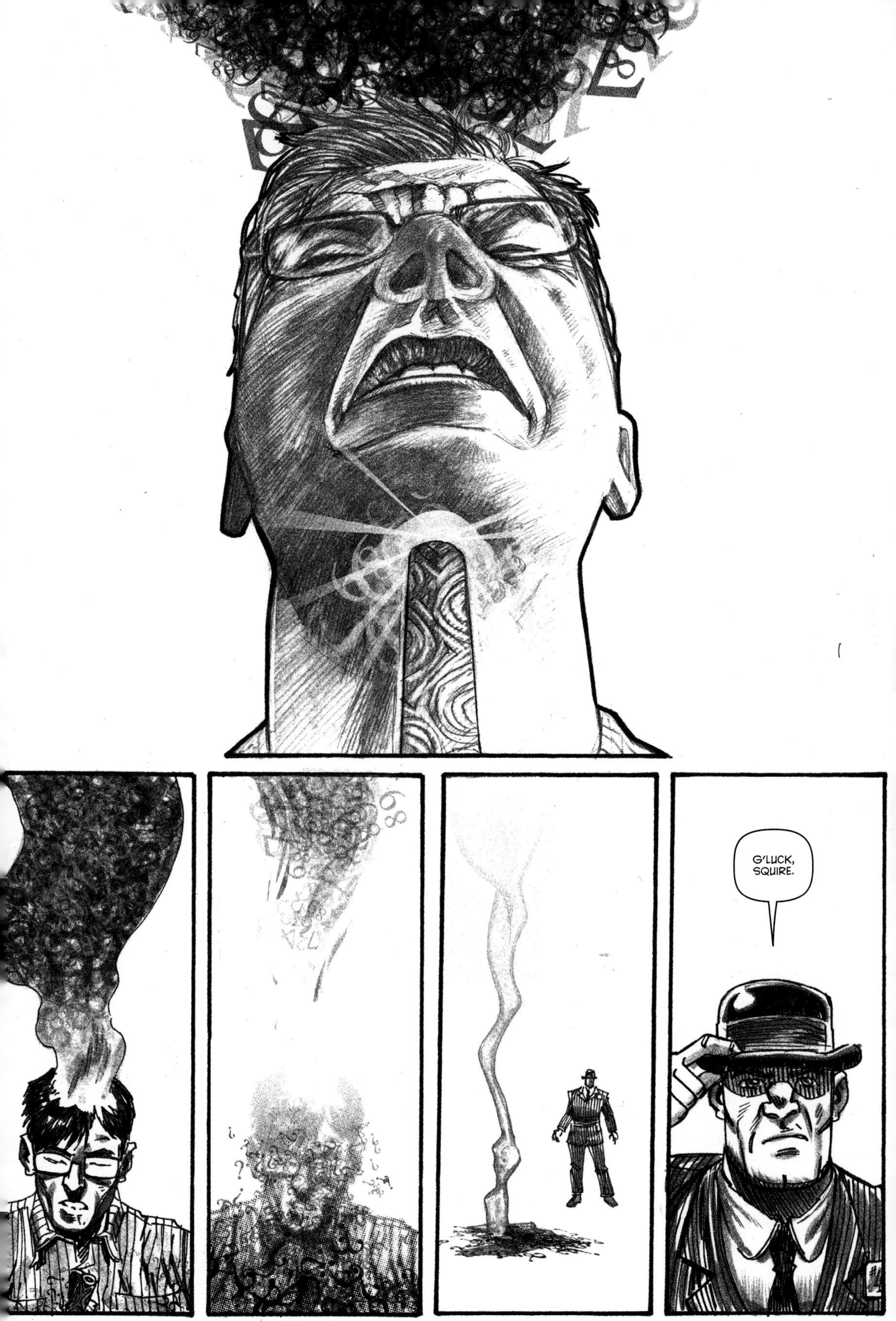
G'LUCK, SQUIRE.

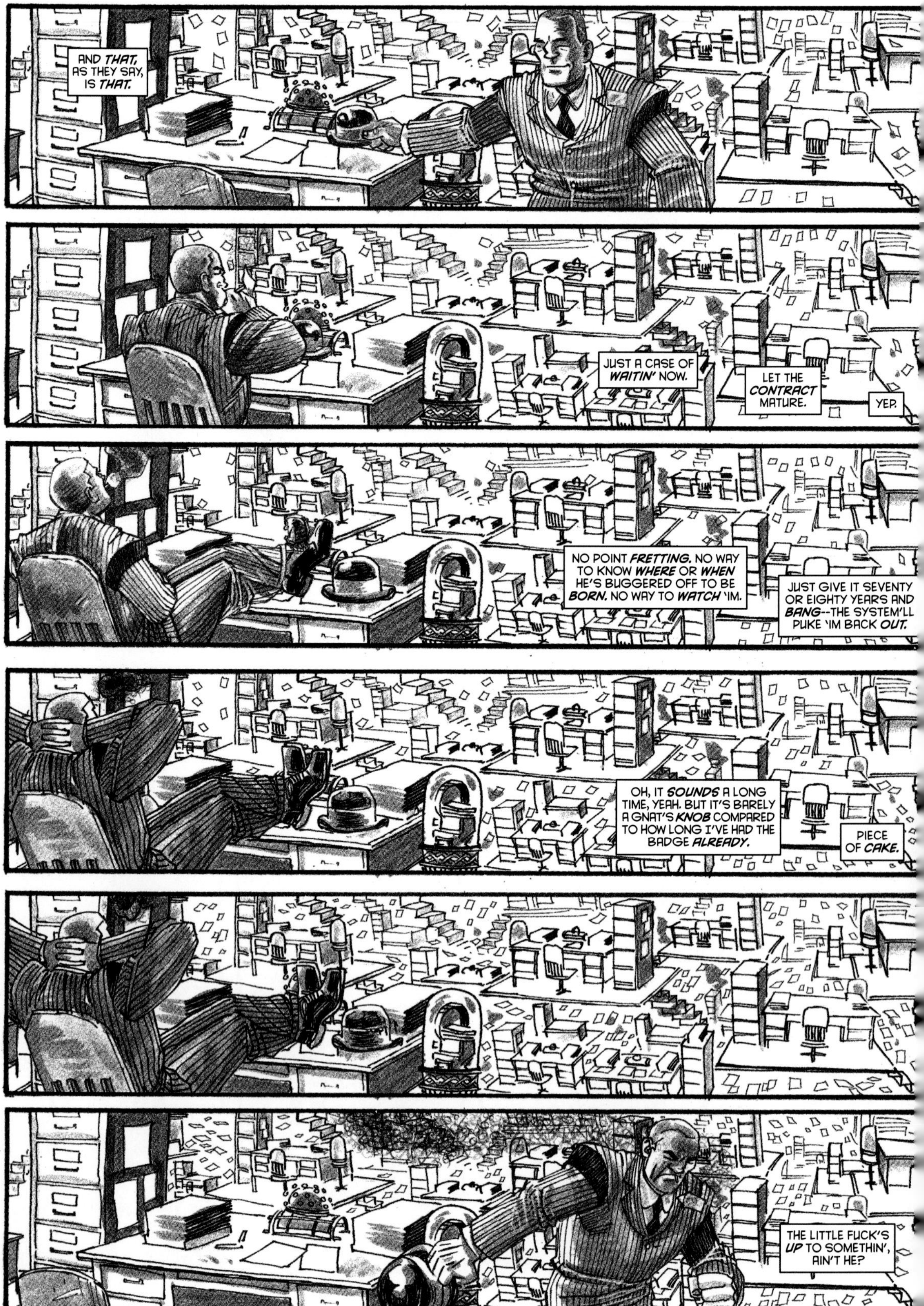
AND THAT, AS THEY SAY, IS THAT.
JUST A CASE OF WAITIN' NOW.
LET THE CONTRACT MATURE.
YEP.
NO POINT FRETTING. NO WAY TO KNOW WHERE OR WHEN HE'S BUGGERED OFF TO BE BORN. NO WAY TO WATCH 'IM.
JUST GIVE IT SEVENTY OR EIGHTY YEARS AND BANG--THE SYSTEM'LL PUKE 'IM BACK OUT.
OH, IT SOUNDS A LONG TIME, YEAH. BUT IT'S BARELY A GNAT'S KNOB COMPARED TO HOW LONG I'VE HAD THE BADGE ALREADY.
PIECE OF CAKE.
THE LITTLE FUCK'S UP TO SOMETHIN', AIN'T HE?

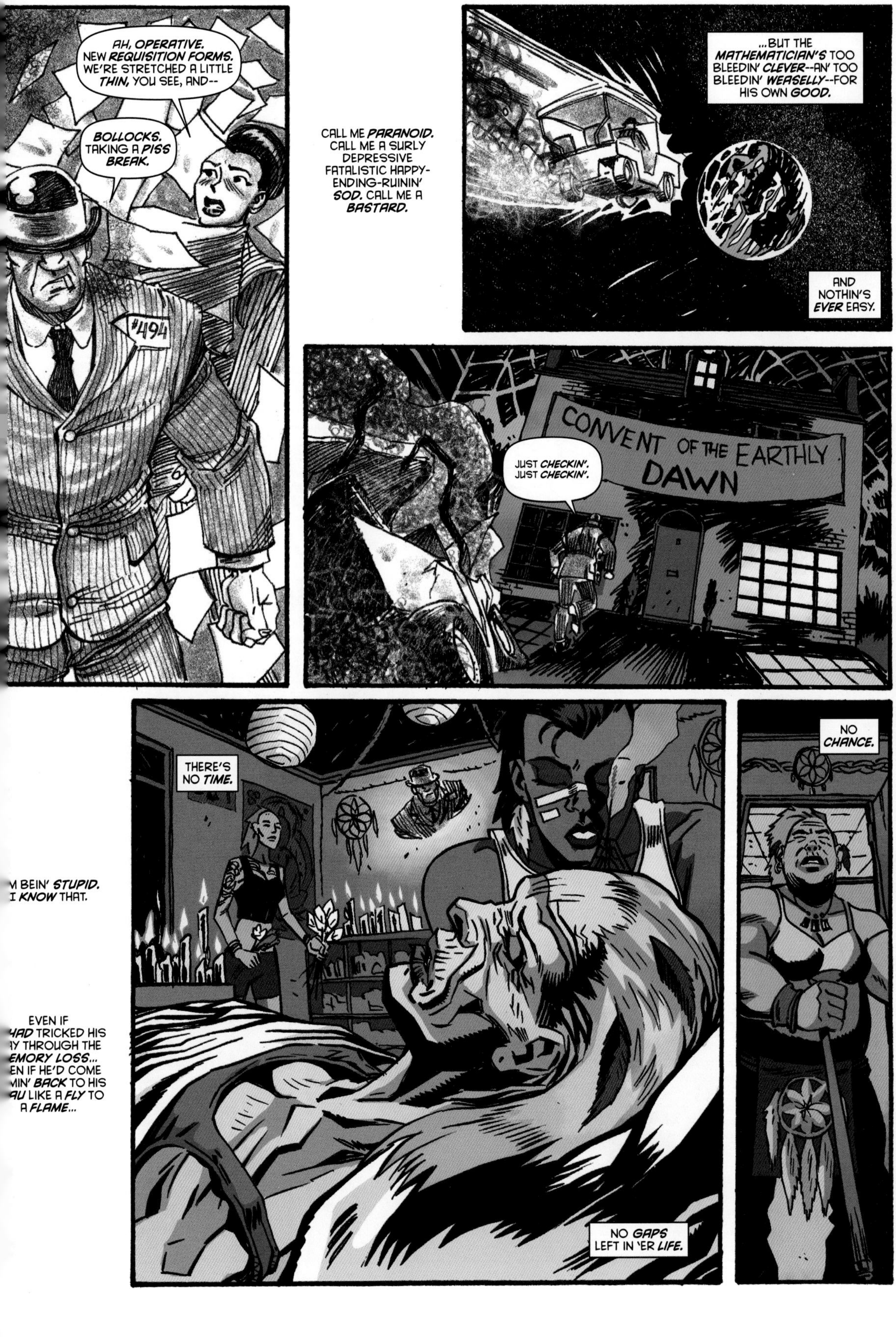

AH, OPERATIVE. NEW REQUISITION FORMS. WE'RE STRETCHED A LITTLE THIN, YOU SEE, AND--
BOLLOCKS. TAKING A PISS BREAK.
#494
CALL ME PARANOID. CALL ME A SURLY DEPRESSIVE FATALISTIC HAPPY-ENDING-RUININ' SOD. CALL ME A BASTARD.
...BUT THE MATHEMATICIAN'S TOO BLEEDIN' CLEVER--AN' TOO BLEEDIN' WEASELLY--FOR HIS OWN GOOD.
AND NOTHIN'S EVER EASY.
CONVENT OF THE EARTHLY DAWN
JUST CHECKIN'. JUST CHECKIN'.
M BEIN' STUPID. I KNOW THAT.
EVEN IF HAD TRICKED HIS Y THROUGH THE EMORY LOSS... EN IF HE'D COME MIN' BACK TO HIS AU LIKE A FLY TO A FLAME...
THERE'S NO TIME.
NO GAPS LEFT IN 'ER LIFE.
NO CHANCE.

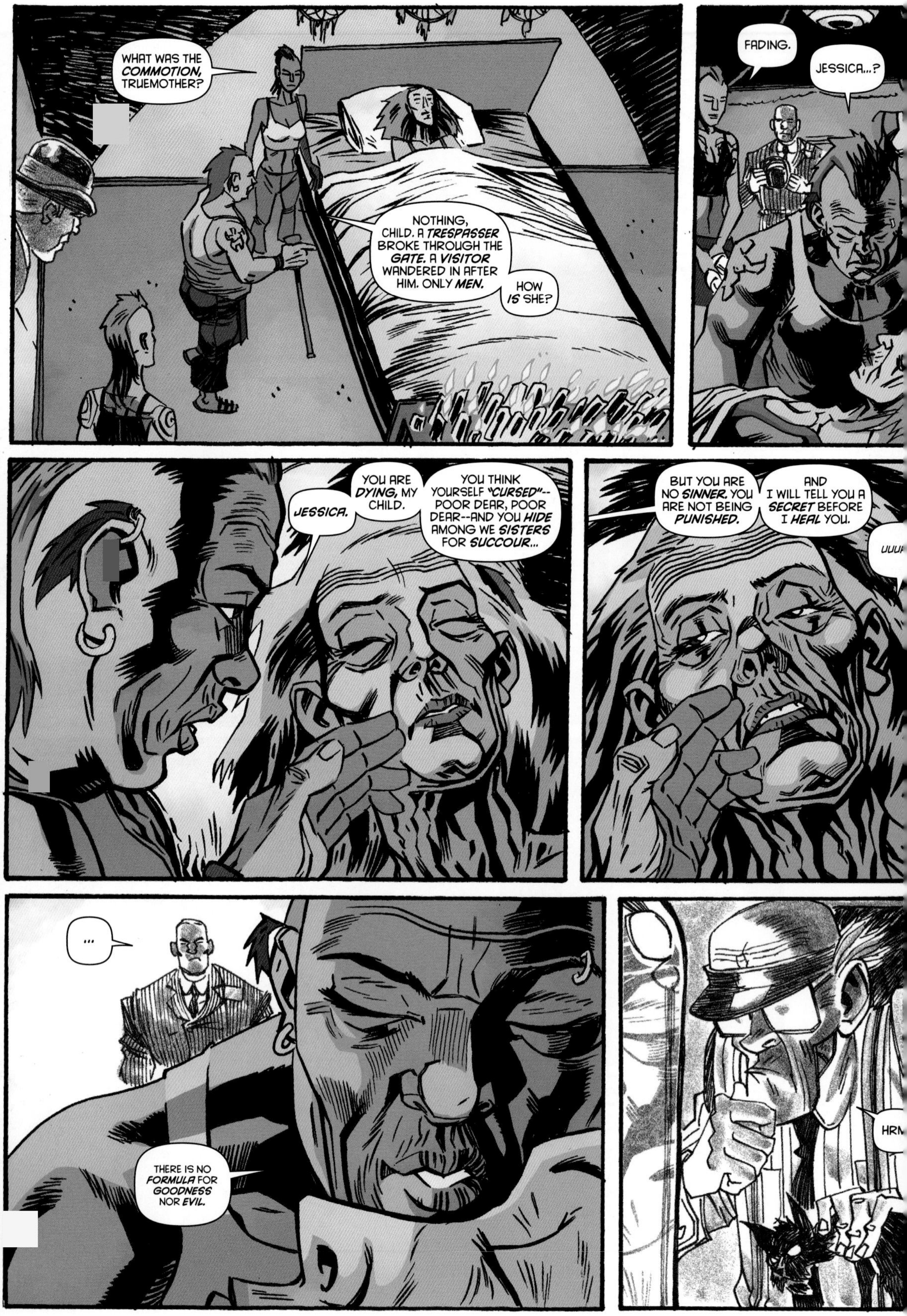
WHAT WAS THE *COMMOTION,* TRUEMOTHER?
NOTHING, CHILD. A *TRESPASSER* BROKE THROUGH THE *GATE.* A *VISITOR* WANDERED IN AFTER HIM. ONLY *MEN.*
HOW *IS* SHE?
FADING.
JESSICA...?
JESSICA.
YOU ARE *DYING,* MY CHILD.
YOU THINK YOURSELF *"CURSED"*--POOR DEAR, POOR DEAR--AND YOU *HIDE* AMONG WE *SISTERS* FOR *SUCCOUR...*
BUT YOU ARE NO *SINNER.* YOU ARE NOT BEING *PUNISHED.*
AND I WILL TELL YOU A *SECRET* BEFORE I *HEAL* YOU.
...
THERE IS NO *FORMULA* FOR *GOODNESS* NOR *EVIL.*

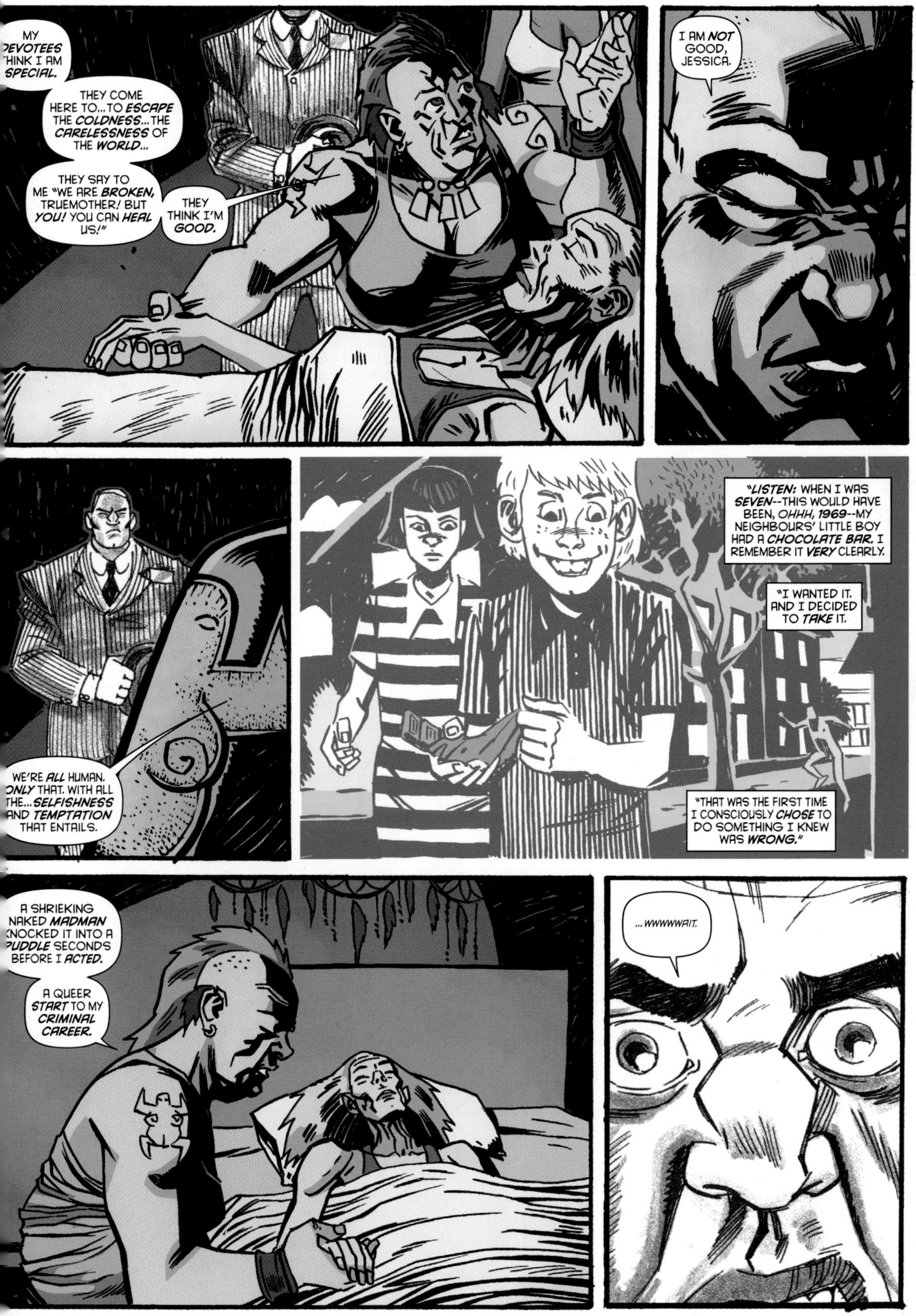
MY DEVOTEES THINK I AM SPECIAL.
THEY COME HERE TO...TO ESCAPE THE COLDNESS...THE CARELESSNESS OF THE WORLD...
THEY SAY TO ME "WE ARE BROKEN, TRUEMOTHER! BUT YOU! YOU CAN HEAL US!"
THEY THINK I'M GOOD.
I AM NOT GOOD, JESSICA.
WE'RE ALL HUMAN. ONLY THAT. WITH ALL THE...SELFISHNESS AND TEMPTATION THAT ENTAILS.
"LISTEN: WHEN I WAS SEVEN--THIS WOULD HAVE BEEN, OHHH, 1969--MY NEIGHBOURS' LITTLE BOY HAD A CHOCOLATE BAR. I REMEMBER IT VERY CLEARLY.
"I WANTED IT. AND I DECIDED TO TAKE IT.
"THAT WAS THE FIRST TIME I CONSCIOUSLY CHOSE TO DO SOMETHING I KNEW WAS WRONG."
A SHRIEKING NAKED MADMAN KNOCKED IT INTO A PUDDLE SECONDS BEFORE I ACTED.
A QUEER START TO MY CRIMINAL CAREER.
...WWWWWAIT.

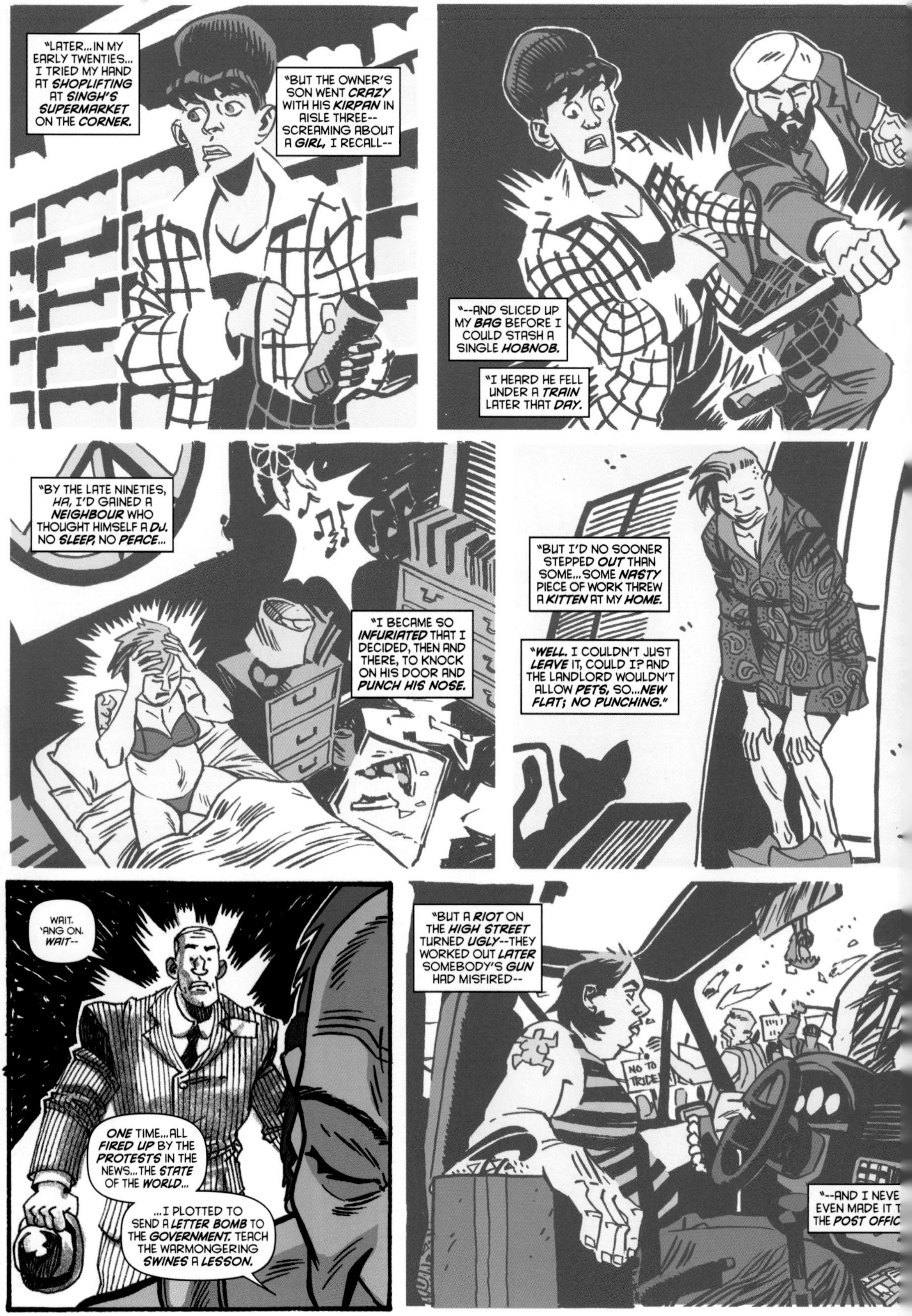
"LATER... IN MY EARLY TWENTIES... I TRIED MY HAND AT SHOPLIFTING AT SINGH'S SUPERMARKET ON THE CORNER.
"BUT THE OWNER'S SON WENT CRAZY WITH HIS KIRPAN IN AISLE THREE-- SCREAMING ABOUT A GIRL, I RECALL--
"--AND SLICED UP MY BAG BEFORE I COULD STASH A SINGLE HOBNOB.
"I HEARD HE FELL UNDER A TRAIN LATER THAT DAY.
"BY THE LATE NINETIES, HA, I'D GAINED A NEIGHBOUR WHO THOUGHT HIMSELF A DJ. NO SLEEP, NO PEACE...
"I BECAME SO INFURIATED THAT I DECIDED, THEN AND THERE, TO KNOCK ON HIS DOOR AND PUNCH HIS NOSE.
"BUT I'D NO SOONER STEPPED OUT THAN SOME... SOME NASTY PIECE OF WORK THREW A KITTEN AT MY HOME.
"WELL. I COULDN'T JUST LEAVE IT, COULD I? AND THE LANDLORD WOULDN'T ALLOW PETS, SO... NEW FLAT; NO PUNCHING."
WAIT. 'ANG ON. WAIT--
ONE TIME... ALL FIRED UP BY THE PROTESTS IN THE NEWS... THE STATE OF THE WORLD...
...I PLOTTED TO SEND A LETTER BOMB TO THE GOVERNMENT. TEACH THE WARMONGERING SWINES A LESSON.
"BUT A RIOT ON THE HIGH STREET TURNED UGLY--THEY WORKED OUT LATER SOMEBODY'S GUN HAD MISFIRED--
NO TO TRIDE
"--AND I NEVE EVEN MADE IT T THE POST OFFIC

I HAVE [B]OME...*GOODER*, [JESS]ICA. *SAINTLIER*. *PURER*.

AND [A]L[L] THROUGH [N]OTHING BUT *CHANCE*.

EVEN WHEN I LEARNT I COULD *USE* MY...MY *CLEANSING INFLUENCE* TO HELP *OTHERS*--AND CHOSE TO ESTABLISH THIS *REFUGE*--

--STILL MY *ROTTEN SELF* WAS NEVER *FAR AWAY*.

"THE HEAD OF THE *BOROUGH COUNCIL* QUIBBLED AT MY *PLANNING APPLICATION*--NOTHING MORE *SINISTER*--AND I WENT TO GIVE HER A PIECE OF MY *MIND*.

"OH, I'M NOT *DEFINITELY* GOING TO USE THE *KNIFE* IN MY *BAG*, BUT...*WELL*..."

[I] DIDN'T [HE]R *ANYWAY*. [D] TAKEN THE [D]AY *OFF*.

[BUT] SOMEONE HAD [STA]MPED ON HER *FOOT* [AT A] *FUNERAL* THE DAY [BE]FORE AND BROKE [THRE]E *BONES*. CHANCE, [C]HANCE, *CHANCE*.

WHY...EVEN *TODAY*, JESSICA. EVEN TODAY I *ATTEMPTED* TO *SIN*.

I HOPED TO GIVE YOU *MORPHINE*. TO TAKE AWAY THE *PAIN*. TO PUSH YOU OVER THE *EDGE*. TO PUT YOU OUT OF YOUR *MISERY*.

UUUHHH...

"BUT THERE WAS NONE *LEFT*."

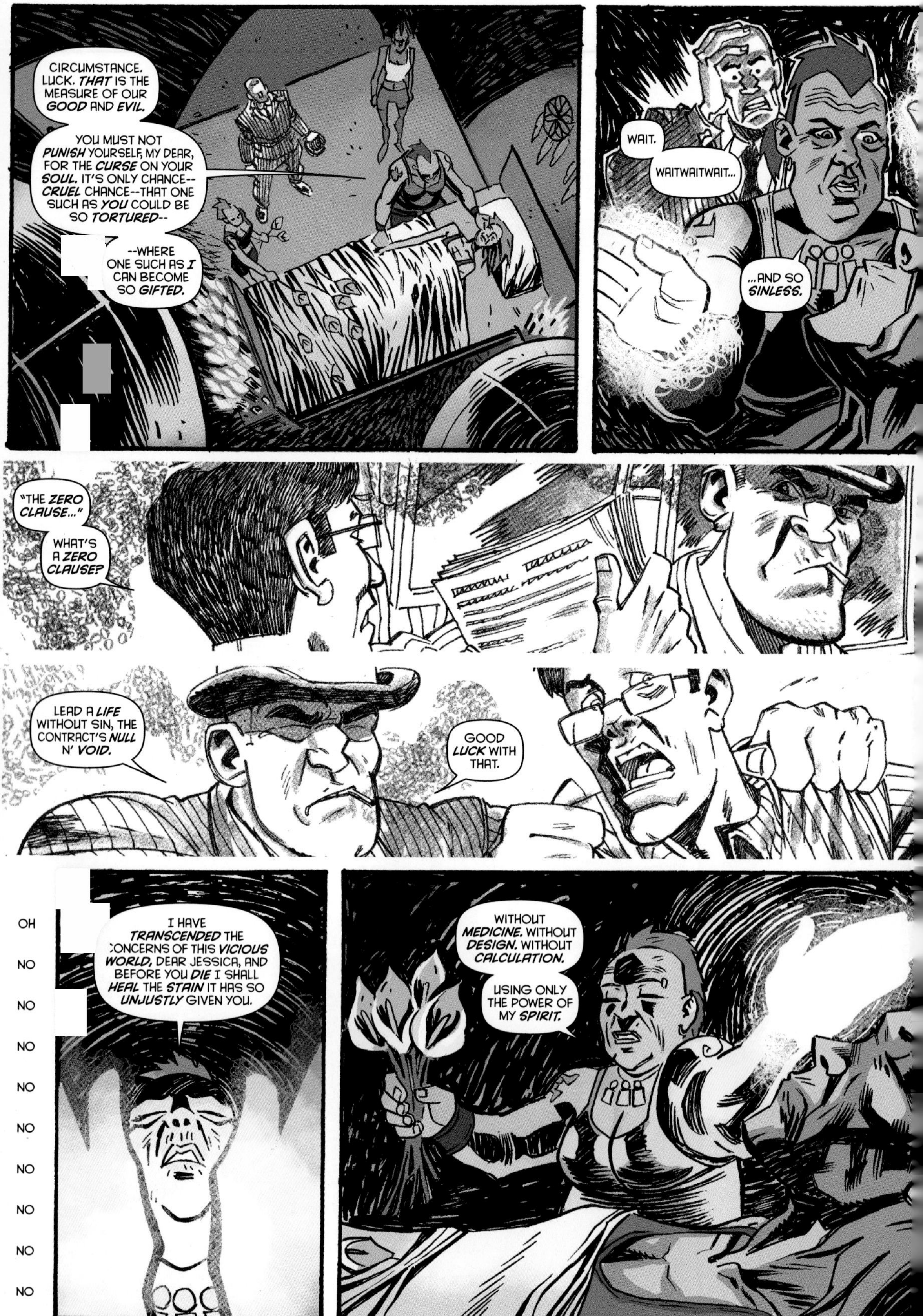
CIRCUMSTANCE. LUCK. THAT IS THE MEASURE OF OUR GOOD AND EVIL.
YOU MUST NOT PUNISH YOURSELF, MY DEAR, FOR THE CURSE ON YOUR SOUL. IT'S ONLY CHANCE-- CRUEL CHANCE--THAT ONE SUCH AS YOU COULD BE SO TORTURED--
--WHERE ONE SUCH AS I CAN BECOME SO GIFTED.
WAIT.
WAITWAITWAIT...
...AND SO SINLESS.
"THE ZERO CLAUSE..."
WHAT'S A ZERO CLAUSE?
LEAD A LIFE WITHOUT SIN, THE CONTRACT'S NULL N' VOID.
GOOD LUCK WITH THAT.
OH
NO
NO
NO
NO
NO
NO
NO
NO
NO
I HAVE TRANSCENDED THE CONCERNS OF THIS VICIOUS WORLD, DEAR JESSICA, AND BEFORE YOU DIE I SHALL HEAL THE STAIN IT HAS SO UNJUSTLY GIVEN YOU.
WITHOUT MEDICINE. WITHOUT DESIGN. WITHOUT CALCULATION.
USING ONLY THE POWER OF MY SPIRIT.

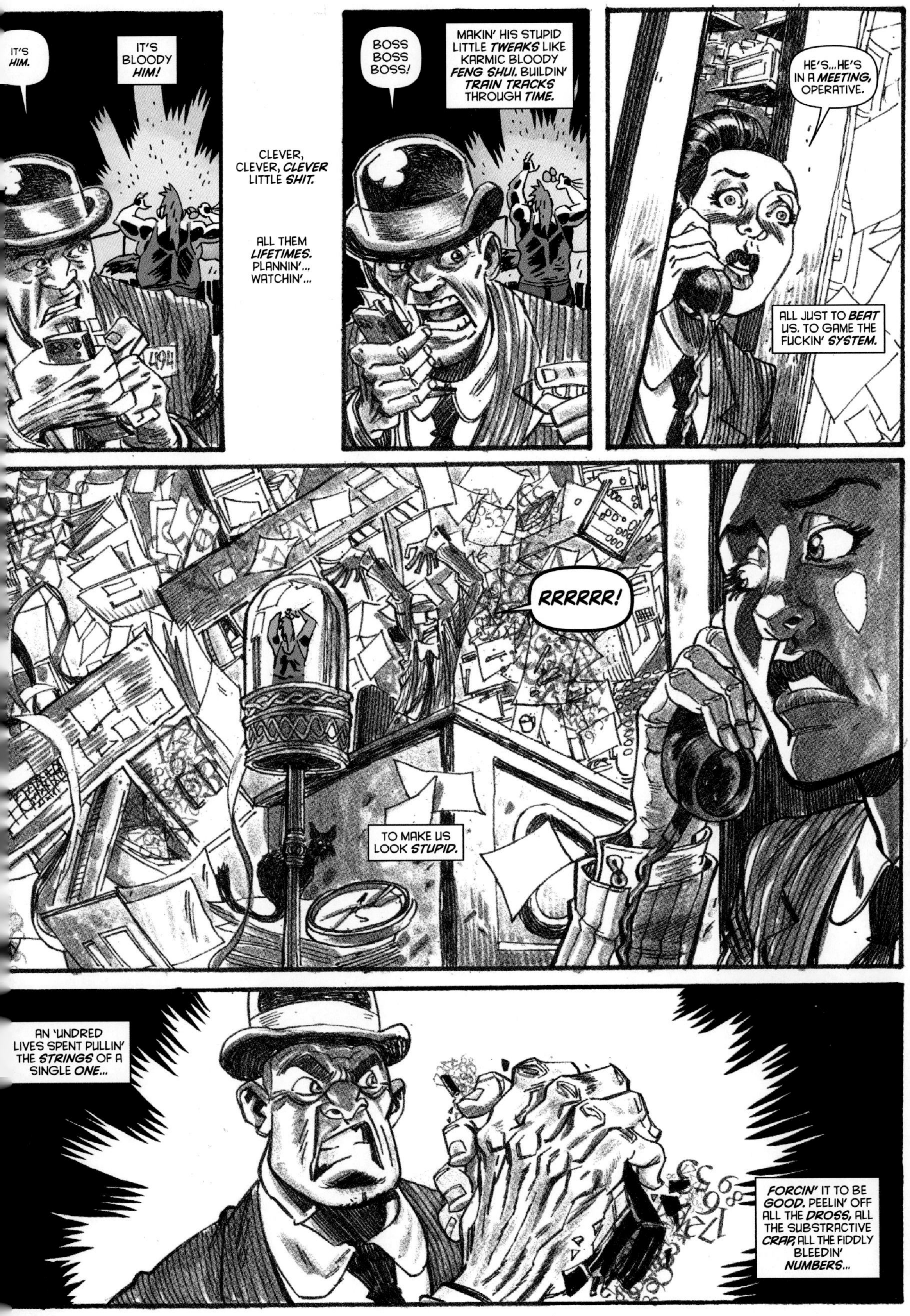

IT'S HIM.
IT'S BLOODY HIM!
CLEVER, CLEVER, CLEVER LITTLE SHIT.
ALL THEM LIFETIMES. PLANNIN'... WATCHIN'...
BOSS BOSS BOSS!
MAKIN' HIS STUPID LITTLE TWEAKS LIKE KARMIC BLOODY FENG SHUI. BUILDIN' TRAIN TRACKS THROUGH TIME.
HE'S...HE'S IN A MEETING, OPERATIVE.
ALL JUST TO BEAT US. TO GAME THE FUCKIN' SYSTEM.
RRRRRR!
TO MAKE US LOOK STUPID.
AN 'UNDRED LIVES SPENT PULLIN' THE STRINGS OF A SINGLE ONE...
FORCIN' IT TO BE GOOD. PEELIN' OFF ALL THE DROSS, ALL THE SUBSTRACTIVE CRAP, ALL THE FIDDLY BLEEDIN' NUMBERS...

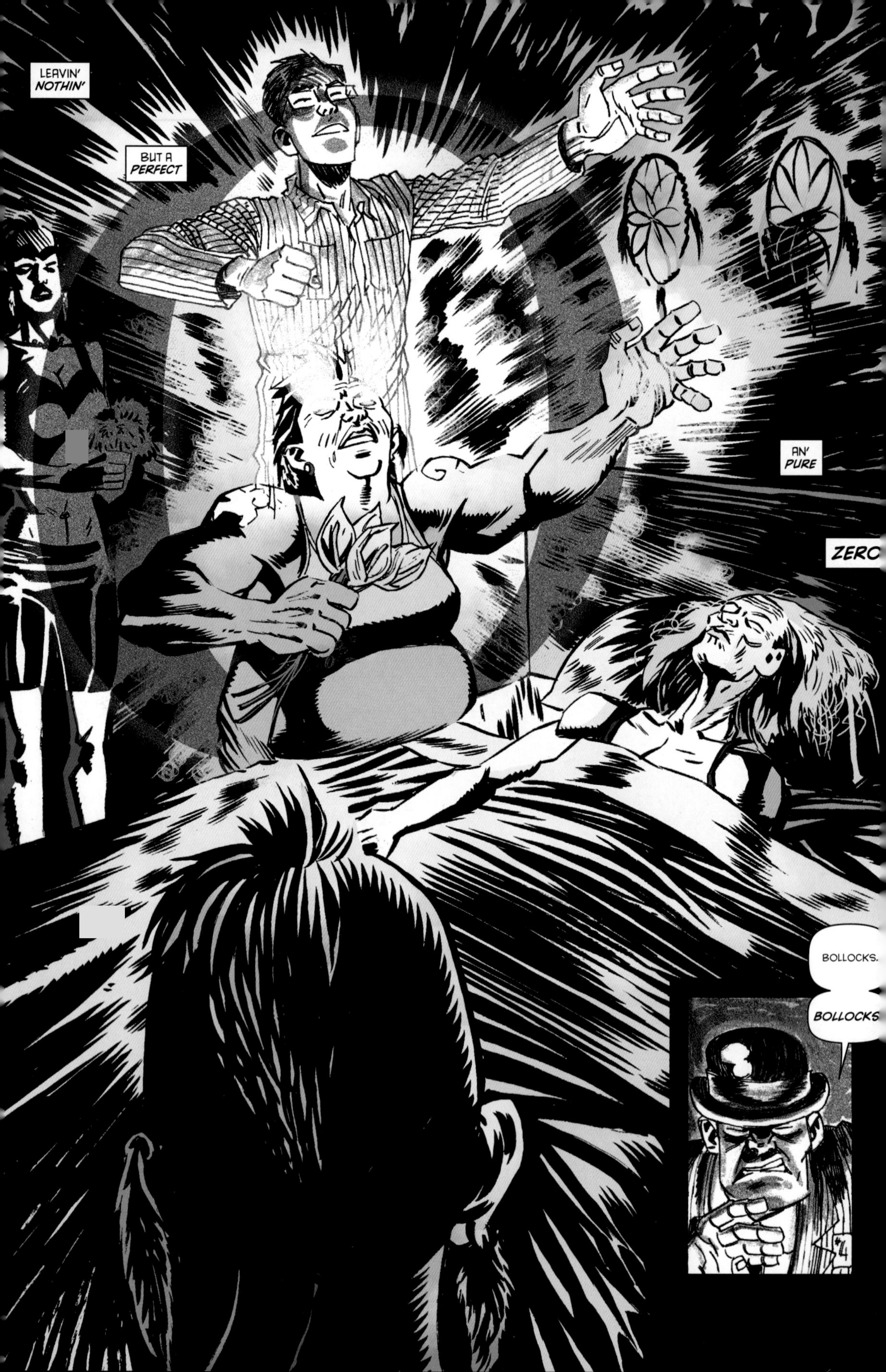
LEAVIN' NOTHIN'
BUT A PERFECT
AN' PURE
ZERO
BOLLOCKS.
BOLLOCKS

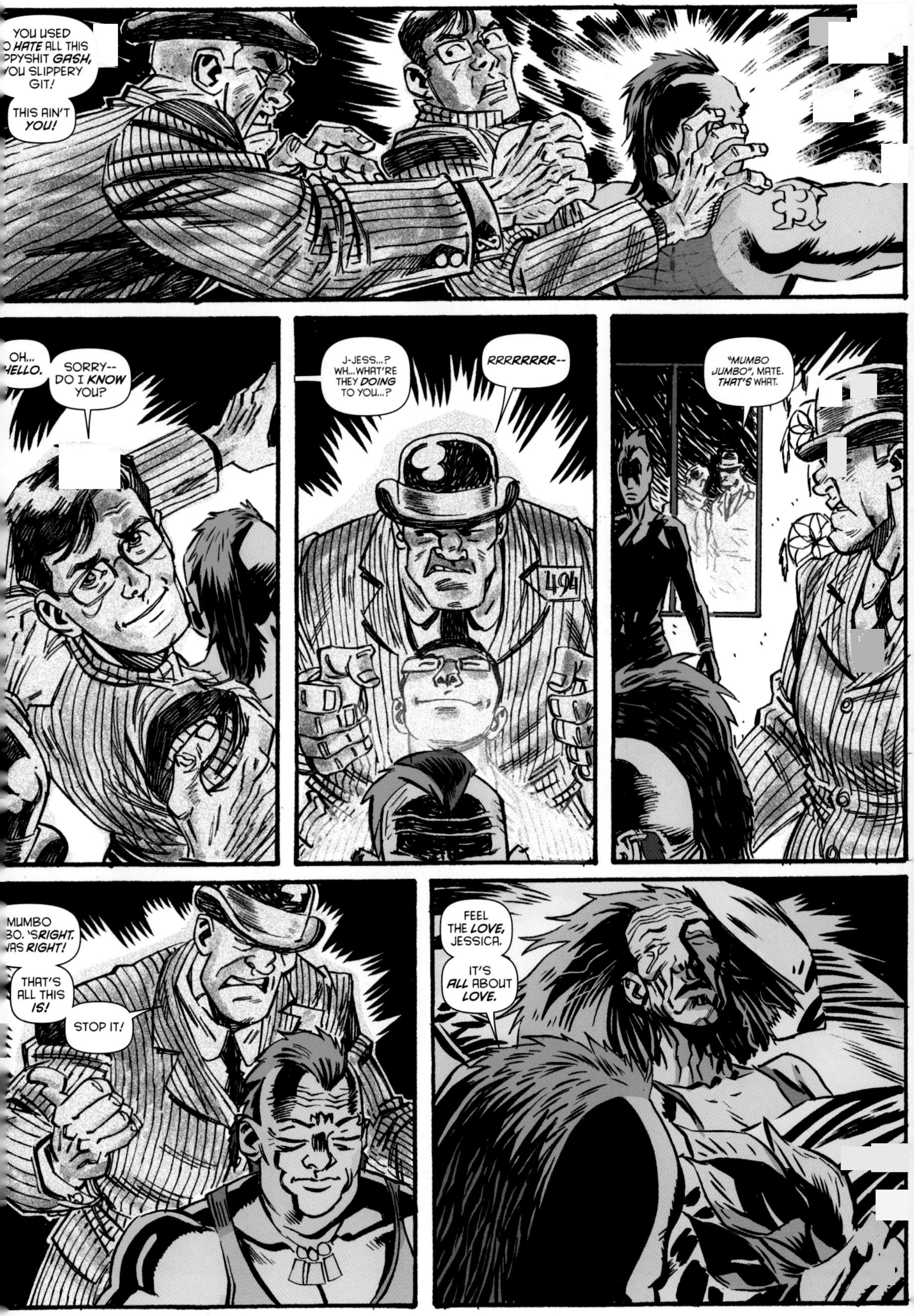
YOU USED O HATE ALL THIS PPYSHIT GASH, YOU SLIPPERY GIT!
THIS AIN'T YOU!
OH... HELLO.
SORRY-- DO I KNOW YOU?
J-JESS...? WH...WHAT'RE THEY DOING TO YOU...?
RRRRRRRR--
"MUMBO JUMBO", MATE. THAT'S WHAT.
MUMBO BO. 'SRIGHT. WAS RIGHT!
THAT'S ALL THIS IS!
STOP IT!
FEEL THE LOVE, JESSICA.
IT'S ALL ABOUT LOVE.

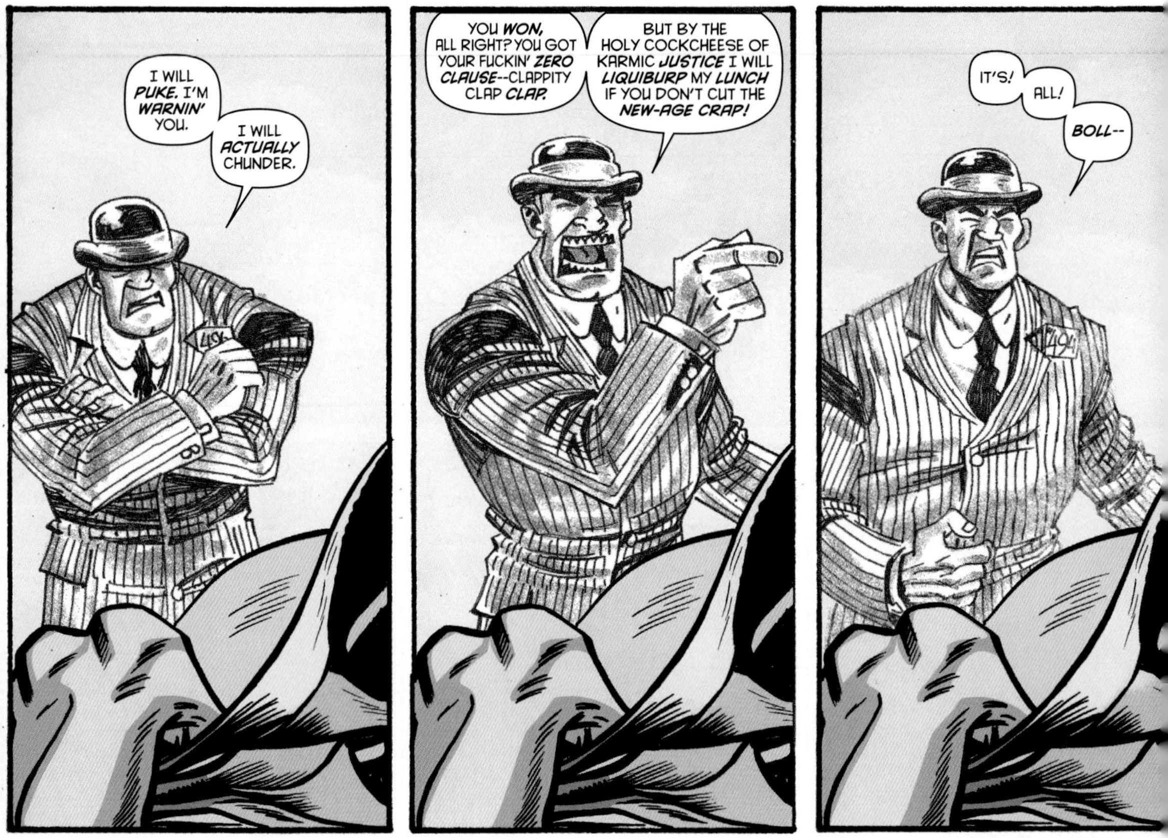
I WILL PUKE. I'M WARNIN' YOU.
I WILL ACTUALLY CHUNDER.
YOU WON, ALL RIGHT? YOU GOT YOUR FUCKIN' ZERO CLAUSE--CLAPPITY CLAP CLAP.
BUT BY THE HOLY COCKCHEESE OF KARMIC JUSTICE I WILL LIQUIBURP MY LUNCH IF YOU DON'T CUT THE NEW-AGE CRAP!
IT'S!
ALL!
BOLL--

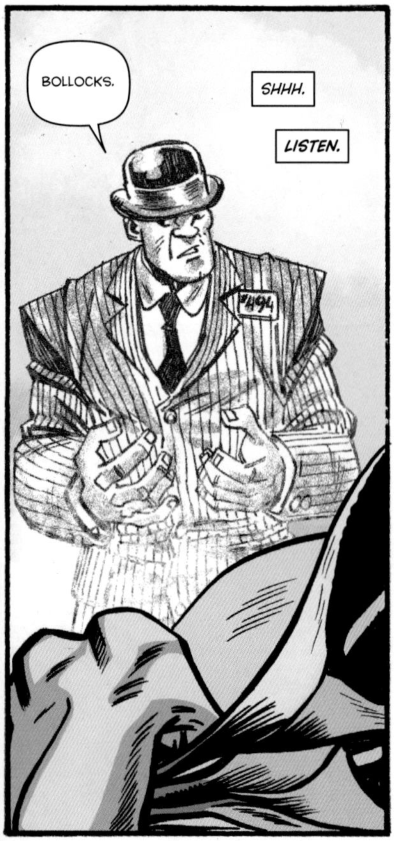
BOLLOCKS.
SHHH.
LISTEN.

JESSICA SPENT HER WHOLE LIFE IN PAIN.

OVER AND OVER AGAIN, *MEN* HAVE APPEARED. THEY'VE *LOVED* HER WITH A *PASSION*...WITH A WHITE-HOT *FLAME* SO FUCKIN' *INTENSE* IT CAN'T BE *RESISTED* OR *IGNORED*...

...AND THEN THEY *DIED.*

AND *SHE,* BEIN' A *FUZZY-BRAINED* SORT...BEIN' A *HIPPY* AN' A *SPIRITUALIST* AN' FUNDAMENTALLY *UNMATHEMATICAL*... *SHE* THOUGHT SHE WAS *CURSED.*

AND WE ALL KNEW HOW *STUPID* THAT WAS, DIDN'T WE?

A-HO-HO-HO.

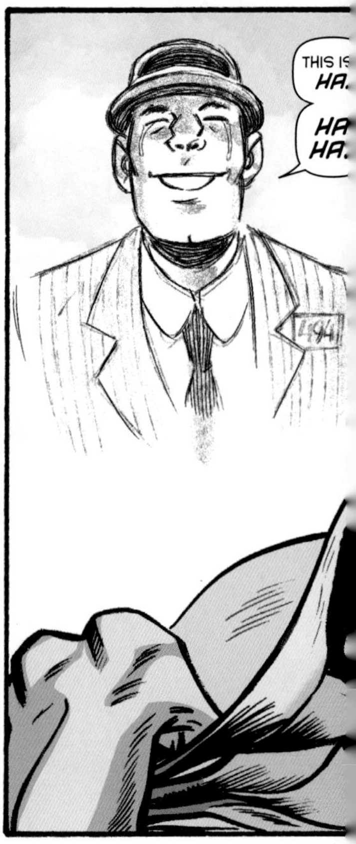
THIS IS

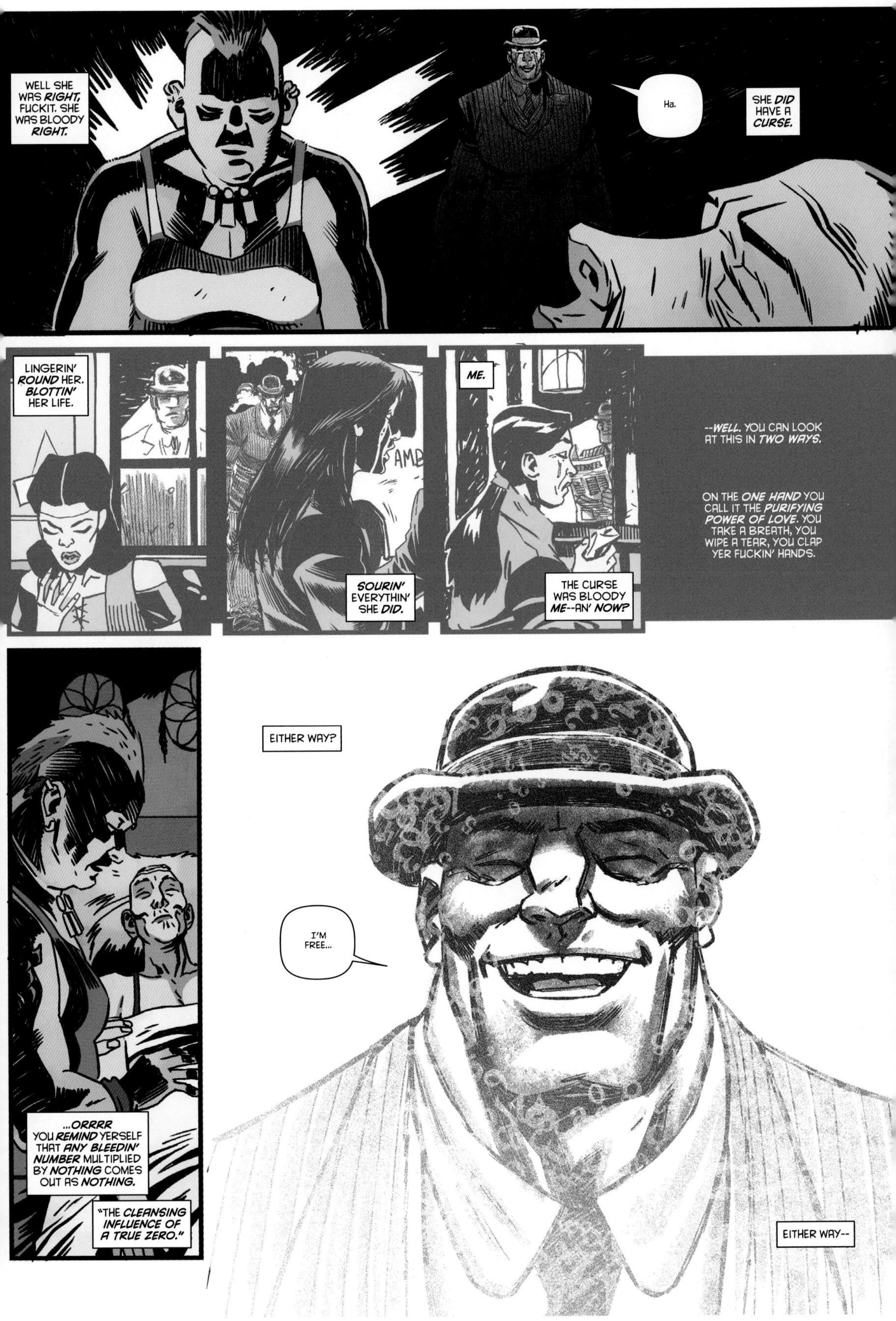

WELL SHE WAS RIGHT, FUCKIT. SHE WAS BLOODY RIGHT.
Ha.
SHE DID HAVE A CURSE.
LINGERIN' ROUND HER. BLOTTIN' HER LIFE.
SOURIN' EVERYTHIN' SHE DID.
ME.
THE CURSE WAS BLOODY ME--AN' NOW?
--WELL. YOU CAN LOOK AT THIS IN TWO WAYS.
ON THE ONE HAND YOU CALL IT THE PURIFYING POWER OF LOVE. YOU TAKE A BREATH, YOU WIPE A TEAR, YOU CLAP YER FUCKIN' HANDS.
...ORRRR YOU REMIND YERSELF THAT ANY BLEEDIN' NUMBER MULTIPLIED BY NOTHING COMES OUT AS NOTHING.
"THE CLEANSING INFLUENCE OF A TRUE ZERO."
EITHER WAY?
I'M FREE...
EITHER WAY--

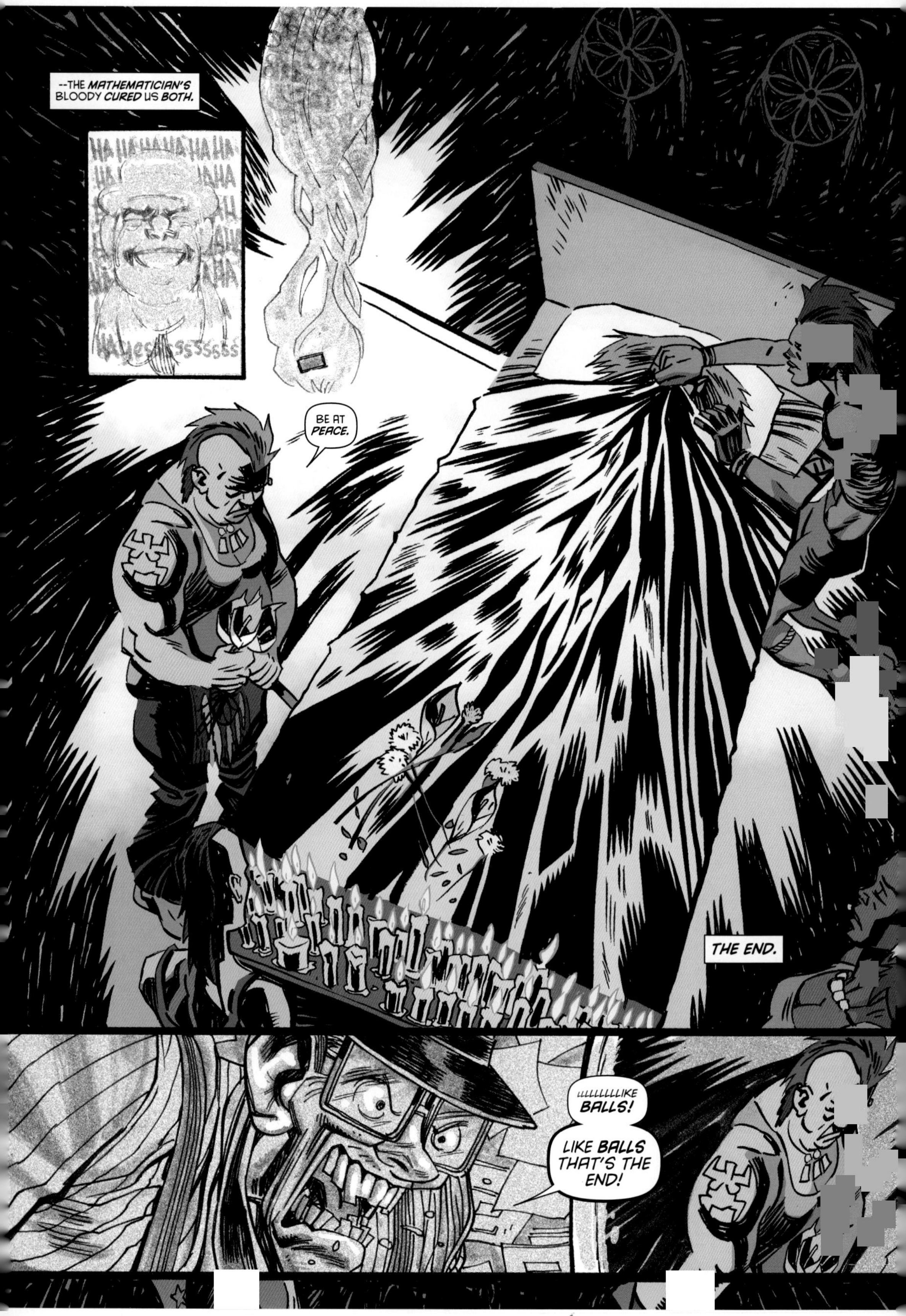
--THE MATHEMATICIAN'S BLOODY CURED US BOTH.
BE AT PEACE.
THE END.
LLLLLLLLLLIKE BALLS!
LIKE BALLS THAT'S THE END!

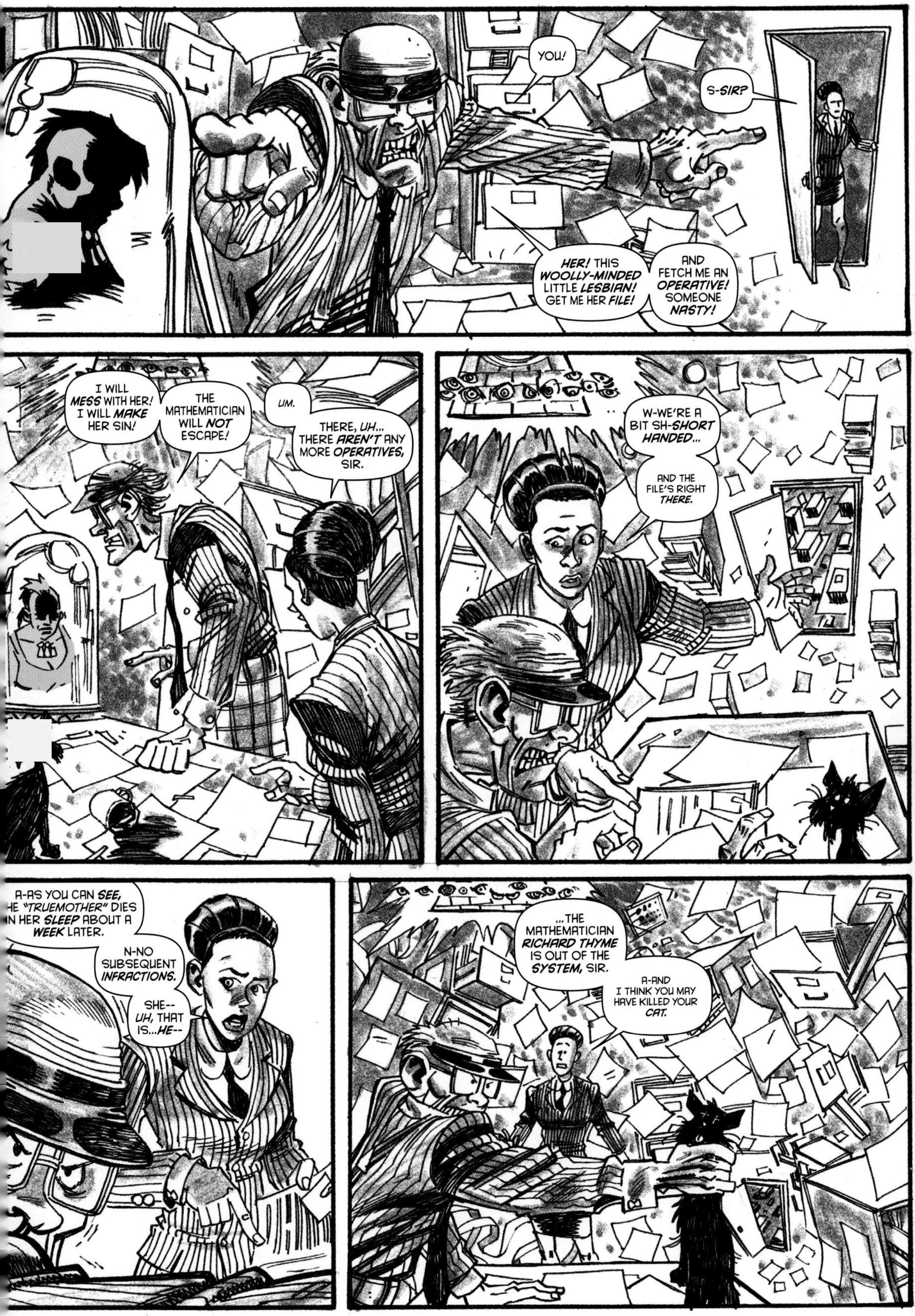
YOU!
S-SIR?
HER! THIS WOOLLY-MINDED LITTLE LESBIAN! GET ME HER FILE!
AND FETCH ME AN OPERATIVE! SOMEONE NASTY!
I WILL MESS WITH HER! I WILL MAKE HER SIN!
THE MATHEMATICIAN WILL NOT ESCAPE!
UM.
THERE, UH... THERE AREN'T ANY MORE OPERATIVES, SIR.
W-WE'RE A BIT SH-SHORT HANDED...
AND THE FILE'S RIGHT THERE.
A-AS YOU CAN SEE, HE "TRUEMOTHER" DIES N HER SLEEP ABOUT A WEEK LATER.
N-NO SUBSEQUENT INFRACTIONS.
SHE-- UH, THAT IS...HE--
...THE MATHEMATICIAN RICHARD THYME IS OUT OF THE SYSTEM, SIR.
A-AND I THINK YOU MAY HAVE KILLED YOUR CAT.

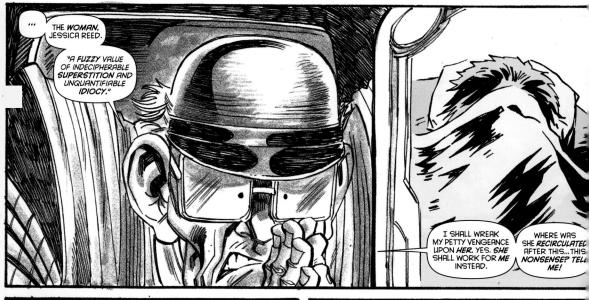

... THE *WOMAN*. JESSICA REED.

"A FUZZY VALUE OF INDECIPHERABLE SUPERSTITION AND UNQUANTIFIABLE IDIOCY."

I SHALL WREAK MY PETTY VENGEANCE UPON *HER*. YES. *SHE* SHALL WORK FOR *ME* INSTEAD.

WHERE WAS SHE *RECIRCULATED* AFTER THIS... THIS *NONSENSE? TELL ME!*

UM.

THE... *UH*. THE SYSTEM DOESN'T SEEM TO *KNOW*, SIR.

I-IT'S AS IF THE *ALGORITHM* WAS *UNBALANCED* AT SOURCE...

DON'T BE *RIDICULOUS*. THE *WENCH* COULD BARELY COUNT TO *TEN!* HOW COULD *SHE* ITERATE HER OWN *RECIRCULATION?*

YOU MUST B MIST--

WHAT...*UH*. WHAT YOU *DOIN'?*

J-JUST...MAKING *ARRANGEMENTS*.

FIND HER.

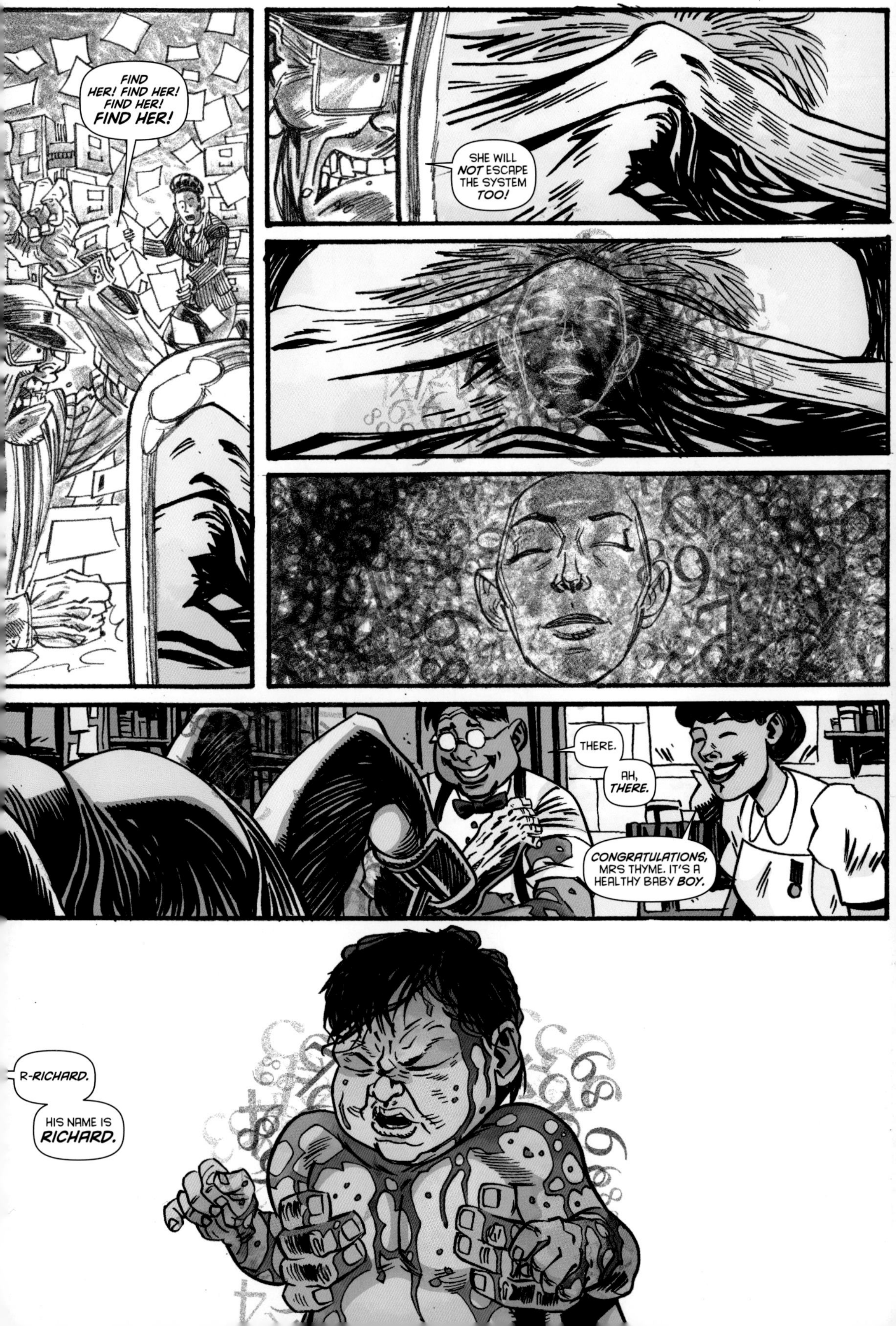
FIND HER! FIND HER! FIND HER! FIND HER!
SHE WILL NOT ESCAPE THE SYSTEM TOO!
THERE.
AH, THERE.
CONGRATULATIONS, MRS THYME. IT'S A HEALTHY BABY BOY.
R-RICHARD.
HIS NAME IS RICHARD.

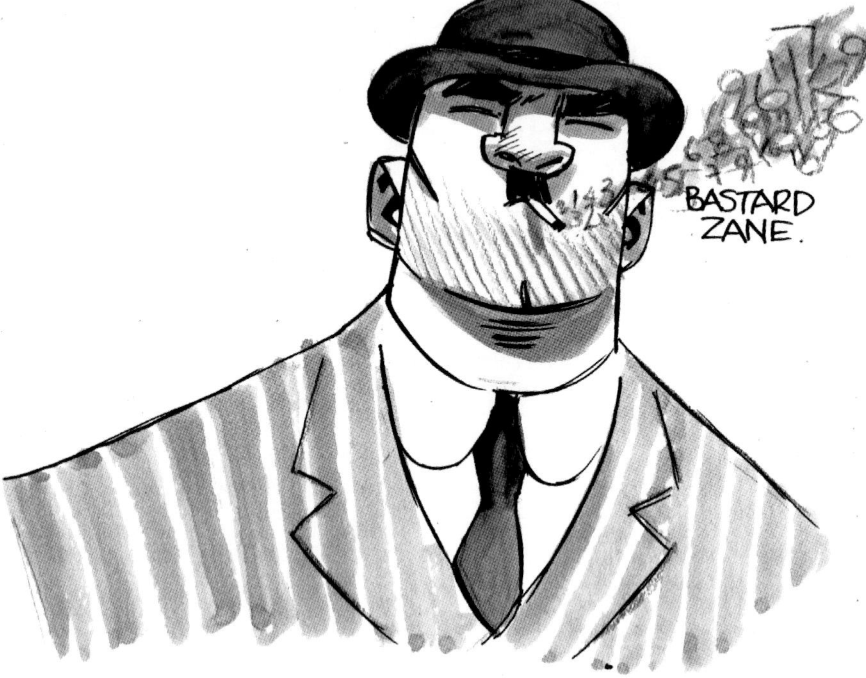
BASTARD
ZANE.

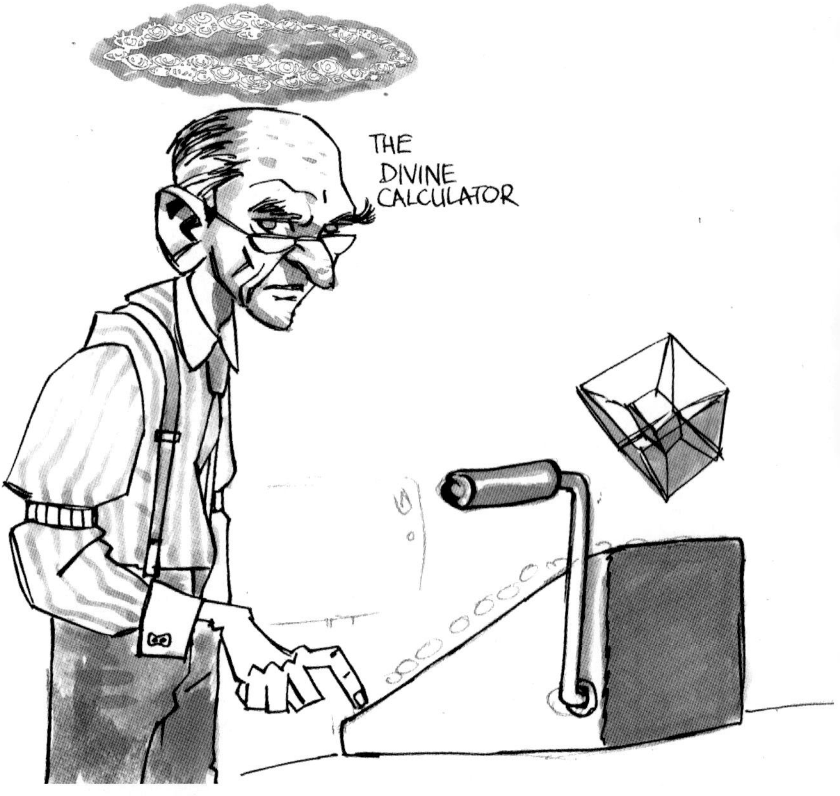
THE
DIVINE
CALCULATOR

Early designs for Zane and the Divine Calculator
by P.J. Holden

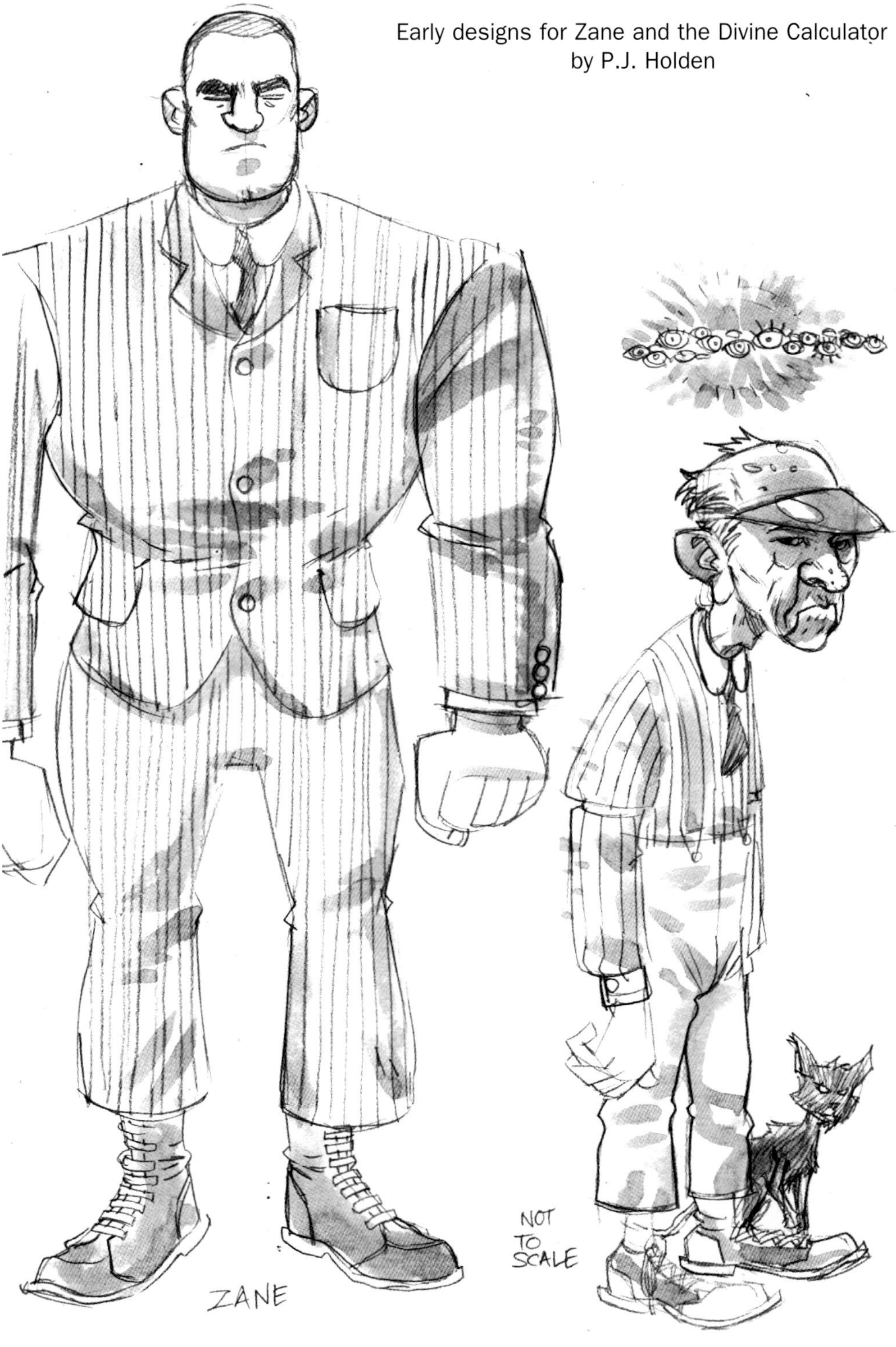
ZANE
NOT TO SCALE

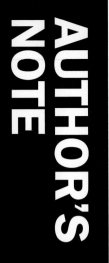

AUTHOR'S NOTE

Listen: people keep asking me what *Numbercruncher* is. Generally I can stammer-out a string of muddled genre-types on demand – *it's a time-twisting romantic thriller crime-noir metaphysical sci-fi black comedy, natch* – which demonstrates either the ineffectuality of genre-theory language or that I'm a contrary arsehole with a morbid fear of pigeon-holes.

People also keep asking me what *Numbercruncher*'s about. That's a tad harder.

You could say *Numbercruncher*'s about love, I suppose, though it's not really. Love's the fuel, not the engine – and that's probably the wankiest thing I've ever written.

To me *Numbercruncher*'s about living with systems. It's about rules and regulations and things operating *the way they're supposed to*. It's about the inner-workings of the Universe running to spec. And it's about what happens when that system – that tedious predictable joyless fucking set of Known Amounts – comes into contact with something dynamic and alive and mysterious, for which it's laughably unprepared.

Numbercruncher – as you shall see – is an idea about a tiny iota of Chaos infecting an ordered system. (The effects spread forwards in time – reshaping the future. And backwards in time – changing perspectives on the past.) *Numbercruncher*'s an idea about magic disrupting a machine.

Numbercruncher's also the only idea that has ever truly struck me. Bear with me here.

Hippytrippy flashback: knuckle-deep in the Summer of 2009, as I cycled alone along a stretch of picturesque Mediterranean coastline. The least bleak, least bureaucratic, least *Numbercruncher*-y scene imaginable. The sun was sunning, waves were waving, gulls were... gulling... probably... and I was filled with a miraculous sense of solitary well-being. Also I had wine in my waterbottle. On reflection that didn't help when – typically – the idea hit halfway round a particularly sharp corner. Wobblement ensued. Swearing followed. As did four pissed-up Spaniards in a battered Mini-Moke singing along to Roxy Music. Had they been driving just a fraction faster *Numbercruncher* might have killed me.

When I say it's the only idea which has ever struck me, "struck" is the operative word.

Listen: in my experience most ideas build-up over time – like embarrassing infections: accretions of mental bric-a-brac that expand and multiply until they reach critical mass. They're the gibbering asexual fertilisations of the mind: wisdom

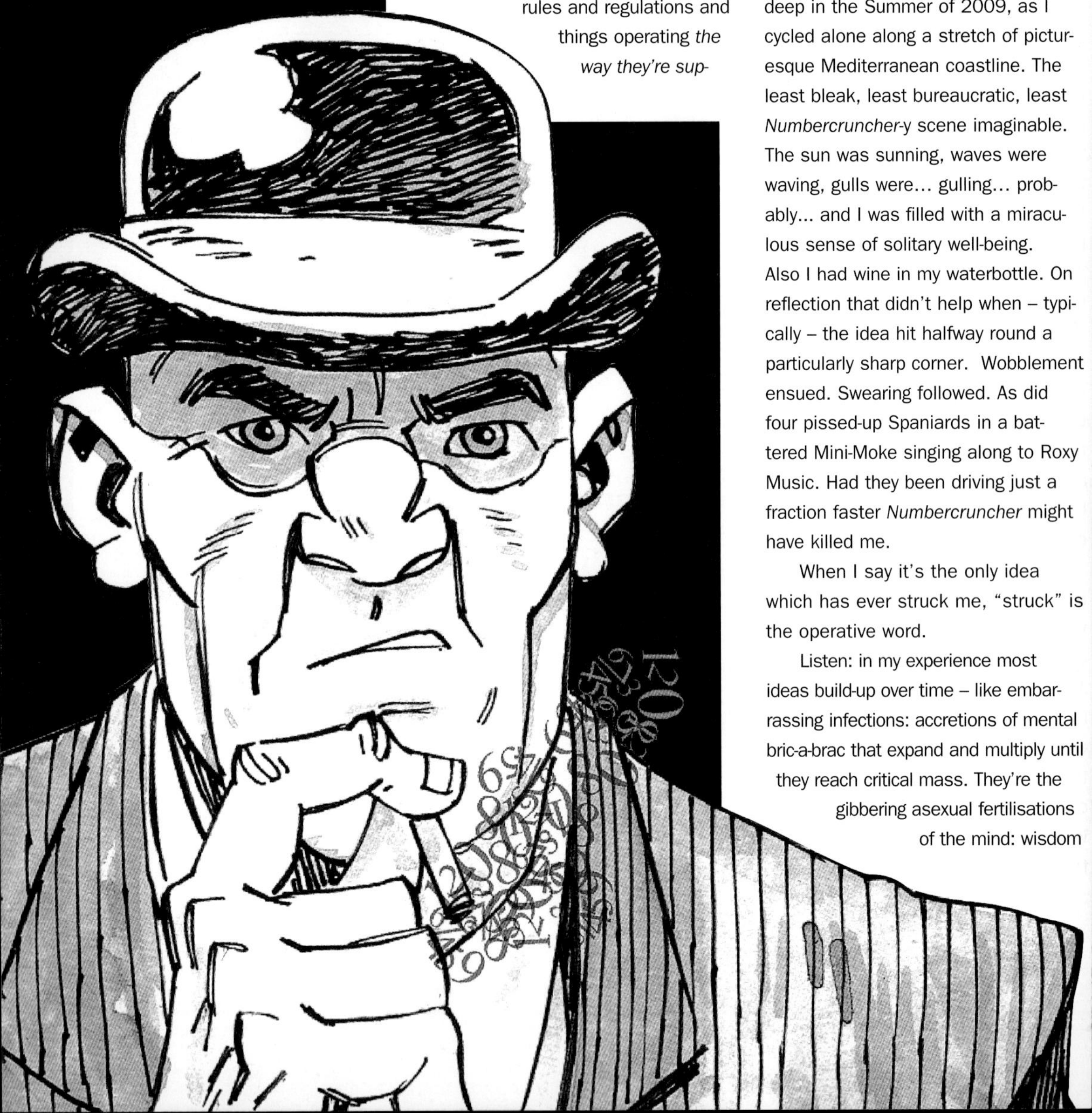

> "...a man, dying young, meddles with divine pow-ers so he can be rein-carnated within his lover's lifetime."

plus rumour; facts mutated by imperfect memory, chimeric mash-ups of partial thought. It's all rather humdrum in those terms. Only when the pressure's right do they come oozing forth: far too late to be anything like a surprise.

Well *this* one was. This one arrived fully formed: *a man, dying young, meddles with divine powers so he can be reincarnated within his lover's lifetime. Rule-bending occurs. A karmic bailiff is dispatched to destroy the romance. An intricate time-travelling love story ensues, but all told from the point of view of the bastard sent to stop it.* The twists, the turns, the details: I can't mention them here because I'd kind of like it if you show up next month to see what happens, but yeah... They were all there, that day on the road.

Numbercruncher's one of those stories where *everything matters*. Everything links up, no matter how inconsequential it may've seemed when you first saw it. Thinking back to that day in the sun, I'm not sure if *Numbercruncher* could ever have happened if it didn't arrive the way it did. And the toughest part? The toughest part was trying to explain it to others afterwards. How does one elevator-pitch a story where every detail relies on every other? How does one spaff out a coke-fuelled Hollywood equation – *"it's like X meets Y – but on acid!"* – when the equation's five lines long and covered in mathematical symbols?

(In the face of these problems PJ and I are indebted to the splendid folks at the *Judge Dredd Megazine*, who first ran *Numbercruncher* – despite my inability to explain what it was about – and later to Steve White and the team at Titan for putting so much energy and belief into the expanded, coloured, retooled, resexed, reawesomed artefact you now hold.)

Here's a weird thing. When I look back, now, to that moment on the road in the sun... I find myself wondering if it really happened that way at all. I wonder if I'm not romanticising... story-ising... myth-making... being infected by a cultural trend about What It Means to have an idea.

See, I think it pleases us all to imagine ideas are somehow Holy; revelatory; epiphanic (which, according to the wiggly line on my screen is not a real word – I'm outraged). It reassures us to envisage ideas as tangible thunderbolts from The Outside: penetrating the boring coiling dog food of our brains. *Yeah, sure,* we admit, *we're all just meat computers – but here's something Other: something profound and new, reaching into the mind like a light!*

You want to know want an idea *really* is, oh delightful sexy reader, in the popular imagination?

An idea is a tiny iota of Chaos infecting an ordered system. (The effects spread forwards in time – reshaping the future. And backwards in time – changing perspectives on the past). An idea is magic disrupting a machine...

Stop me if you've heard this before.

Si Spurrier, 2013

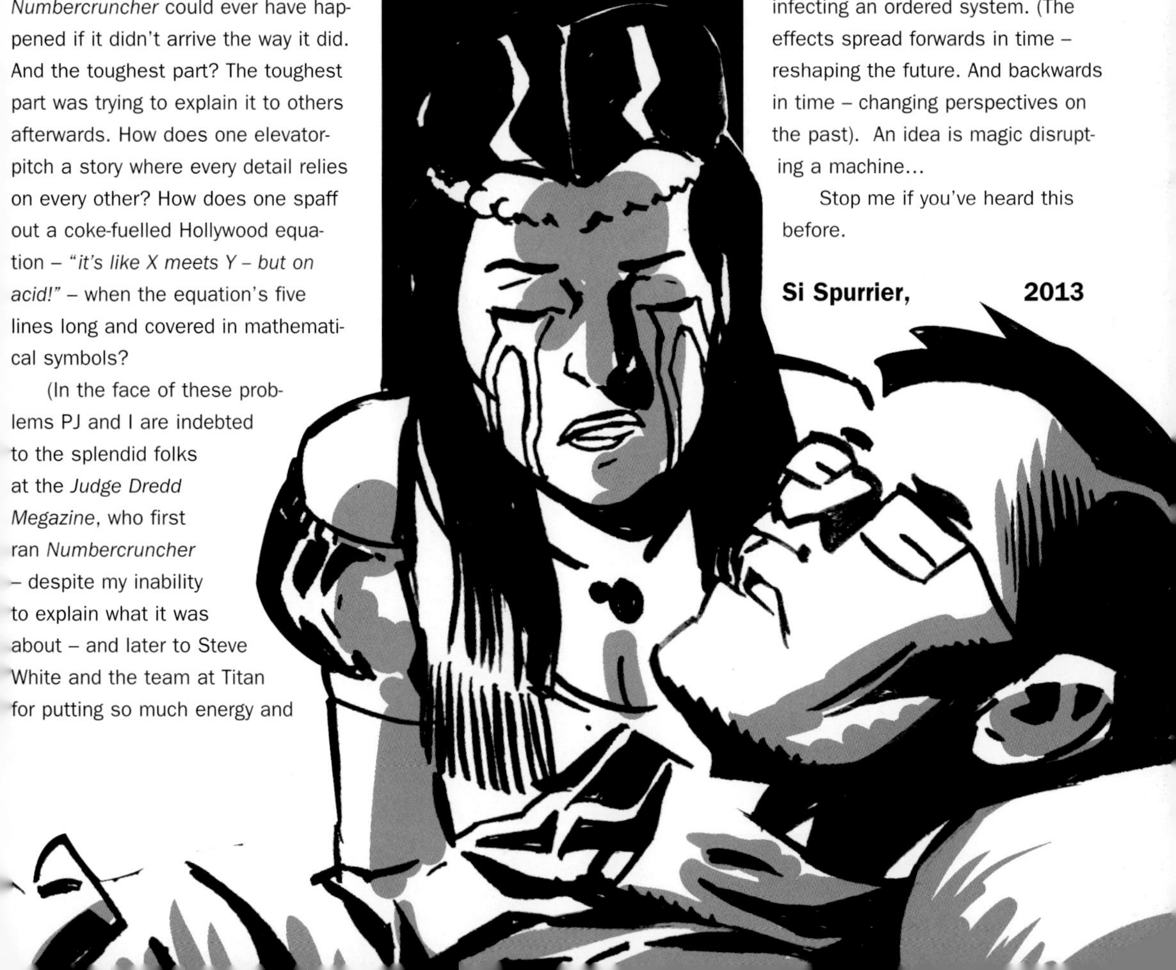

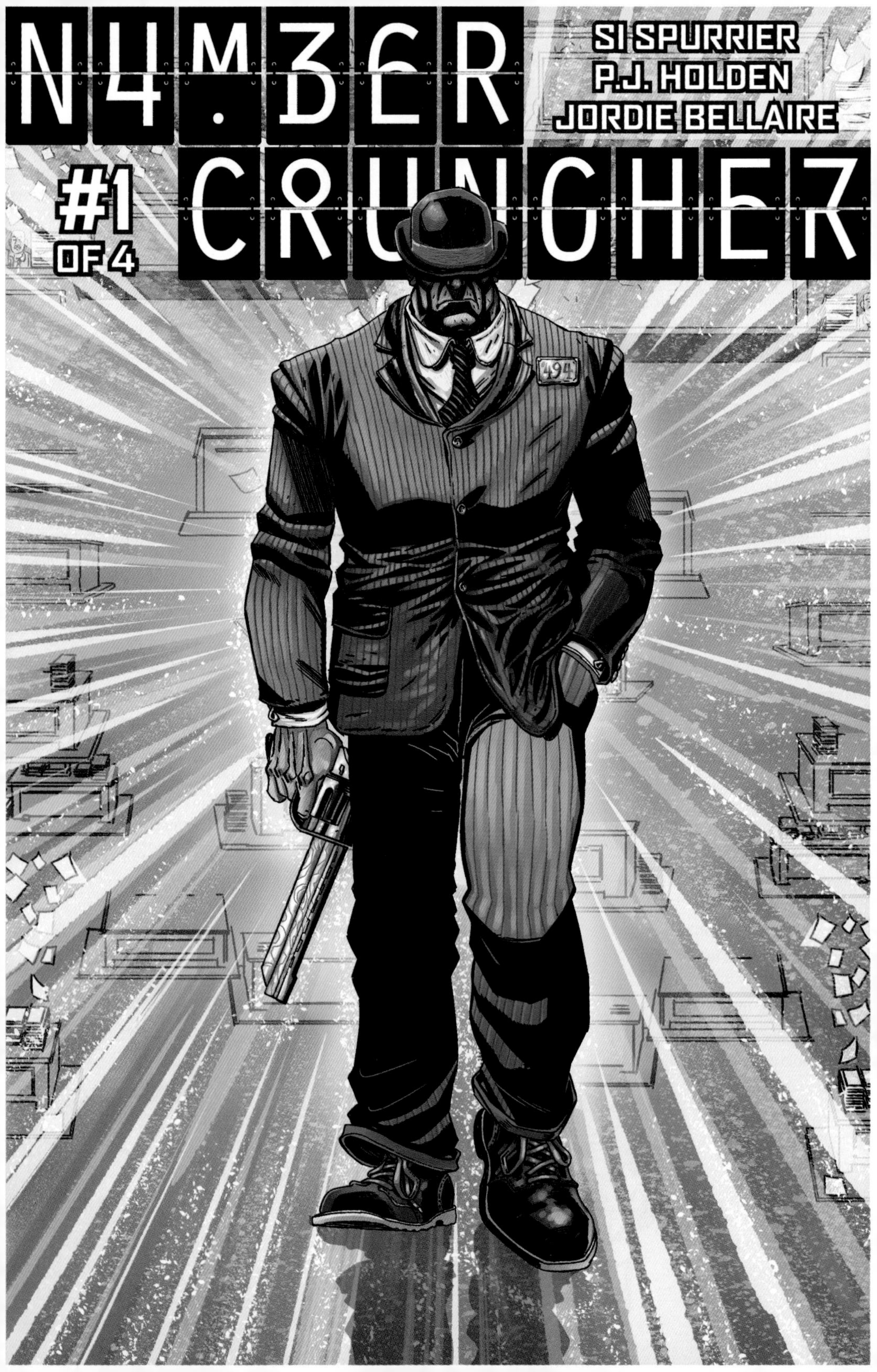
N4M3ER CRUNCHER
SI SPURRIER
P.J. HOLDEN
JORDIE BELLAIRE
#1 OF 4
494

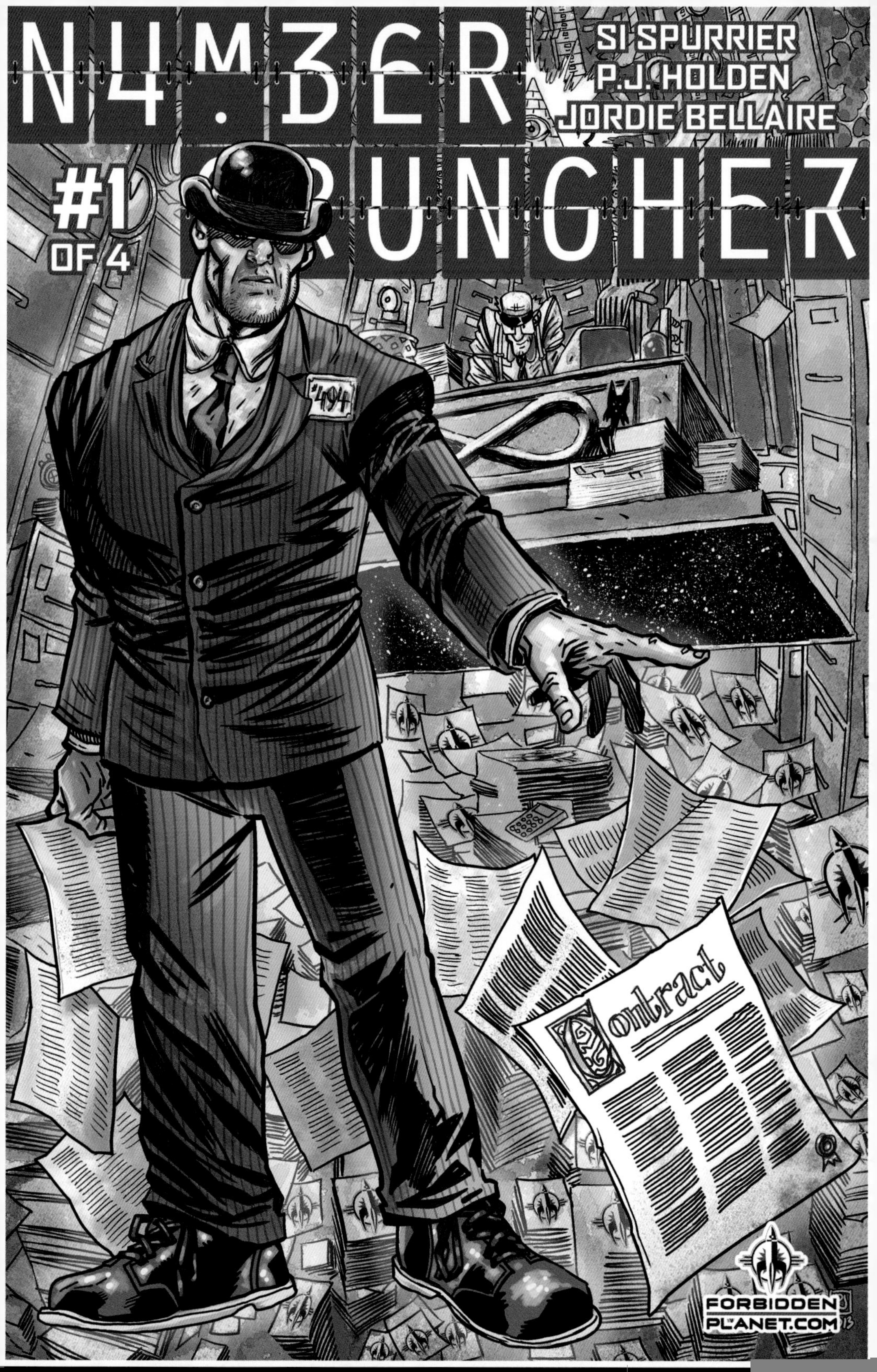

NUMBER CRUNCHER
SI SPURRIER
P.J. HOLDEN
JORDIE BELLAIRE
#1 OF 4
Contract
FORBIDDEN PLANET.COM

A COMIC FOR
TALKING TO GOD

Brian Truitt, from *USA Today*, chats with Si Spurrier and PJ Holden.

BT: How did the concept for *Numbercruncher* come about between you two and how did you end up with Titan Comics?

PJ: *Everything originated with Si, really.*

SS: Life, the Universe, all wisdom, good and evil, etc etc.

The whole coming-up-with-it part of *Numbercruncher* is slightly weird for two reasons: first, I can remember exactly where I was when it hit me (cycling alone along a craggy patch of empty shoreline on a Mediterranean Island), when normally I'd default to "in the bath" or "bit-by-bit"; and second, it arrived in the highly unusual form of an *idea*. That probably sounds stupid (*how else* would it arrive, Si?) but that's actually really rare: a plot hitting you like that, fully formed. Normally it'll be… say… a cool character, or a little vignette, or a theme or message that matters to you, around which you set out to build a story, like an oyster wrapping a little grain of shit in shiny, shiny mucus.

Ah, the romance of writing.

But no, this time round the bare bones of the story landed like a nuke: *guy dies young, but he's so totally in love that he decides to cheat the rules of reincarnation so he can return to his lover. The Universe tries to stop him, but—*

Well, I can't say much more without giving things away for the later parts of the story. But it's twisty, it's turny, it bounces and coils round about 50 years of history, there are a crapload of big conceptual surprises along the way, and *all of it* sprang to life, fully formed, that day on the bicycle by the sea.

The second stage, which is always the fun part, was simply to slap some flesh on the bones. Which required a suitably unhinged artist. Cue Mr. Holden:

PJ: *I think I had some sense of how to attack the visuals (based entirely on my love of the* classic A Matter of Life and Death - *a film similarly set in the real world and the afterlife) and my job was, largely to keep up with Si, who seemed to have the entire thing mapped out.*

SS: As for the publishing route… PJ and I both launched our careers through the UK powerhouse comic *2000AD*, so when they announced they'd be running a slot in their monthly sister-title for creator-owned projects we jumped at the chance. Fortune decreed that – just as the serialization ended – Titan started planning its sexy new international comics arm – Titan Comics – and we once again seized the moment. The beautiful part about *Numbercruncher* finding its home at Titan for worldwide release and trade collection is that these guys, like *2000AD*, characterize exactly the kind of dynamic, open-minded, genre-defying excitement the project embraces. People have asked me before to describe what sort of story *Numbercruncher* is… The best I can do is *"metaphysical time-twisting black-comedy romantic crime noir thriller"*, or "Eternal Sunshine of the Spotless Mind *meets* A Matter of Life and Death *by way of* Lock, Stock and Two Smoking Barrels *and* Inception"… both of which are possibly the worst elevator-pitches ever. It's only down to the likes of Titan that something so unusual can be given the chance it deserves.

Why mathematics as a main theme and the core conceit of your afterlife here, with rules and contracts and such?

SS: Frankly, it started out as a requirement of the plot. I wanted our 'hero' to be a normal Joe: someone without superpowers or big muscles or military training, a guy who uses his natural cleverness to literally break the rules of the Universe. Certain options presented themselves, but mostly they're the hackneyed nonsense you'd expect: cabbalistic deals, sorcery, latter-day Faustian pacts. So I started thinking about it all in more modern terms. Y'know who gleefully breaks the rules of reality everyday? Quantum theorists, existential physicists and mathematicians. It's like Zane says during episode one: *"It's not about fire and brimstone, or ponces with frocks and harps, or clouds or virgins or eternal-bleedin'-carousing in the halls of our forefathers – it's all about numbers."*

That in itself threw up a really lovely thematic slant on the whole story. If our central character manages to get one over on those who control the Laws Of The Universe, using nothing but his intuitive mathematical brilliance, it follows that the Universe must be a kinda number-fixated place. And suddenly this whole wonderful world suggests itself – of accountants, mealy-mouthed tax collectors, form-stampers, guys with calculators and tickertapes, jobsworths and – yes – *numbercrunchers*.

And hey, for a story whose central notion is about the power of love and life, what a wonderful and subversive notion! That the machinery behind the scenes – the afterlife, the choirs of angels, even the Supreme Being at the heart of it all – are these grey, dismal, penny-pinching asshole tax collectors.

PJ: *For my part, again it was Si's conceit and I tried to run with it as much as possible in the artwork, there's a lot of numbers and fractals and some genuinely complex mathematical formulates laid into it (there's also a lot of gibberish formulas, I'm not a mathematician!)*

Does the first series center on Thyme and Zane?

SS: It does, yeah. (There's no second series planned as

yet – this is a self contained, twisty beast with a very definite ending).

PJ: *It's really a battle of wits between Thyme and Zane. Thyme is subtle and smart and playing the long game, Zane is... Well, Zane is not that.*

SS: Heh heh heh, perfectly put.

Interestingly, I tend to regard Richard Thyme as the hero but Zane as the protagonist. That's in the sense that even though we're all generally programmed to be on the side of love and joy and cleverness – i.e. the mathematician – the story's dramatic tension comes from the fact we never quite know what he's up to. I felt in this case we could have our cake and eat it: the story worked a lot better if we were cheering just a teensy bit for the thuggish 'bad' guy, and seeing it all through his eyes.

To me, Zane's kind of the perfect anti-hero. He exists purely to *prevent* the happy ending from occurring, but his motives are so rational, and he's so guiltily likeable, that we find ourselves uncomfortably rooting for him. That's one of my favorite things about this series: the fact that the two main characters – perfect enemies though they may be – have perfectly sympathetic reason for behaving the way they do. Zane wants to escape an eternity of servitude; Thyme wants to be with his lady love. The Universe decrees that only one or the other of them gets their way.

Is Thyme a personal character for either of you guys?

PJ: *I think Thyme's all consuming love is very seductive and the fact he'll go to the end of time to be with the woman he loves is something you sort of want to be part of your character.*

But he's far smarter than me, that's for sure.

SS: I can totally imagine PJ in those pyjamas, mind you, so there's a connection there. And there's a page later on – end of episode three, I think – where Thyme's expression is *so* PJ it's not true.

In my wanky writerly way, for me Thyme's halfway between the archetypal trickster-god/wheeler-dealer figure – the character you want to succeed even though you don't know what he's thinking – and the eternal romantic everyman. He represents the power of love, the power to beat the odds. He's a genre-breaking, übermodern avatar of the old 'Beating Death At Chess' trope.

He comes across as a bit of a smug prick, at times, so... yeah. Nothing like me. Nothing like me at all. *cough*

What inspired Zane, both in terms of personality and design?

PJ: *The design was, pretty much as described by Si – and came out in the first drawing I did of him. I wanted to give him a little comedy toothbrush moustache but that was pretty much vetoed right away! He's a fun character to draw, a sort of dimwitted rhino of a man.*

SS: Yeah, I still don't know why I had such a reaction to the moustache. Maybe it feels like a layer of alienation too

far...? Like, enormous metaphysical undead thug he may be, but a Hitler 'tache? How will readers *ever* relate to that?

I know, I know, it's crazy.

Character-wise, I wanted him to be the perfect counterpoint to the mathematician. He's not smart, he's not sneaky, he's simple and crude and straightforward. I love that archetype – think Marv from *Sin City* – who come across as dumb and violent and good for nothing but breaking heads, but have hidden depths and a rough poetry all of their own.

The Divine Calculator and his world is an interesting one. Did he go through some different iterations before finalizing him?

SS: Character-wise, he was there as soon as the mathematics/accountancy angle arose: this nasty little taxman type, with no understanding of love or compassion. He's basically a manifestation of the Universe: constantly becoming more and more complex, throwing up new rules and new tyrannies to preserve a doomed quest for order.

He's a prick, basically. A petty, snide, toxic, weasely little prick. Behold your god and tremble!

PJ: *Again, Si's description allowed me to create the character in one pass – he pretty much didn't change from initial design to me drawing the book. Of course, since doing it, I've watched* Carousel, *and discovered that sort of old accountant type (peaked cap, sleeve holders) is an archetypal angel in some movies. Lots of the design came about because I wanted to fill his office and the afterlife with detail, paper flying about, filing cabinets everywhere, and some Google-fu turned up this great old abandoned typewriter design that I ended up using for Zane's typewriter.*

And there is a lot of math going on with the numbers and symbols. Is that enjoyable to let yours imaginations go crazy and embrace the most math-y place ever?

SS: Yeah, absolutely. I mean, from a story point of view it's never more than a surface layer – we never really get into any genuine fiddly math (imagine trying to sell *that* book) – but it acts as a byword for the antagonistic elements of the narrative: order, rules, stagnation...

But it was a visual challenge from the outset. The foundation-notion is that everything in this story-universe is made of – and underwritten by – numbers. I mean, that's true in the real world – *everything* is mathematics – but the beauty of comics is that you can visualize these abstract notions in beautiful ways. Which is where PJ came in.

PJ: *I do love numbers and maths, it's always fascinated me, the fact that numbers – without any sort of will or desire of their own, set the boundaries for everything we can do – and it was fun to play in a world where reciting a specific mathematic formula will get you an appointment with the afterlife's Divine Calculator.*

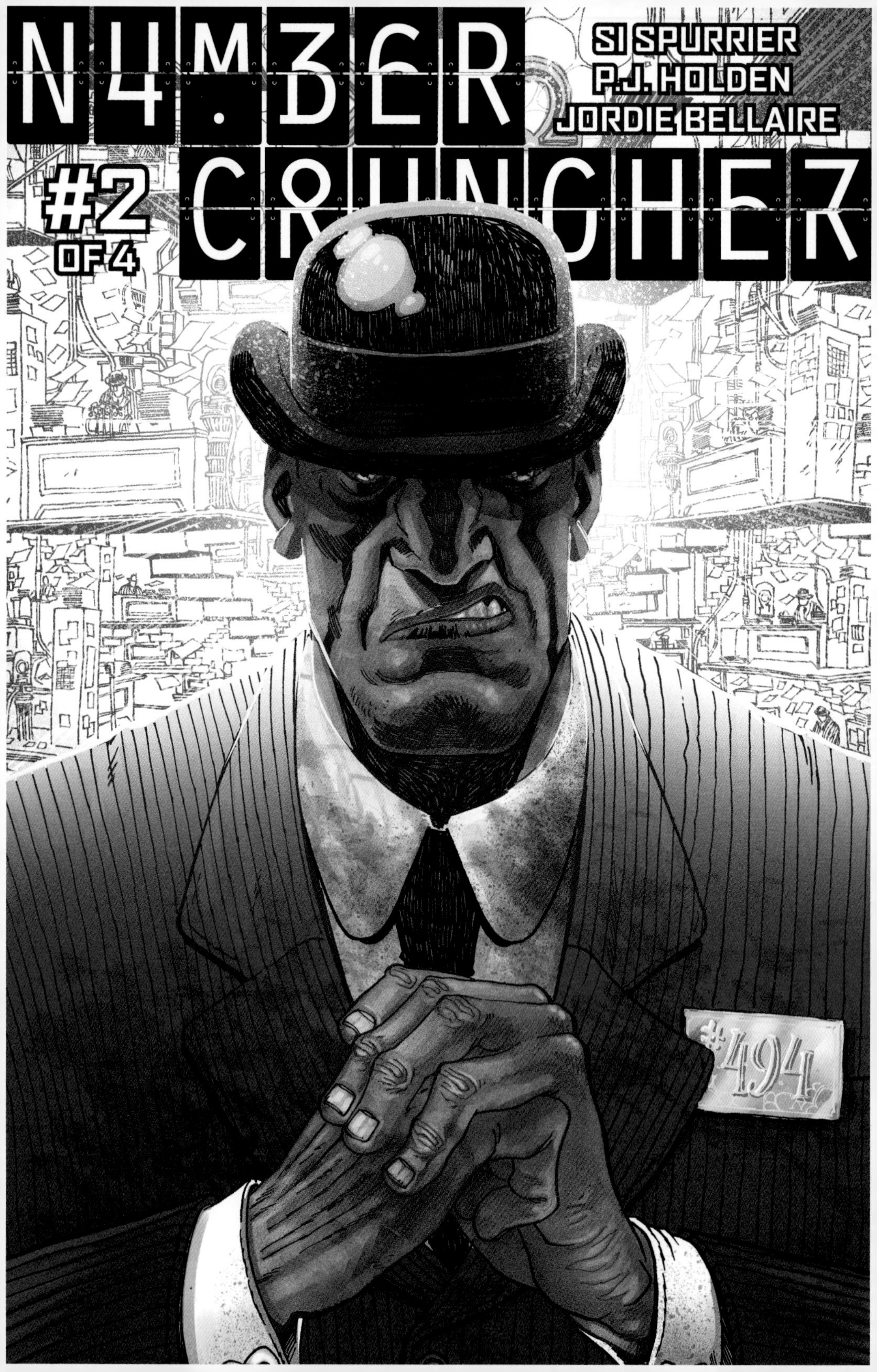

N4M3ER
CR8UNCHER
#2
OF 4
SI SPURRIER
P.J. HOLDEN
JORDIE BELLAIRE
#494

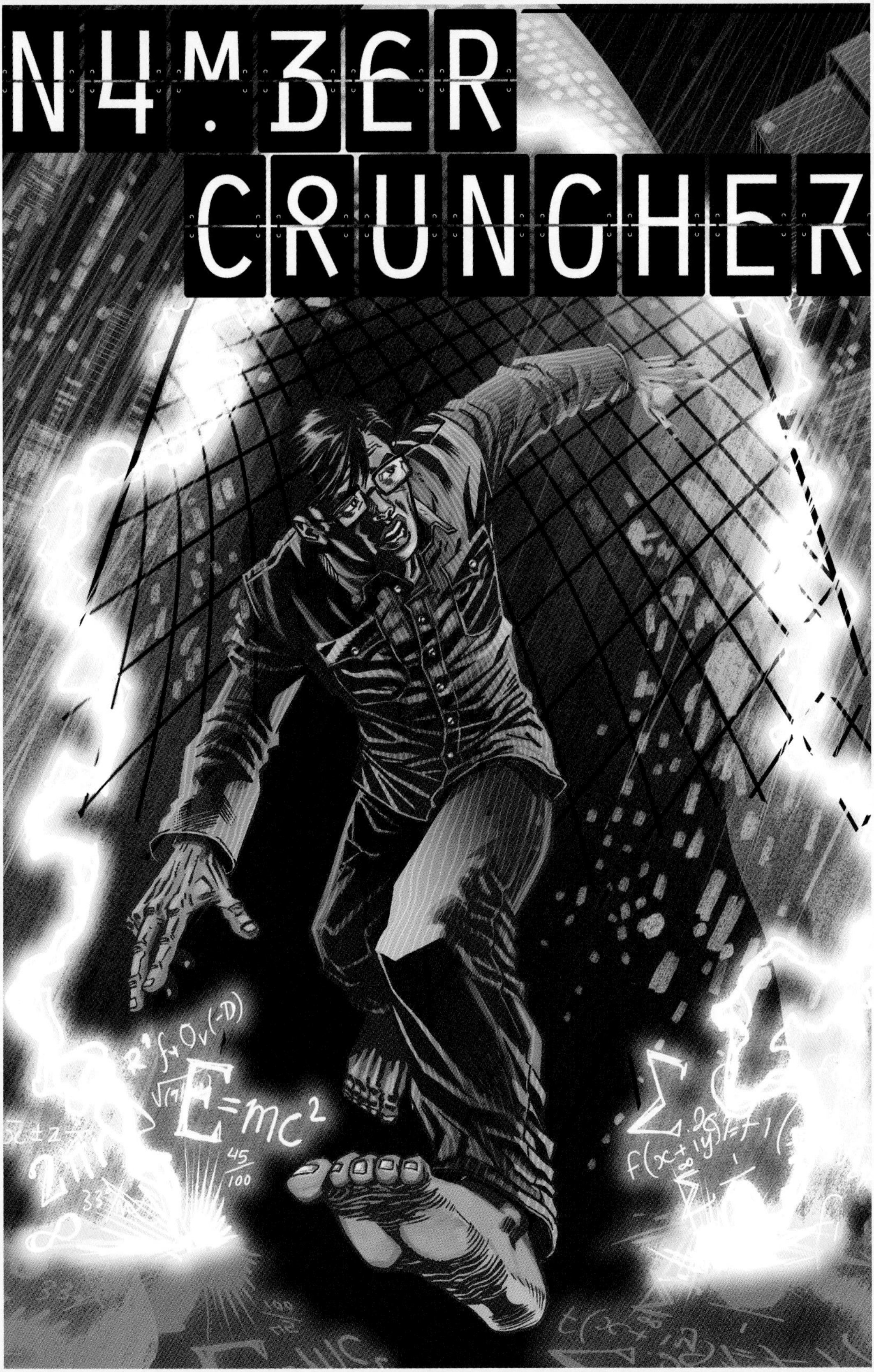
N4M3ER
CRUNCHER
$E=mc^2$

Unused, never-before-seen cover for #2 by P.J. Holden

WORKING FLAT-OUT

Behind the scenes of Jordie Bellaire's coloring process.

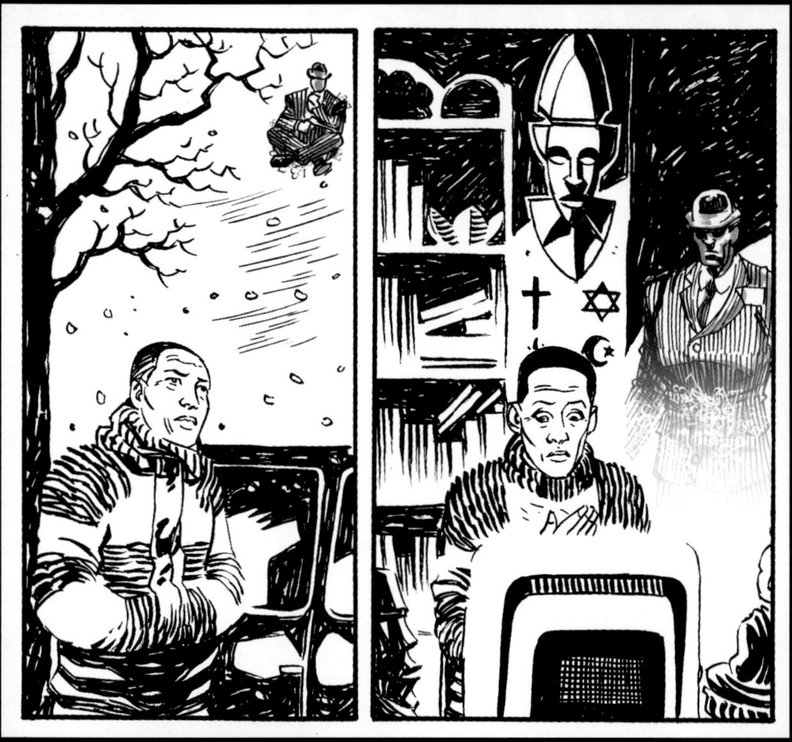

PAGE INCARNATION NUMBER
It all begins with Si's script anc PJ's fantastic art. In a story suc as this, where color (or its lack is key to the storytelling and division of scenes, Jordie's colo complement the linework witho overwhelming it or seeking to displace it. The coloring proces becomes one of creating atmosphere and clarity.

That's clarity of scenes – at a glance, you can spot the divisio between the 'real' world, and Zane's – and clarity of storytell ing; the subtle gradations that guide you to characters' faces, point your eye towards importa parts of the scene – or obfusca them, as with Zane fading into the dark on the opposite page.

PAGE INCARNATION NUMBER 2
Flat colors are added on a separate layer in Photoshop. 'Flatting' is primarily about separating out all the large areas of color (especially on art that has a lot of open or unfinished lines), rather than choosing the 'right' hues or final shades.

Depending on the colorist, flats can range from 'representative' and close to final – as here – to flat colors that are wildly disassociated from reality, so that the colorist isn't distracted by the palette on the page.

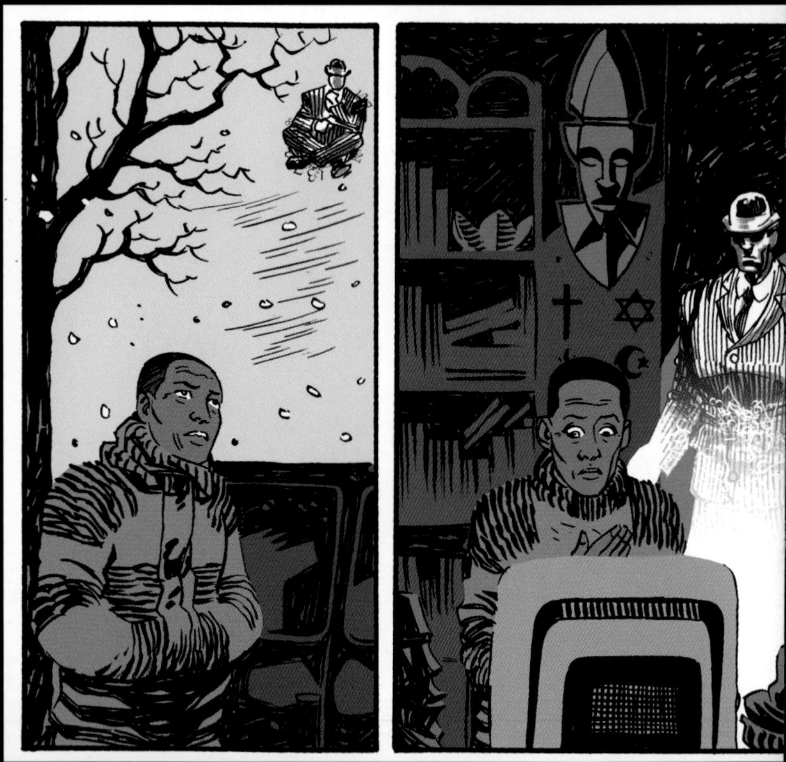

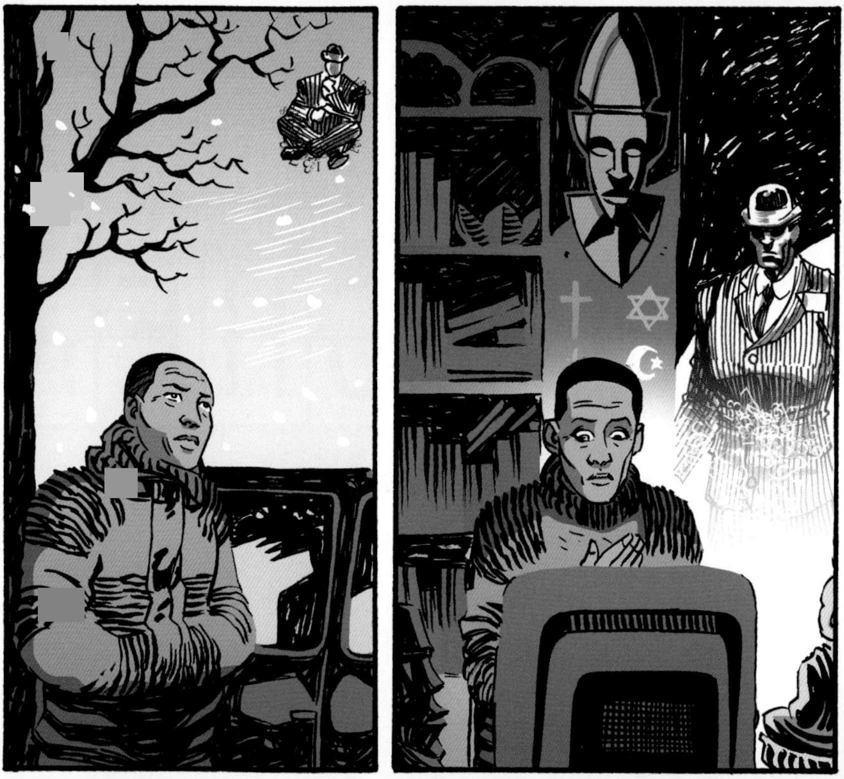

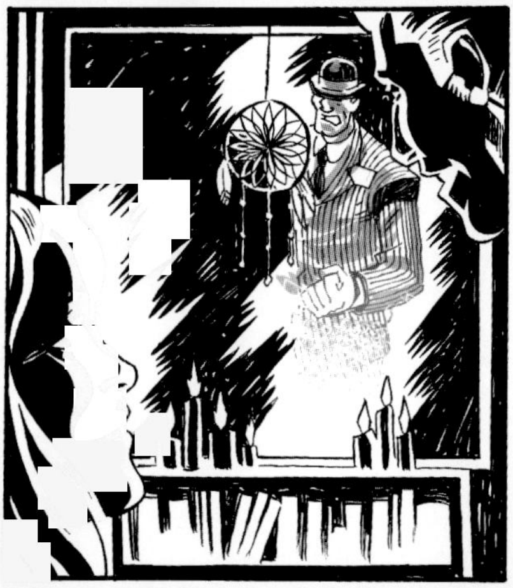

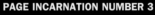

PAGE INCARNATION NUMBER 3

Once the flat colors are in place, then rendering or, 'the fun bit' can begin. This is everything from choosing final colors – in the panel above, you can see how Jordie has chosen a cool blue and grey, to pop the warm central figure forward, over the browns and greys of the original flats – to adding subtle gradients and 'color holds', which is where a black line is knocked back to a color, as with the white flurries of snow, above, and the flames of the candles below. ■

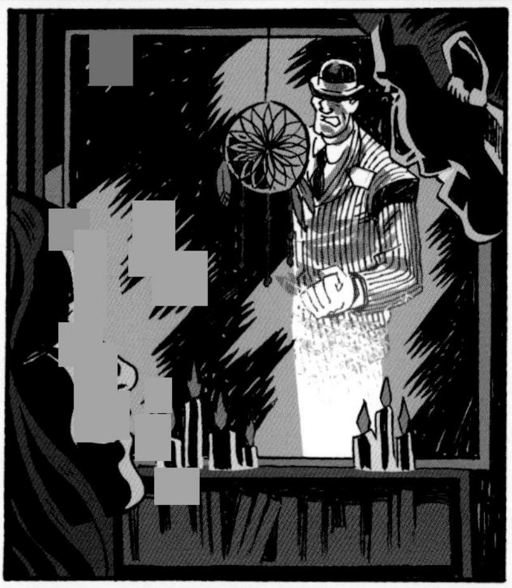

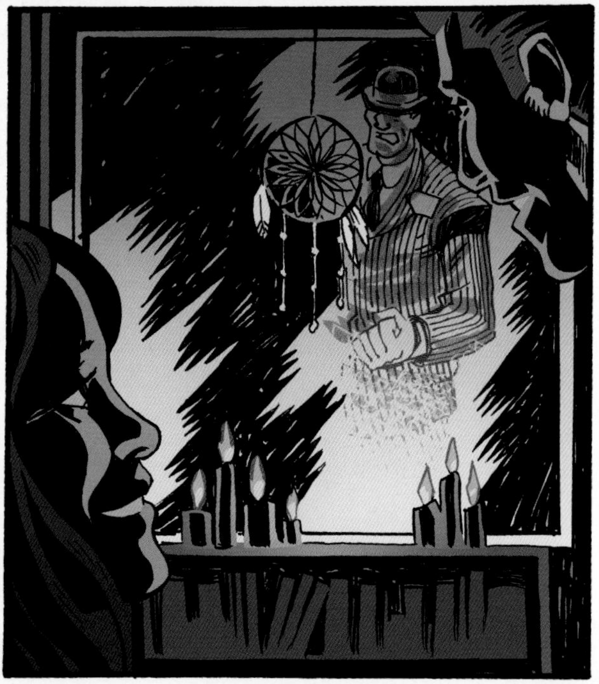

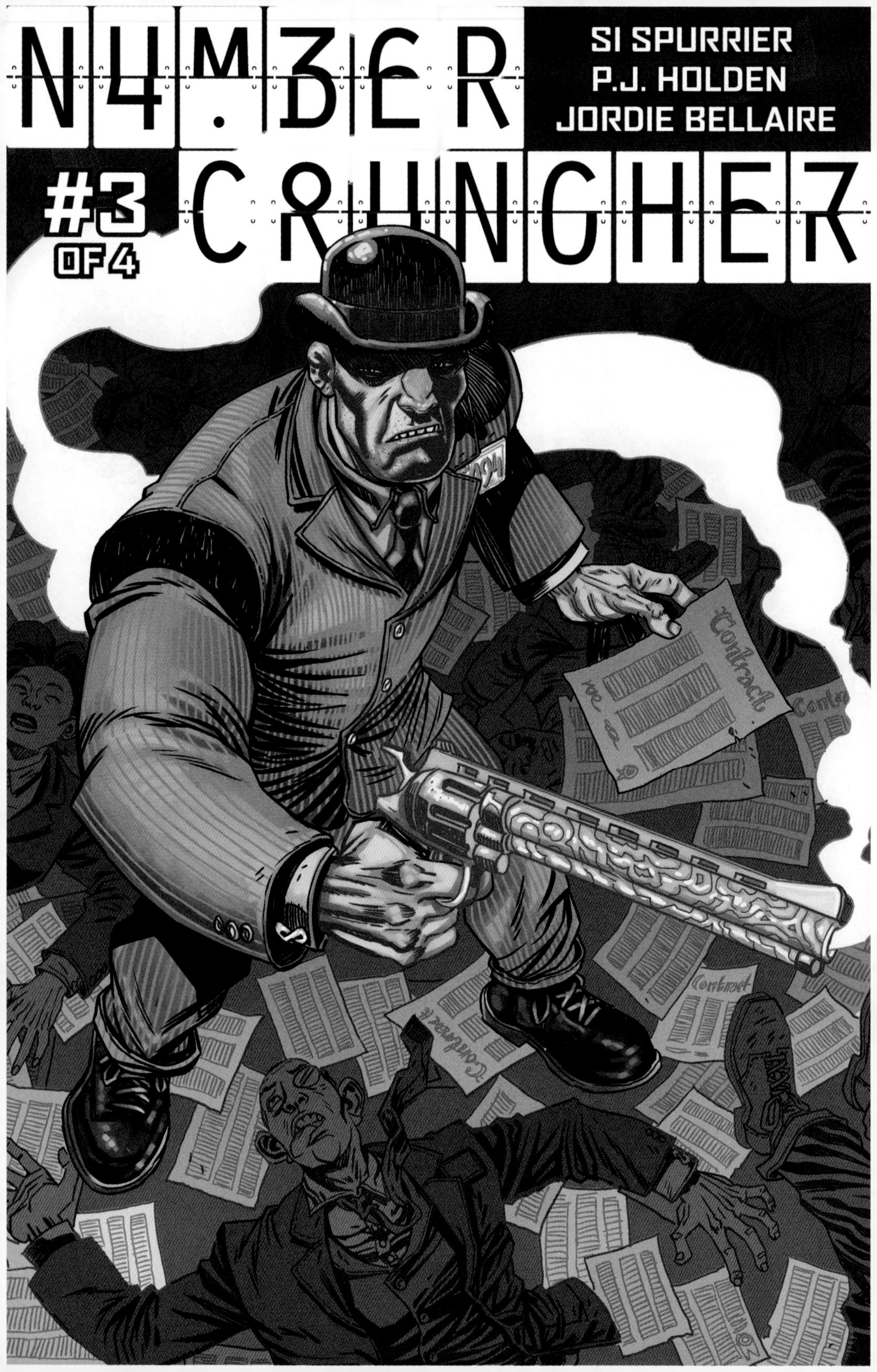
NUMBER
CRUNCHER
#3 OF 4
SI SPURRIER
P.J. HOLDEN
JORDIE BELLAIRE
Contract

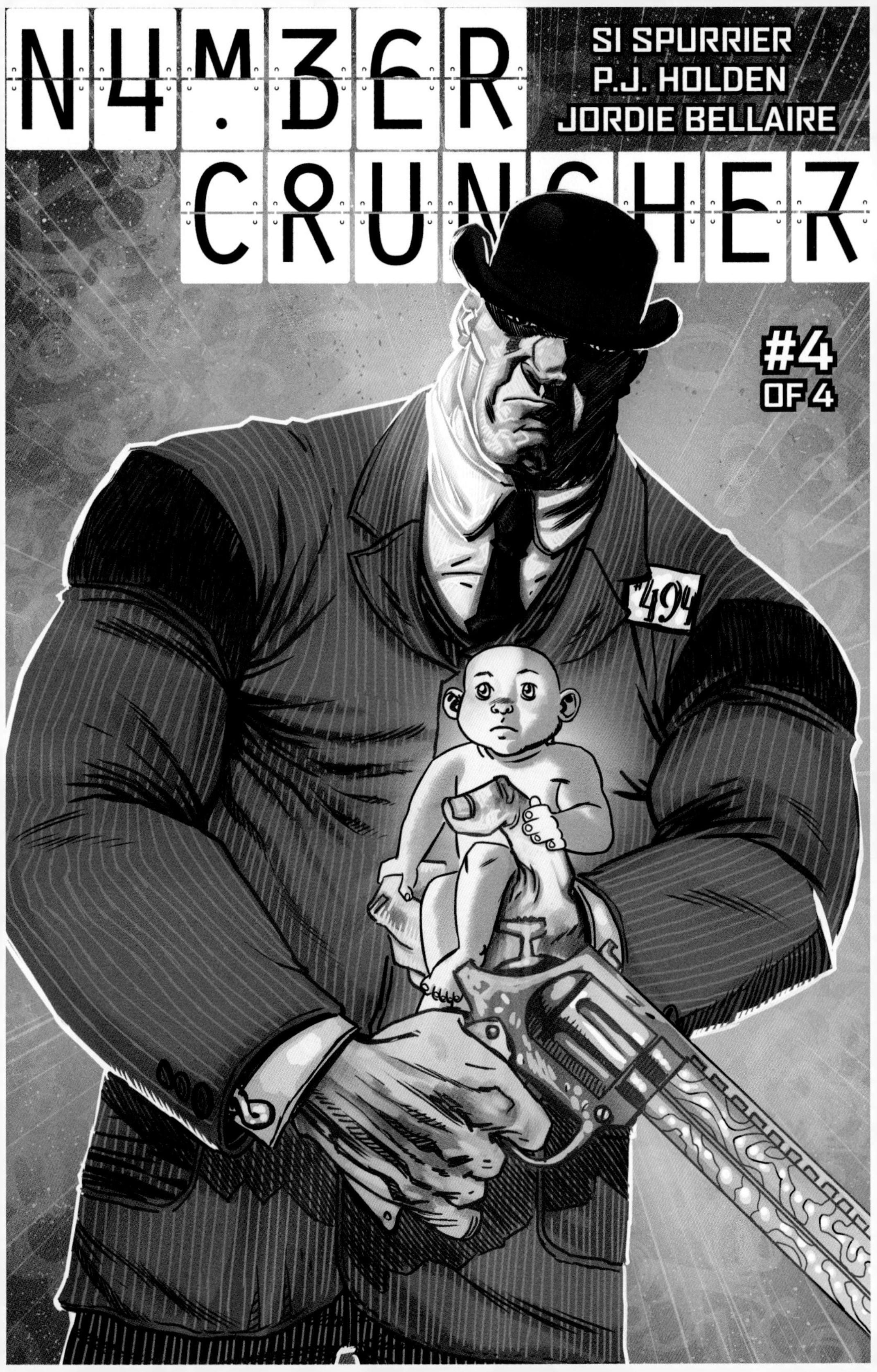
N4M.3ER
CRUNCHER
SI SPURRIER
P.J. HOLDEN
JORDIE BELLAIRE
#4
OF 4
#494

BIRTH PLACEMENT

A cover comes to life.

Nothing jumps off a cover like a big man with a big gun holding a small baby. Just ask John Woo.

PJ Holden did a beautiful job bringing the cover of *Numbercruncher* #4 to life, so we thought we'd offer up a little insight into the whole process that brought his artwork to the finished page.

SKETCH

PJ initially did four concepts for the cover. Following a long period of deliberation, diplomacy in action, hardball politics and bitter rancour, the *Numbercruncher* team finally settled on concept D (it was a close run thing with C, but there were dissenting voices that felt threatening a baby with a gun would not be a popular choice in some quarters...).

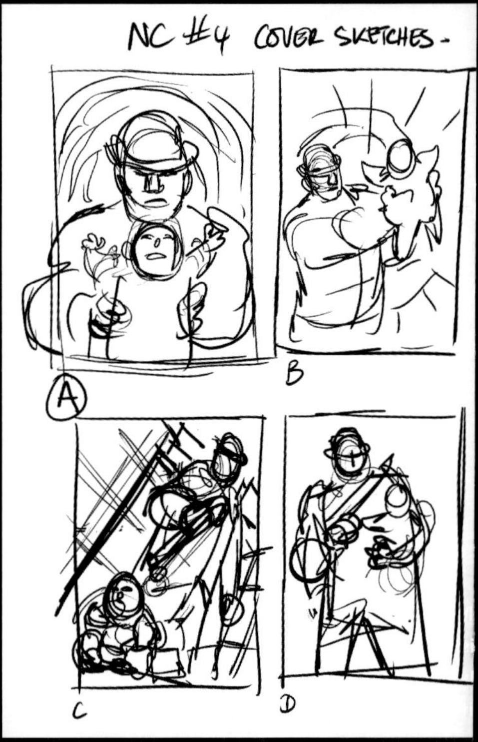
NC #4 COVER SKETCHES -
A
B
C
D

COVER ROUGH

PJ then supplied a rough – a basic color image of the cover to give the team an idea of how the cover was developing. So far, so good.

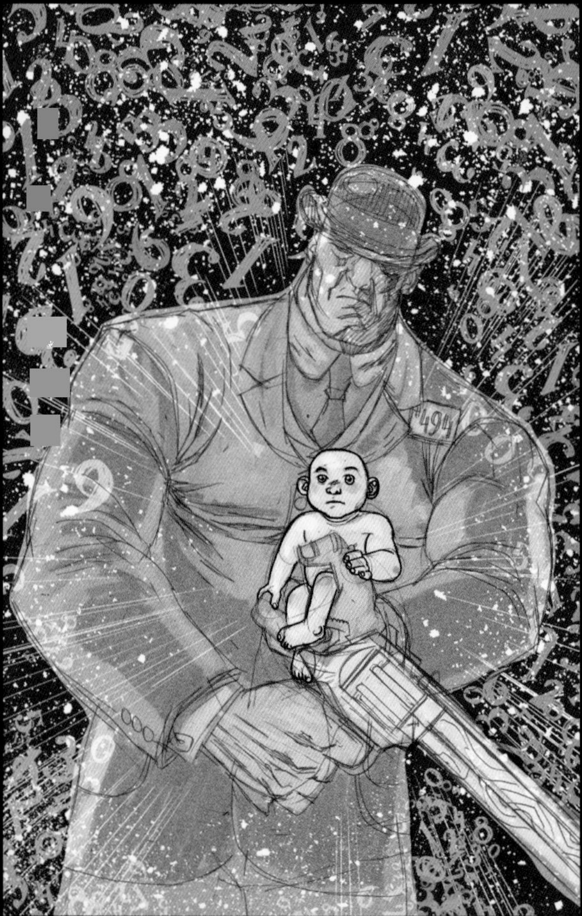
494

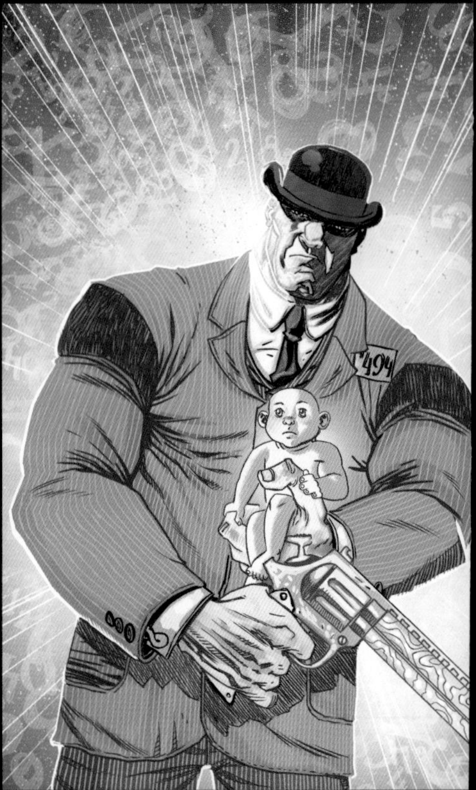
494

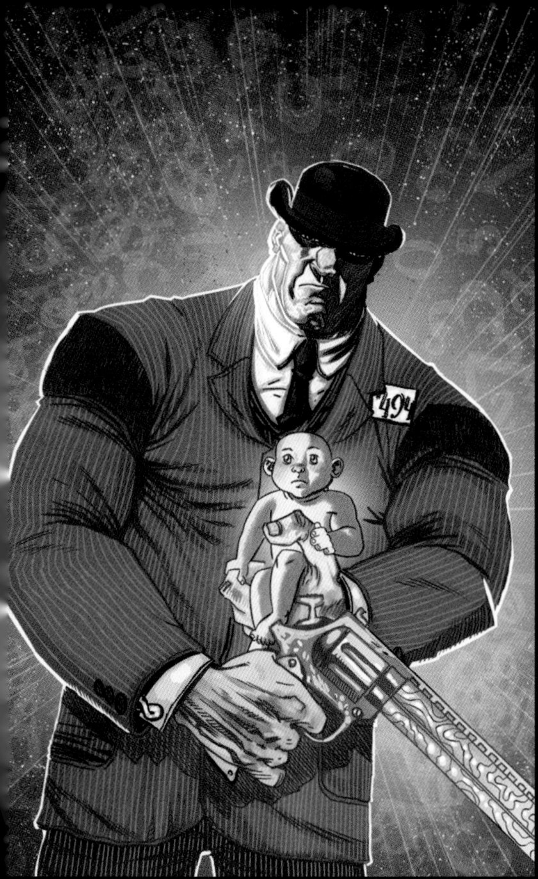

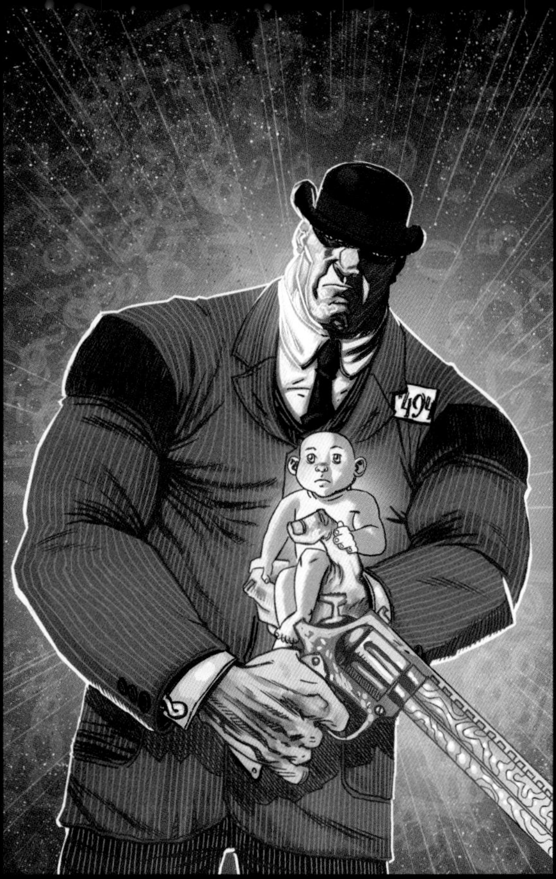

MOST THERE...

s was the more or less the final version. The y amendment after this was making the baby ttle pinker so that he looked, well, more baby-e; and playing with the background color until found one everyone could agree on. ■

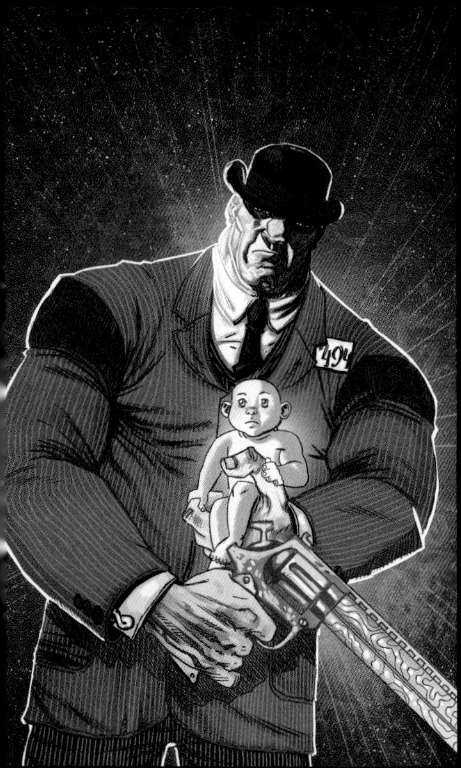

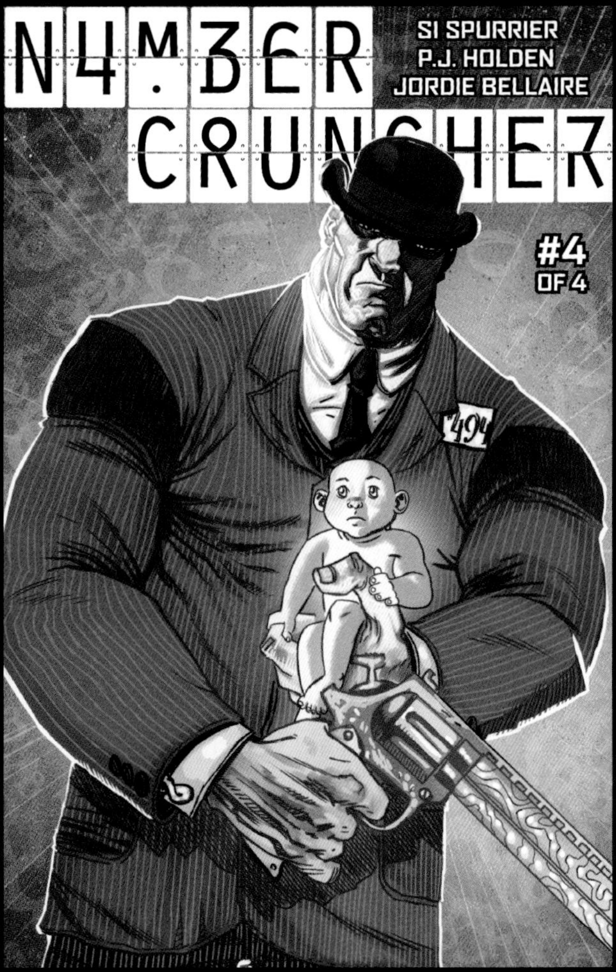
N4M3ER
CRUNCHER
SI SPURRIER
P.J. HOLDEN
JORDIE BELLAIRE
#4
OF 4

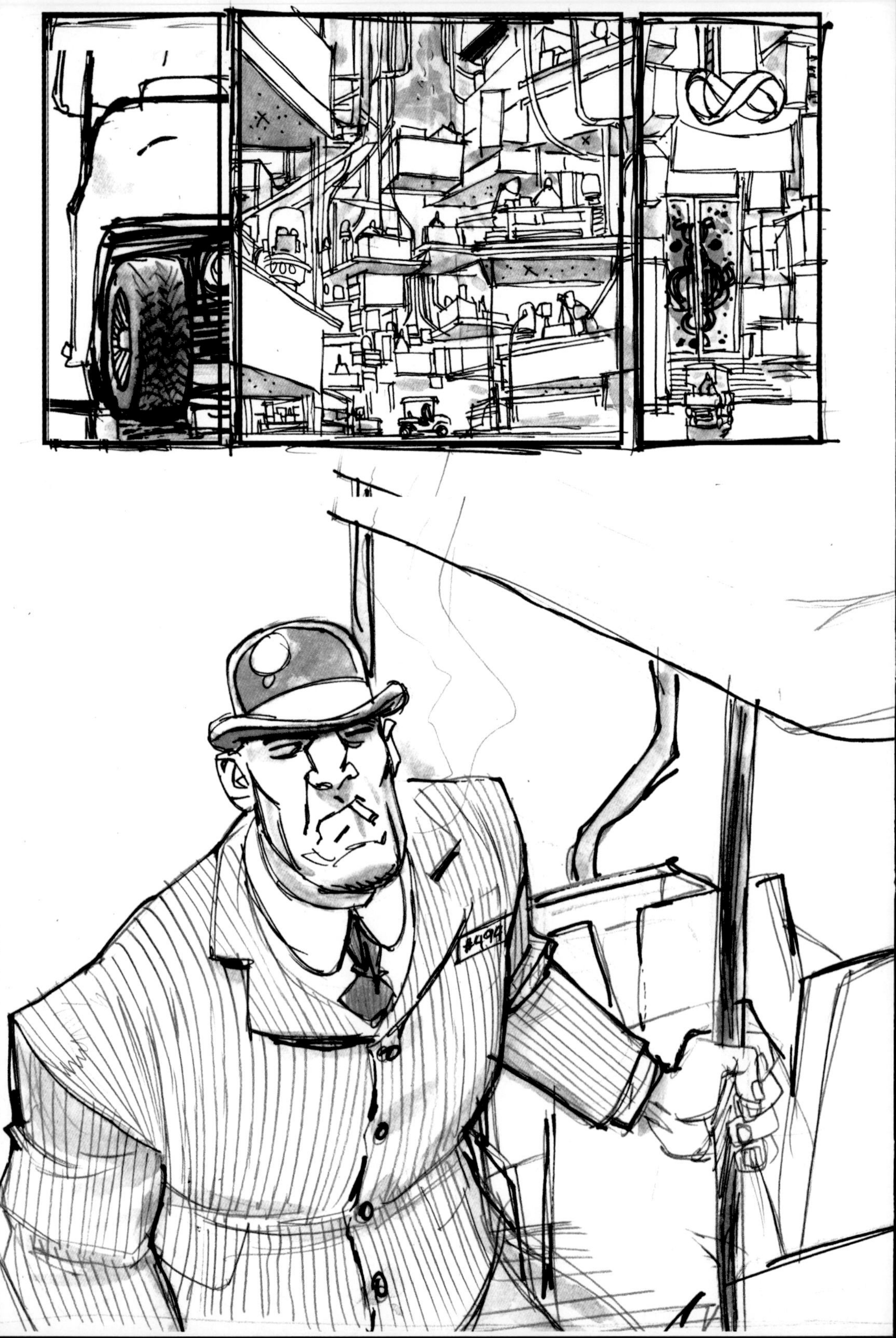
#494

Page 2 pencil art by P.J. Holden

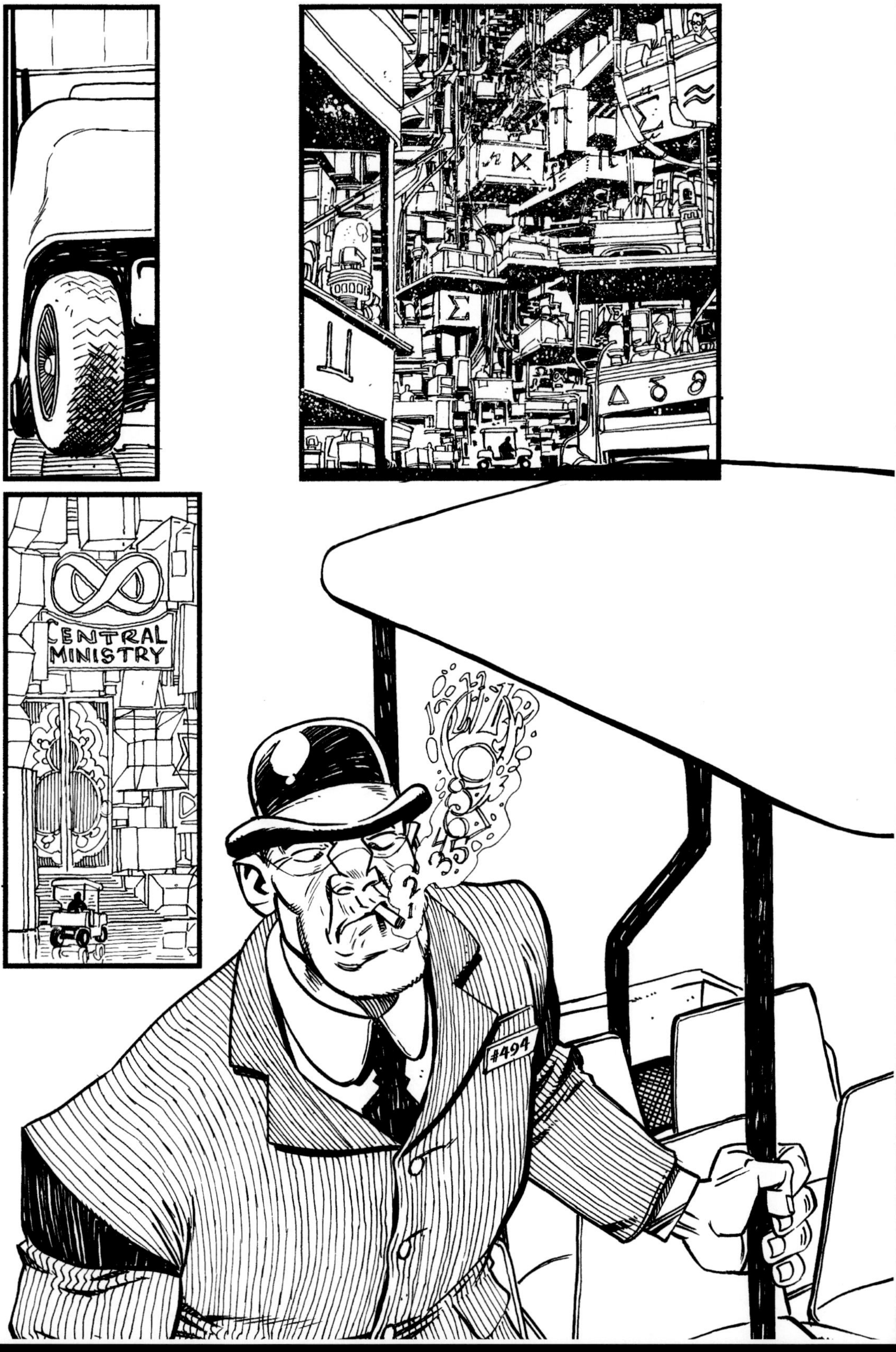
CENTRAL MINISTRY
#494

Page 2 inked art by P.J. Holden

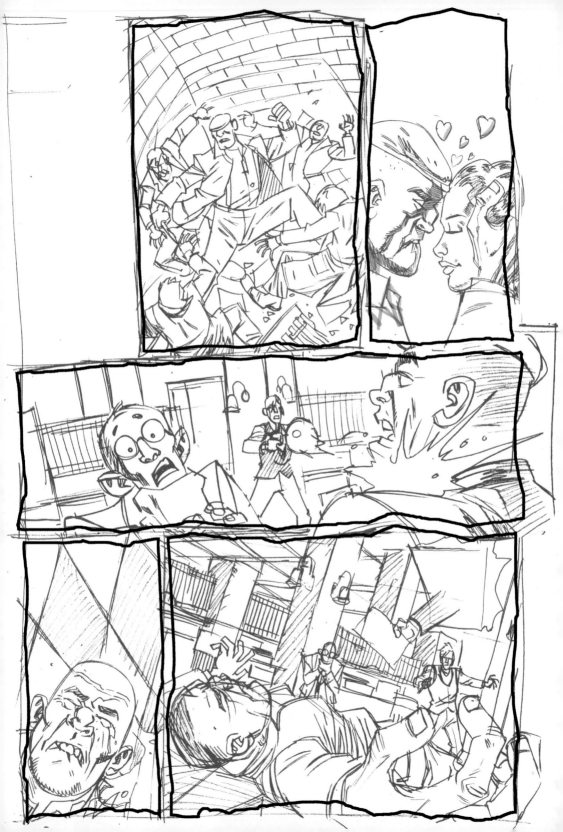

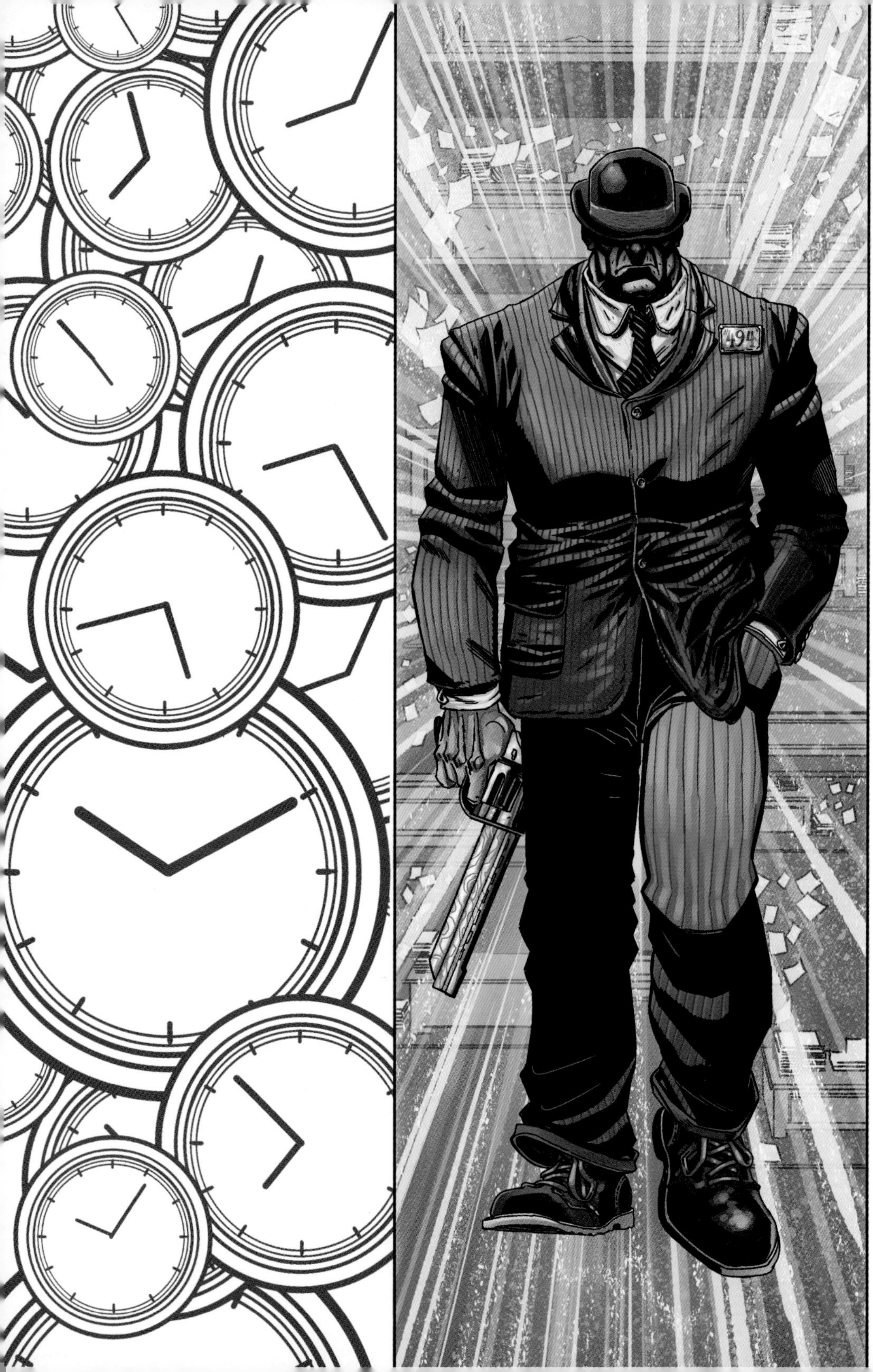
494

CREATORS' BIOGRAPHIES

SI SPURRIER

Si cut his teeth as a writer on Britain's flagship sci-fi comic, *2000AD*, writing numerous strips including *Judge Dredd*, *Lobster Random* and *The Simping Detective*; he also recently worked as one of the co-writers on the critically acclaimed *Trifecta* storyline. Currently he is writer on Marvel's *X-Men Legacy*, Avatar's *Crossed: Wish You Were Here*, and *Six-Gun Gorilla* for BOOM! He lives in London and also cooks.

PJ HOLDEN

PJ Holden has been a regular on *2000AD* and *Judge Dredd Megazine* since 2001, working on numerous strips including *Judge Dredd*, *Rogue Trooper* and the *86ers*. He also worked on *Battlefields: Happy Valley* with Garth Ennis and *Terminator/Robocop: Kill Human* with Rob Williams, both for Dynamite. He lives in Northern Ireland.

JORDIE BELLAIRE

Jordie is best described as 'prolific'. When not social networking, she somehow manages to color, well, a lot. Her current credits include work for pretty much every major comics publisher on such titles as *Captain Marvel*, *The Rocketeer*, *Ultimate Comics X-Men*, *Quantum & Woody*, *X-Files: Season 10*, *Mara* and *The Manhattan Projects*.

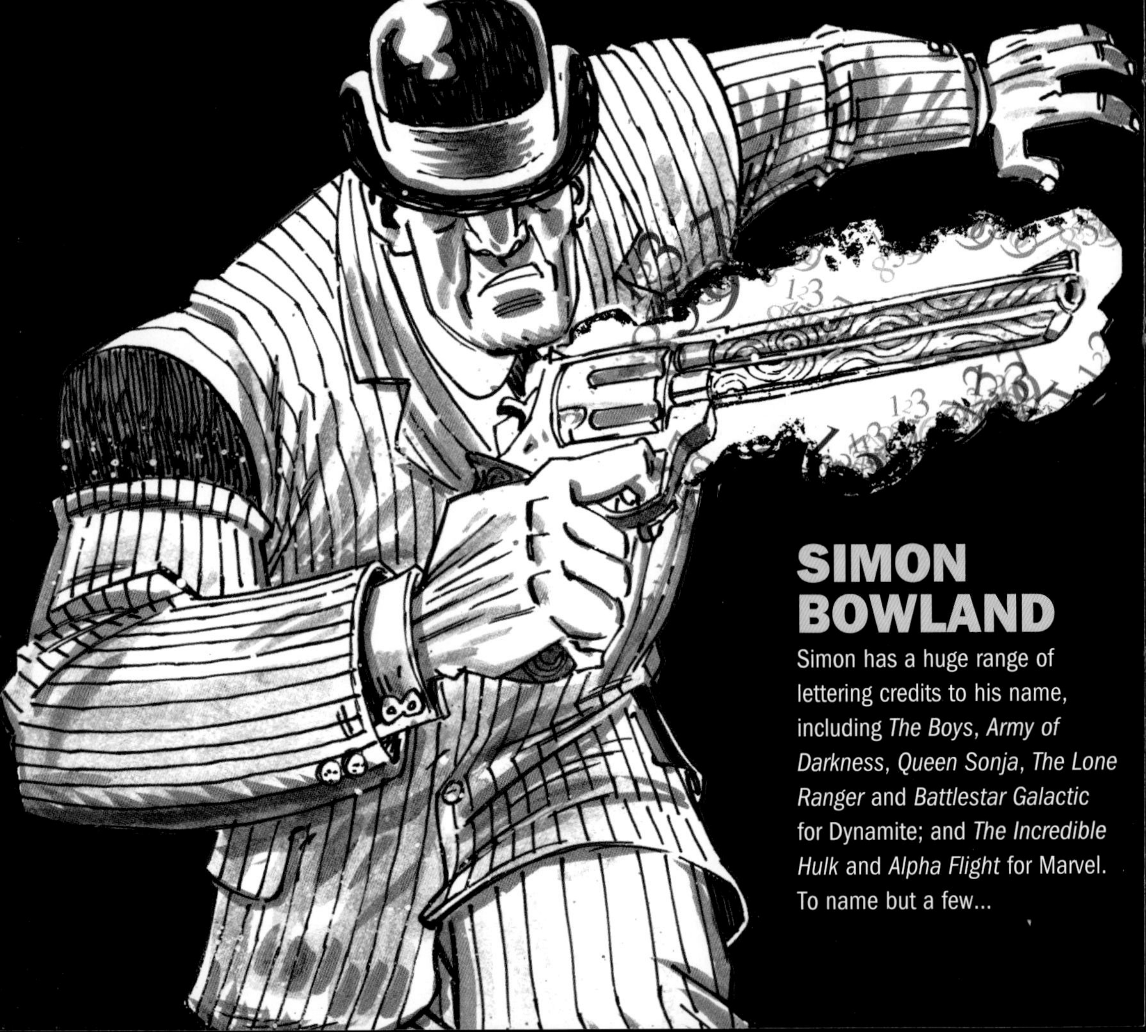

SIMON BOWLAND

Simon has a huge range of lettering credits to his name, including *The Boys*, *Army of Darkness*, *Queen Sonja*, *The Lone Ranger* and *Battlestar Galactic* for Dynamite; and *The Incredible Hulk* and *Alpha Flight* for Marvel. To name but a few...